The Best AMERICAN ESSAYS 1995

Edited and with an Introduction
by JAMAICA KINCAID

ROBERT ATWAN,
Series Editor

D0067882

HOUGHTON MIFFLIN COMPANY

BOSTON • NEW YORK 1995

For information about this and other Houghton Mifflin trade and reference books and multimedia products, visit The Bookstore at Houghton Mifflin on the World Wide Web at http://www.hmco.com/trade/.

ISSN 0888-3742
ISBN 0-395-69184-2
ISBN 0-395-69183-4 (pbk.)

Printed in the United States of America
QUM 10 9 8 7 6 5 4 3 2 1

Contents

Foreword

AS FAR AS I KNOW, Emily Dickinson never wrote a single essay. She dashed off hundreds of stunning letters to family and friends (letters full of domestic details and anxious horror), and these are the closest we get in prose to her enigmatic life. In nearly two thousand poems — those other letters to a world that never wrote to her — she clearly searched for a level of expression that challenged the imprisoning conventions of everyday syntax:

> They shut me up in Prose —
> As when a little Girl
> They put me in the Closet —
> Because they liked me "still" —

Poetry offered a way out of the closet, an alternative to being "shut up" literally and figuratively. It furnished her with a sharp instrument to hold at bay the nameless terrors of childhood.

This year's collection of essays takes us into a world of closets and secrets and childhood terrors, where — as Charles Simic's "memory fragments" reveal — poetry becomes utterly necessary. Not surprisingly, many of this year's contributors are poets and novelists who have been confronting such themes throughout their distinguished careers. As essayists, they are acutely aware of how conventional prose can muffle the voice, dampen the emotional range, and simplify human identity to a point where it can be painlessly and trivially defined by mere political assertion. Surely such identities have grown, to borrow H. L. Mencken's term, into one of the chief literary rackets of our time.

Though Dickinson didn't write essays, her poetry could easily serve as a primer for the genre: in poem after poem, we find no unearned abstractions, few compositional comforts, no racketeering in ready-made identities. In short, we find writing that seems almost physically alive, pulsating with life. Such vitality informs this collection. An essay such as Maxine Kumin's "Jicama, Without Expectation" is so immersed in sensuous detail — sights, smells, physical sensations — that the boundary line between reading and living begins to decompose, like those mulched pages of the *New York Times* Kumin ritually adds to her garden.

In these essays boundary lines get blurred: the line between life and death, male and female, prose and poetry, truth and fiction, positive and negative. This collection introduces us to a world where, in W. S. Di Piero's words, we find all about us a "constantly melting and recomposing amalgam of images." On a rainy winter night in Rome, Joseph Brodsky, sitting near the equestrian statue of Marcus Aurelius, recalls a passage from the *Meditations* he had memorized in boyhood: "The universal nature out of the universal substance, as if it were wax, now moulds the figure of a horse, then melting this down uses the material for a tree, next for a man, next for something else; and each of these things subsists for a very short time."

In front of Burl's, a Los Angeles restaurant, an eight-year-old Bernard Cooper experiences a moment of sexual confusion when he encounters two flamboyantly dressed transvestites. All normal gender boundaries dissolve. "Any woman might be a man," he thinks as he sees, sitting behind the plate glass window of Burl's (an anagram of "blurs"), his parents, who no longer securely seem "the embodiments of woman and man."

In Diana Kappel-Smith's lovely meditation on the natural world, salt becomes a metaphor for the mysterious ways the world and the human body are tied together, all things "inextricably mixed." Yet salt is above all a concrete reality: you can lick it, taste it; it's an inseparable part of our physical being. Salt leads Kappel-Smith to a realization about the ways of knowing: "Perhaps it's a matter of semantics, but to me the word 'understand' means to possess physical knowledge; it means to have a corporeal grasp, a surety that the body owns. A purely cerebral construct is 'not understanding.'" The possession of physical knowledge: that phrase captures one of the dominant themes of this collection.

One hazard of the essay form is that the writer can too easily turn into a talking head. We may kindly overlook an author's voluntary disembodiment in philosophical and academic essays; but the personal essayist had better not become a ghost writer. The center of "auto-bio-graphy" isn't "self" or "writing," it's "life" in the fullest physical meaning of that powerful ancient Greek word. As William H. Gass puts it: "Autobiography is a life writing its life." And even on that topic Emily Dickinson, as W. S. Di Piero reminds us, offers essayists some professional advice: "Tell all the Truth but tell it slant." But that's another story altogether.

The Best American Essays features a selection of the year's outstanding essays, essays of literary achievement that show an awareness of craft and a forcefulness of thought. Hundreds of essays are gathered annually from a wide variety of national and regional publications. These essays are then screened and turned over to a distinguished guest editor, who may add a few personal favorites to the list and who makes the final selections.

To qualify for selection, the essays must be works of respectable literary quality, intended as fully developed, independent essays (not excerpts) on subjects of general interest (not specialized scholarship), originally written in English (or translated by the author) for publication in an American periodical during the calendar year. Publications that want to make sure their contributors will be considered each year should include the series on their subscription list (Robert Atwan, *The Best American Essays*, P.O. Box 416, Maplewood, New Jersey 07040).

For this year's volume, I'd like to thank a good friend, Bruce Forer, for the advice and encouragement he has generously provided since the series was launched in 1986. I remain deeply indebted to my editors at Houghton Mifflin, Janet Silver, Wendy Holt, and Liz Duvall, for countless helpful suggestions and for the extraordinary effort they make on behalf of this series. Several periodicals are being featured this year for the first time; I'd like to welcome them and the editors who make sure I see them: H. Emerson Blake (*Orion*), Lee Gutkind (*Creative Nonfiction*), Bret Israel (*The Los Angeles Times Magazine*), Hilda Raz (*Prairie Schooner*), Frederick Smock (*The American Voice*), and Ronald Spatz (*The Alaska*

Quarterly Review). I especially want to thank Ann Kjellberg, who was the American editor of *Artes* (a new periodical of literature, art, and music), for her kind assistance over the years.

It was a great pleasure and honor to work with Jamaica Kincaid, whose contributions to our contemporary literature are surely unsurpassed and whose gift for crossing boundaries can be felt throughout this volume.

R. A.

Introduction

AN ESSAY! The fixed form or the fixed category of any kind, any definition at all, fills me with such despair that I feel compelled to do or be its opposite. And if I cannot do its opposite, if I can in fact complete the task that is the fixed form, or fill the fixed category, I then deny it, I then decline to participate at all. Is this a complex view? But I believe I have stated it simply: anything that I might do, anything that I might be, I cannot bear to be enclosed by, I cannot bear to have its meaning applied to me.

The Essay: and this is not a form of literary expression unfamiliar to me. I can remember being introduced to it. It was the opinions and observations of people I did not know, and their opinions and observations bore no relationship to my life as I lived it then. But even now, especially now, I do not find anything peculiar or wrong about this; after all, the opinions and observations of people you do not know are the most interesting, and even the most important, for your own opinions and observations can only, ultimately, fix you, categorize you — the very thing that leads me to dissent or denial.

To choose a good essay, then, from among a number of essays is something I am quite able to do. A good essay for me is an essay that pleases me. And this isn't to say that pleasing myself is my sole aspiration in this world, but how else can I make a judgment about anything, including an essay?

I must have been taught the principles of the essay, for surely it must have such a thing, principles; that is, a certain integrity that must not be violated. I do not remember them. I remember the principles involved in writing a letter. I was taught them. A letter has six parts: the sender's address should be written in the upper right-hand corner of the paper, underneath that should be the date, on the next line but over on the left should be the name and address of the recipient of the letter, underneath that should be the greeting or salutation, then comes the body of the letter, and last is the yours truly, the closing. *What are the principles involved in writing a letter?* would have been a question asked of me many times as a part of an exam, and passing the exam itself was a way for other people to know whether I was worth the effort being expended on me and whether I should be given access to certain parts of the world. An example of my letter-writing ability had to be demonstrated: a letter to an imaginary friend living in another part of the colonial empire.

An essay too has principles: you state, you build on your statement, you sum up. How awful that sounds to me now, how dry, how impossible. I could not see it then, but I can see it now: this definition was meant to be a restriction, and it worked very well; for how could I express any truth about myself or anything I might know in the form of state, build, and sum up when everything about me and everything I knew existed in a state of rage, rage, and more rage. I came into being in the colonial situation. It does not lend itself to any literary situation that is in existence. Not to me, anyway.

The examples of this literary form, the essay, that were shown to me when I was being taught its principles were written by men of substantial standing in their societies, men who had the time to contemplate an idea, who knew that their opinions might influence events in their day. It wasn't difficult to notice that unethical men, living in times of ethical scarcity, were preoccupied with ethics and not as they might practice ethical behavior but as an exercise in contemplation. And so too with the idea of freedom. They, these men, seemed to have thought hard and long before writing volumes on the idea of freedom, that state of being not a slave, while surrounded by people who were enslaved, or dependent on the labor of people who were enslaved. On being given these essays to study and then to imitate not the content, only the style, I did not have these thoughts. I had a feeling when reading them: I felt angry, I felt sad, I felt I could never have command over words, I felt I would never have an idea, I felt no matter how big I got, I would always remain small.

I did not know then how really useful it would become to have read the thoughts of Francis Bacon, how his ideas, the language he used, would be one of the many sources from which I come, and so without it a part of me could not exist. The phrase "capable of perpetual renovation" appears in Bacon's essay "The Advancement of Learning." He was referring then to the revolution in knowledge occurring in his time. When I first read it many years ago, this idea of "perpetual renovation," I did not grasp any meaning in it that would apply to me. I suspect that Francis Bacon did not know that someone like me would find comfort in it. But it must be this perpetual renovation that leads me to say that if there is a form to the essay, if there is a fixed way to execute it, that way does not satisfy me now, not its form, not its luxurious content.

The luxurious content: and why should I call "The Advancement of Learning" luxurious? Sitting in a room that is one of many in a large house, as a citizen of a prosperous country, which is to say a country whose actions in the world have been successful and so they are the best and correct ones, I now understand the meaning of contemplation: it is to think about something related to you or related to something far removed from you, but its resolution is not urgent to you, its resolution is not like a thorn in the side of your body whose removal would offer an obvious contrast. Someone for whom learning, the world of knowledge, is such an unquestioned existence can speak of its possibilities, its depths, its unlimitedness; someone for whom existence means existing physically from day to day might find summing up the world through the use of the imagination, summoning up the world solely through the mind, a luxury, an enviable act out of the ordinary and so therefore to be dismissed. Just for instance, as I am writing this, I have come across a quote by a man who lived to be one hundred years old and at that grew tired of living and so he starved himself to death. He said, "Death is either a transition or an awakening. In either case it is to be welcomed, like every other aspect of the life process." But I am forty-six years of age and I don't see death in that way at all: my own death now would be among the last things I would welcome: living is urgent, not to be taken for granted. Desiring its opposite, death, is a luxury.

The essays I selected here have no visible theme, again they only pleased me, which is to say that I loved reading them and had that childish pleasure while reading them that everything else apart from reading was labor (and labor is quite different from work, one being forced, the other a source of realization; I say this not with any universal certainty, it is only my opinion). "Burl's," the essay by Bernard Cooper about a boy discovering his homosexuality, was the most familiar and yet the strangest. I know what it is like to discover who you really are, or really might be; on the other hand, I am not yet homosexual (I put it this way because I don't like to close the door on anything). The essays are mostly by writers I have always admired — Edna O'Brien, Cynthia Ozick, Harold Brodkey, William H. Gass, Henry Louis Gates, Joseph Brodsky, Elaine Scarry, Edward Hoagland, James A. McPherson — writers whose voices I am familiar with in a pleasing way and so I suspect wanted to hear yet again. But then there were writers whose prose I had never read before and was thrilled to read for the first time — Josephine Foo — and writers whose work I knew only through their poems so I was not familiar with them in this form (the essay) at all — Maxine Kumin, Charles Simic.

Ideally, the essays are supposed to be arranged in alphabetical order, to show that I do not prefer one over the other, for that would no doubt cause some hurt feelings, and why should people who have done nothing except write something that I like have their feelings hurt? They are arranged alphabetically then, except I chose to begin with the essay on Marcus Aurelius by Joseph Brodsky and end with an essay on the end of the century (which makes me feel as if I have come to the end of a large landmass) by Elaine Scarry. I chose to do this because Marcus Aurelius reminds me of my earliest memories of learning, for as a child in a school I had to memorize the history of the Romans and their influence on Britain, and because at the very end of the century I hope to be alive, and if I am not, I believe poetry, the work of it (not the labor, it is not labor, I believe so), will be.

As I write this, it is the middle of the night, it is hot, the curtains are drawn open in the room in which I write. A moth so large banged up against the mesh window screen that it caused the screen to make a shuddering sound. It was attracted to the light from my lamp. The great essay about the moth has been written and I can see no room for renovation.

JAMAICA KINCAID

The Best
AMERICAN
ESSAYS
1995

JOSEPH BRODSKY

Homage to Marcus Aurelius

FROM ARTES

I

While antiquity exists for us, we, for antiquity, do not. We never
did, and we never will. This rather peculiar state of affairs makes
our perspective on antiquity somewhat invalid. Chronologically
and, I am afraid, genetically speaking, the distance between us is
too immense to imply any causality: we look at antiquity as if out
of nowhere. Our vantage point is similar to that of an adjacent
galaxy's view of ourselves; it boils down, at best, to a solipsistic
fantasy, to a vision. We shouldn't claim more, since nothing is less
repeatable than the highly perishable cellular mix known as an
individual human being: the same goes for the context within
which one acts. What would an ancient Roman, were he to wake up
today, recognize? A cloud on high, blue waves, a woodpile, the horizontality of the bed, the verticality of the wall — but no one by face,
unless of course those he encountered were stark naked, which is
to say beheaded. Yet even on a beach or in our own bedchambers
we produce poor replicas — tanning quickly and showing agility
alien to marbles'. Finding himself in our midst, he at best would
have a sensation similar to that of a moon landing, i.e., not knowing what is before him: the future, or the past? a landscape or a
ruin? These things, after all, have great similarity. Ask a painter.

II

The twentieth is perhaps the first century that looks at this statue
of a horseman [Marcus Aurelius] with slight bewilderment. Ours

is the century of the automobile, and our kings and presidents drive, or else they are driven. We don't see many horsemen around, save at equestrian shows or races. One exception is perhaps the British consort, Prince Philip, as well as his daughter, Princess Anne. But that has to do not even so much with their royal station as with the name Philip, which is of Greek origin and means "philo-hippoi": lover of horses. It is so much so that Her Royal Highness was married — until recently — to Captain Mark Phillips of the Royal Guards, an accomplished steeplechaser himself. You may even add to that Prince Charles, the heir to the British crown, an avid polo player. But that would be it. You don't see leaders of democracies, or, for that matter, the few available tyrannies, mounted. Not even military commanders receiving parades, of which these days there are fewer and fewer. The last, I suppose, was a Russian, Marshal Zhukov, on May 9, 1945, when Germany was defeated, and Stalin himself, son of the Caucasus Mountains though he was, couldn't climb the white stallion. Horsemen have left our precincts almost entirely. To be sure, we still have our mounted police; and there is perhaps no greater joy for a New Yorker than to watch one of these Lochinvars in the saddle issuing a traffic ticket to an illegally parked car while his hackney is sniffing at the victim's hood. But when we erect monuments to our leaders and public heroes these days, there are only two feet resting on the pediment. The car took over, and you don't put a cast-iron leader of democracy atop a granite Rolls-Royce — although this could be a great boost to that firm's currently flagging fortunes. But the competition is fierce in this industry, and rival companies may object to the free publicity. The Russians of course couldn't care less for a free market, and in St. Petersburg there is indeed a monument to Lenin atop an armored car, actually made by Rolls-Royce (circa 1916). And some people in California are given to going to the eternal rest along with their vehicles, or asking for their marble replicas for tombstones. But they of course are not heads of state, although their fortunes could easily match some nations' budgets. Anyhow, the horse disappears and with it, its rider. You spot them nowadays through your windshield only in some rural areas or else in the hearts of our capitals, but then they are immobile. Very often, in either case, you don't know their names: trudging along or standing still, equestrians are in the first place monuments to the past, and it is the horse that does it. A four-legged hieroglyph of the past? Well, perhaps, since a horse is used to symbolize quite a lot: empires, virility, nature. Actually, there is a whole etiquette of equestrian statuary, and when a horse for instance rears up under the rider, it means that the latter died in battle. If all of its four hooves rest on the pediment, that suggests he died in his four-poster. If one leg is lifted high up in the air, then the implication is that he died of battle-related wounds; if not so high up, that he lived long enough, trotting as it were through his existence. You can't do that with a car. Besides, a car, even a Rolls, doesn't bespeak one's uniqueness, nor does it elevate one above the crowd the way a horse does. Roman emperors in particular used to be depicted on horseback not in order to commemorate their preferred mode of transportation but precisely to convey their superiority: their belonging, often by birth, to the equestrian class. In the parlance of the time, "equestrian" presumably meant "high up" or "high born." An equus, in other words, in addition to carrying an actual rider, was saddled with a lot of allusions. So it indeed may represent the past; which is not worse than representing the animal kingdom, for that's where the past came from. Maybe this is what Caligula had in mind after all when he introduced his horse to the Senate: as a representative of the animal kingdom, or of the past. Since antiquity seems to have made this connection already. Since it seems to have had far more truck with the past than with the future.

III

What the past and the future have in common is our imagination, which conjures them. And our imagination is rooted in our eschatological dread: the dread of thinking that we are without precedence or consequence. The stronger that dread, the more detailed our notion of antiquity or of Utopia. Sometimes — actually, all too often — they overlap, as when antiquity appears to possess an ideal order and abundance of virtues, or when the inhabitants of our Utopias stroll through their marble well-governed cities clad in togas. Marble is to be sure the perennial building material of our antiquity and Utopia alike. On the whole, the color white permeates our imagination all the way through its extreme ends, when its version of the past or the future takes a metaphysical or religious turn. Paradise is white, so are ancient Greece and Rome. This predilection is not so much an alternative to the darkness of our fancy's source as a metaphor for our ignorance, or simply a reflection of the material our fancy normally employs for its flight: paper. A crumpled paper ball on its way to the wastebasket could easily be taken for a splinter of a civilization, especially with your glasses off.

IV

I first saw this bronze horseman indeed through a windshield, of a taxi, some twenty years ago, almost in a previous incarnation. I'd just landed in Rome for the first time, and was on my way to the hotel where a distant acquaintance of mine had made a reservation. The hotel bore a very un-Roman name: it was called Bolivar. Something equestrian was already in the air, since the great libertador is normally depicted atop his rearing horse. Did he die in battle? I couldn't remember. Presently we were stuck in the evening traffic in what looked like a cross between a railroad station's square and the end of a soccer game. I wanted to ask the driver how far we were from the hotel, but my Italian was good only for "Where are we?" "Piazza Venezia," he blurted, nodding to the left; "Campidoglio," a nod to the right. And with another nod: "Marco Aurelio," followed by what was no doubt an energetic reference to the traffic. I looked to the right. "Marco Aurelio," I repeated to myself, and felt as if two thousand years were collapsing, dissolving in my mouth thanks to the Italian's familiar form of this emperor's name. Which always had for me an epic, indeed imperial sway, sounding to me like a caesura-studded, thundering announcement by history's own major-domo: Marcus! — caesura — Aurelius! The Roman! Emperor! Marcus! Aurelius! This is how I had him in high school, and the major-domo was our own stumpy Sarah Isaakovna, a very Jewish and very resigned lady in her fifties, who taught us history. Yet for all her resignation, when it came to uttering the names of Roman emperors, she'd straighten up, assuming an attitude of grandeur, and practically shout up, well above our heads, into the peeling-off stucco of the classroom's wall adorned with its portrait of Stalin: Caius Julius Caesar! Caesar Octavian

Augustus! Caesar Tiberius! Caesar Vespasianus Flavius! The Roman Emperor Antoninus Pius! And then — Marcus Aurelius! It was as though the names were bigger than she herself, as though they were swelling up from inside to be released into a far greater space than her own body or, for that matter, the room, the country, the times themselves could contain. She reveled in those odd-sounding foreign names, in their unpredictable succession of vowels and consonants, and that was, frankly, contagious. A child loves that sort of thing — strange words, strange sounds — and that's why, I suppose, history is best taught in childhood. At the age of twelve one may not grasp the intrigue, but a strange sound suggests an alternative reality. "Marcus Aurelius" certainly did to me, and that reality proved to be quite vast: larger, in fact, than that emperor's own. Now apparently came time to domesticate that reality; that's what, I suppose, I was in Rome for. "Marco Aurelio, eh?" I said to myself, and turned to the driver: "Where?" He pointed to the top of a huge waterfall of marble steps leading uphill, now right in front of us, and as the car sharply swerved to gain some minuscule advantage in the sea of traffic, I momentarily beheld a floodlit pair of horse's ears, a bearded head, and a protruding arm. Then the sea swallowed us up. Half an hour later, at the entrance to the Bolivar, my valet-pack in one hand, my money in another, I asked the driver in a sudden surge of fraternity and gratitude — after all, he was the first person I had spoken with in Rome and he had also brought me to my hotel and didn't even overcharge me, or so it seemed — his name. "Marco," he said, and drove off.

v

The most definitive feature of antiquity is our absence. The more available its debris and the longer you stare at it, the more you are denied entry. Marble negates you particularly well, though bronze and papyri don't fall too far behind. Reaching us intact or in fragments, these things strike us of course with their durability and tempt us to assemble them, fragments especially, into a coherent whole, but they were not meant to reach us. They were, and still are, for themselves. For man's appetite for the future is as limited as his own ability to consume time is, or as grammar, this first casualty of every discourse on the subject of the hereafter, shows.

At best, these marbles, bronzes, and papyri were meant to outlast
their subjects and their makers — but not themselves. Their existence was functional, which is to say, of limited purpose. Time is no
jigsaw puzzle, because it is made up of lives that are finite. And
though perhaps objects-inspired, the idea of the afterlife wasn't
an option until quite late. Anyhow, what is before us are the
leftovers of necessity or vanity, i.e., of considerations always near-
sighted. Nothing exists for the future's sake: and the ancients
couldn't in nature regard themselves as the ancients. Nor should
we bill ourselves as their tomorrow. We won't be admitted into
antiquity: it was well inhabited, in fact overpopulated, as it was.
There are no vacancies. No point in busting your knuckles against
marble.

VI

If we find the lives of Roman emperors highly absorbing, it is
because we are highly self-absorbed creatures. To say the least, we
regard ourselves as centers of our own universes, varying to be sure
in width, but universes nonetheless, and as such having centers.
The difference between an empire and a family, a network of
friends, a web of romantic entanglements, a field of expertise, etc.,
is a difference in volume, not in structure. Also, because the
caesars are so much removed from us in time, the complexity of
their predicament appears to be graspable, shrunk, as it were, by
the perspective of two millennia to almost a fairy-tale scale, with
its wonders and its naiveté. Our address books are their empires,
especially after hours. One reads Suetonius or Aelius or, for that
matter, Psellus, for archetypes even if all one runs is a bike shop
or a household of two. Somehow it is easier to identify with a caesar
than with a consul, or praetor, or lictor, or slave, even though that
is what one's actual station in the modern reality corresponds to.
This has nothing to do with self-aggrandizement or aspirations but
is due to the understandable attraction of king-size (so to speak),
clear-cut versions of compromised virtue, vice, or self-delusion
rather than their fuzzy, inarticulate originals next door or, for that
matter, in the mirror. That's why, perhaps, one looks at their
likenesses, at the marbles especially. For in the end, a human oval
can accommodate only so much. You can't have more than two
eyes or less than one mouth; surrealism wasn't yet invented and

African masks were not yet in vogue. (Or maybe the Romans clung so much to Greek standards precisely because they were.) So in the end you are bound to recognize yourself in one of them. For there is no caesar without a bust, as there is no swan without a reflection. Clean-shaven, bearded, bald, or well coiffed, they all return a vacant, pupil-free marble stare, pretty much like that of a passport photo or the mugshot of a criminal. You won't know what they have been up to; and putting these faces to their stories is what, perhaps, makes them indeed archetypal. It also moves them somewhat closer to us, since, being depicted fairly often, they, no doubt, must also have developed a degree of detachment vis-à-vis their physical reality. In any case, to them a bust or a statue was indeed what a photograph is to us, and the most "photographed" person would obviously be a caesar. There were of course others: their wives, senators, consuls, praetors, great athletes or beauties, actors and orators. On the whole, though, judging by what has survived, men were chiseled more often than women, which presumably reflects who controlled the purse as much as the society's ethos. By either standard, a caesar would be a winner. In the Capitoline Museum you can shuffle for hours through chambers filled up practically to the rafters with rows and rows of marble portraits of caesars, emperors, dictators, augusti hoarded there from all over what used to be the place they ran. The longer one stayed on the job, the more numerous would be one's "photographs." One would be depicted in one's youth, maturity, decrepitude; sometimes the distance between one's busts is no more, it would seem, than a couple of years. It appears that marble portraiture was an industry, and, with its calibrations of decay, something of a mortuary one; the rooms strike you in the end as not unlike a library housing the encyclopedia of a beheading. It is hard to "read," though, because marble is notoriously blank. In a sense, what it also has in common with photography — or, more accurately, with what photographs used to be — is that it is literally monochrome. For one thing, it renders everyone blond. Whereas in their real lives, some of the models — caesars' wives, to say the least, since many of them came from Asia Minor — were not. Yet one is almost grateful to marble for its lack of pigmentation, the way one is grateful to a black-and-white photograph, for it unleashes one's fantasy, one's intuition, so that viewing becomes an act of complicity: like reading.

Aurelius's *Meditations,* perhaps not so much for the depth of its probing as for the respectability the discipline itself gained in the royal embrace. Politics are far more often the pursuit of philosophers than philosophy is the sideshow of kings. Besides, for Marcus Aurelius philosophy was a lot more than a sideshow: it was, as we'd say today, a therapy, or, as Boethius put it later, a consolation. He wasn't a great philosopher, nor was he a visionary; not even a sage; his *Meditations* is at once a melancholy and a repetitive book. The Stoic doctrine at the time had become a doctrine indeed, and though he did write in Greek, he is no match for Epictetus. Most likely a Roman emperor was drawn to this kind of language out of respect for the doctrine's origins, and also perhaps out of nostalgia, in order not to forget the language of civilized discourse; the language, after all, of his youth and pursuits more noble perhaps than those at hand. Add to that, if you will, possible considerations of secrecy, and the benefit of detachment: the purpose and the method of the discipline itself, enhanced here by the very means of expression. Not to mention that his reign simply happened to coincide with a substantial revival of Greek culture in Rome, the first Renaissance, if you will, owing no doubt to the long era of considerable stability historians dubbed the Pax Romana. And historians love Marcus Aurelius precisely because he was the last guardian of that pax. Because his reign effectively and neatly concluded a period of Roman history lasting nearly two centuries that began with Augustus and, to all intents and purposes, ended with our man. They love him because he is the end of the line, and a very coherent one at that: which, for historians, is a luxury. Marcus was a highly conscientious ruler; perhaps because he was appointed to the job, not anointed; because he was adopted into the dynasty, not born to it. And both historians and philosophers love him precisely for carrying out so well the commission for which he thought himself ill suited, and was in fact reluctant to accept. To them, his predicament presumably echoes in some fashion their own: he is as it were a model for those who have to go in this life against their calling. In any case, the Roman Empire gained a lot more from his dual loyalty to duty and philosophy than did the Stoic doctrine (which, in its own turn, comes with Marcus to the end of its own line: ethics). So much so that it's been maintained, often vigorously, that this sort of inner split is a

good recipe for ruling. That it's better if one's spiritual yearnings
have their own outlet and don't interfere too much with one's
actions. This is what the whole philosopher-king business is all
about, isn't it? When your metaphysics gets short shrift. As for
Marcus, however, he dreaded this prospect from the very beginning, dreaded being summoned to Hadrian's court, for all its
comforts and bright perspectives. Perhaps precisely because of
those; a true product of the Greek doctrine, all he aspired to was
"the camp-bed and skin coverlet." Philosophy for him was a manner of dressing as much as it was a manner of discourse: the texture
of existence, not just a mental pursuit. Picture him as a Buddhist
monk then; you won't be much off target, since the "way of life"
was the essence of Stoicism as well; emphatically so, we may add.
The young Marcus must have been apprehensive of the royal
adoption for more reasons than Hadrian's sexual predilections: it
meant a wardrobe as different as the accompanying mental diet.
That he went for it had to do, one imagines, less with royal pressure
than with our man's own misgivings about his intellectual forti-
tude: apparently it's easier to be a king than a philosopher. Anyhow, it came to pass, and here's a monument. The good question,
though, is, to whom? To a philosopher? Or to a king? To both?
Perhaps to neither.

IX

A monument is by and large a vertical affair, a symbolic departure
from the general horizontality of existence, an antithesis to spatial
monotony. A monument never actually departs from this horizontality — well, nothing does — but rather rests upon it, punctuating
it at the same time like an exclamation mark. In principle, a
monument is a contradiction. In this way, it resembles its most
frequent subject: a human being, equally endowed with vertical
and horizontal properties, but eventually settling for the latter. The
durability of the material a monument is usually made of — marble, bronze, increasingly cast iron, and now even concrete — highlights the contradictory nature of the undertaking even further,
especially if a monument's subject is a great battle, a revolution,
or a natural disaster — i.e., an event that took a great toll and was
momentary. Yet even if the subject is an abstract ideal or the

consequences of a momentous event, there is a detectable clash of time frames and notions of viability, not to mention textures. Perhaps given the material's aspiration for permanence, the best subject for a monument is indeed destruction. Zadkin's statue of bombed-out Rotterdam immediately comes to mind: its verticality is functional, since it points at the catastrophe's very source. Also, what could be more horizontal than the Netherlands? And it occurs to one that the monument owes its genealogy to great planes, to the idea of something being seen from afar — whether in a spatial or a temporal sense. That it is of nomadic origin, for at least in a temporal sense we are all nomads. A man as aware of the futility of all human endeavor as our philosopher-king would of course be the first to object to being turned into a public statue. On the other hand, twenty years of what appears to have been practically nonstop frontier combat, taking him all over the place, effectively turned him into a nomad. Besides, here's his horse.

X

The Eternal City is a city of hills, though. Of seven of them, actually. Some are natural, some artificial, but negotiating them is an ordeal in any case, especially on foot and especially in summer, although the adjacent seasons' temperatures don't fall too far behind. Add to that the emperor's rather precarious health; add to that its not getting any better with age. Hence, a horse. The monument sitting at the top of the Capitoline actually fills up the vacuum left by Marcus's mounted figure, which, some two thousand years ago, occupied that space quite frequently, not to say routinely. On the way to the Forum, as the saying goes. Actually, on his way from it. Were it not for Michelangelo's pedestal, the monument would be a footprint. Better yet a hoofprint. The Romans, superstitious like all Italians, maintain that when the bronze Marcus hits the ground, the end of the world will occur. Whatever the origin of this superstition, it stands to reason if one bears in mind that Marcus's motto was "Equanimity." The word suggests balance, composure under pressure, evenness of mental disposition; literally: equation of the animus, i.e., keeping the soul — and thus the world — in check. Give this formula of the Stoic posture a possible misspelling, and you'll get the monument's definition: Equinimity. The horseman tilts, though, somewhat, as if leaning toward his subjects, and his hand is stretched out in a gesture that is a cross between a greeting and a blessing. So much so that for a while some insisted that this was not Marcus Aurelius but Constantine, who converted Rome to Christianity. For that, however, the horseman's face is too serene, too free of zeal or ardor, too uninvolved. It is the face of detachment, not of love — and detachment is precisely what Christianity never could manage. No, this is no Constantine, and no Christian. The face is devoid of any sentiment; it is a postscript to passions, and the lowered corners of the mouth bespeak the lack of illusion. Had there been a smile, you could think perhaps of the Buddha; but the Stoics knew too much about physics to toy with the finality of human existence in any fashion. The face shines with the bronze's original gold but the hair and the beard have oxidized and turned green, the way one turns gray. All thought aspires to the condition of metal; and the bronze denies you any entry, including interpretation or touch. What you've got here, then, is detachment per se. And out of this detachment the emperor leans toward you slightly, extending his right hand either to greet you or to bless you — which is to say acknowledge your presence. For where he is, there is no you, and vice versa. The left hand theoretically holds the reins, which are either missing now or were never there in the first place: a horse would obey this rider no matter what. Especially if it represented nature. For he represents Reason. No, he is no Christian and no Constantine. The face is clearly of the Antonine dynasty, though he wasn't born into it but adopted. The hair, the beard, the somewhat bulging eyes and slightly apoplectic posture, are those of his stepfather turned father-in-law and his very own son. Small wonder that it is so hard to tell the three of them apart among the Ostia marbles. But, as we know nowadays, a period's fashion may easily beat the genes. Remember the Beatles. Besides, he revered Antoninus Pius enough to emulate him in a variety of ways; his appearance could be simply that attitude's spinoff. Also the sculptor, being a contemporary, might have wished to convey the sense of continuum perceived by the historians of the stepfather's and the stepson's reigns: a sense that Marcus himself, needless to say, sought to create. Or else the sculptor just tried to produce a generic portrait of the era, of the perfect ruler, and what we've got here is the fusion of the two best emperors the realm had had since the murder of Domitian — the way he did the horse, whose identity we don't ponder. In all probability, however, this is the author of the *Meditations* himself: the face and the torso slightly tilted toward his subjects fit extremely well the text of that melancholy book, which itself leans somewhat toward the reality of human existence, in the attitude not so much of a judge as of an umpire. In this sense this monument is a statue to a statue: it's hard to picture a Stoic in motion.

XI

The Eternal City resembles a gigantic old brain that long ago gave up any interest in the world — it being too graspable a proposition — and settled for its own crevasses and folds. Negotiating their narrows, where even a thought about yourself is too cumbersome, or their expanses, where the concept of the universe itself appears puny, you feel like a worn-out needle shuffling the grooves of a vast record — to the center and back — extracting with your soles the tune that the days of yore hum to the present. This is the real His Master's Voice for you, and it turns your heart into a dog. History is not a discipline but something that is not yours — which is the main definition of beauty. Hence the sentiment, for it is not going to love you back. It is a one-way affair, and you recognize its Platonic nature in this city instantly. The closer you get to the object of your desire, the more marble or bronze it gets, as the natives' fabled profiles scatter around like animated coins escaped from some broken terra-cotta jar. It is as though here time puts, between bedsheets and mattress, its own carbon paper — since time mints as much as it types. The moment you leave Bolivar or else the equally smelly yet cheaper Nerva, you hit Foro Trajano with its triumphant column tightly wrapped in conquered Dacians and soaring like a mast above the marble ice floe of broken pillars, capitals, and cornices. Now this is the domain of stray cats, reduced lions in this city of reduced Christians. The huge white slabs and blocks are too unwieldy and random to arrange them in a semblance of order or drag them away. They are left here to absorb the sun, or to represent "antiquity." In a sense they do; their ill-matching shapes are a democracy, this place is still a Forum.

And on his way from it, just across the road, beyond pines and cypresses, atop the Capitoline Hill, stands the man who made the fusion of republic and imperial rule probable. He has no company: virtue, like a malady, alienates. For a split second, it is still A.D. 176 or thereabouts, and the brain ponders the world.

XII

Marcus was a good ruler and a lonely man. In his line of work, loneliness of course comes with the territory; but he was lonelier than most. *Meditations* gives you a greater taste of that than his correspondence; yet it is just a taste. The meal had many courses and was pretty heavy. To begin with, he knew that his life had been subverted. For the ancients, philosophy wasn't a byproduct of life but the other way around, and Stoicism was particularly exacting that way. Perhaps we should momentarily dispense here with the very word "philosophy," for Stoicism, its Roman version especially, shouldn't be characterized as love for knowledge. It was rather a lifelong experiment in endurance, and a man was his own guinea pig: he was not a probing instrument, he was an answering instrument. By the time of Marcus, the doctrine's knowledge was to be lived rather than loved. Its materialist monism, its cosmogony, its logic, and its criterion of truth (the perception which irresistibly compels the subject to assent to it as true) were already in place, and for a philosopher life's purpose was to prove the validity of this knowledge by applying it to reality till the end of his days. In other words, a Stoic's life was a study in ethics, since ethics buys nothing except osmosis. And Marcus knew that his experiment was interrupted, or qualified, to a degree he himself wouldn't be able to comprehend; worse still, that his findings — provided there were any — could have no application. He believed Plato, but not to this extent. At any rate, he would be the first to square the common good with individual unhappiness, and that's what *Meditations* is perhaps all about: a postscript to *The Republic.* He knew that as a philosopher he was finished: that concentration was out, that all he could hope for was some time for sporadic contemplation. That the best that his life would amount to would be a few glimpses of eternity, a true surmise now and then. He accepted that, for the sake of the common good no doubt, but hence

Meditations' overriding melancholy or, if you will, pessimism — all the more deep because the man definitely suspected that there was rather more to the story. *Meditations* is a patchy book, borne out by interference. It is a disjointed, rambling internal monologue, with occasional flashes of pedantry as well as of genius. It shows you what he might have been rather than what he was: his vector, rather than an attained destination. It appears to have been jotted down amidst the hubbub and babel of this or that military campaign, successful as they might have been — by the campfire, indeed, and the soldier's cloak played the Stoic philosopher's body coverlet. In other words, it was done in spite of — or, if you will, against — history, of which his destiny was trying to make him a part. A pessimist he perhaps was, but certainly not a determinist. That's why he was a good ruler, why the mixture of republic and imperial rule under him didn't look like a sham. (One may even argue that the larger democracies of the modern world show an increasing preference for his formula. Good examples are contagious, too; but virtue, as we said, alienates. Not to mention that time, wasting its carbon paper on subjects, seems to have very little left for rulers.) To say the least, he was a good caretaker: he didn't lose what he inherited; and if the empire under him didn't expand, it was just as well; as Augustus said, "Enough is enough." For somebody in charge of an entity so vast and for so long (practically thirty-three years, from A.D. 147, when his father-in-law conferred upon him the powers of emperorship, to his death in A.D. 181 near the would-be Vienna), he has surprisingly little blood on his hands. He would rather pardon than punish those who rebelled against him: those who fought him, he would rather subdue than destroy. The laws he made benefited the most powerless: widows, slaves, juniors, although it must be said that he was the first to introduce the double standard in prosecuting criminal offenses by members of the Senate (the office of special prosecutor was his invention). He used the state's purse sparingly and, being abstemious himself, tried to encourage this in others. On several occasions, when the empire needed money, he sold imperial jewels rather than hit his subjects up for new taxes. Nor did he build anything extravagant, no Pantheon or Coliseum. In the first place, because those already existed; secondly, because his sojourn in Egypt was quite brief and he didn't go beyond Alexandria, unlike

Agrippa and unlike Titus and Hadrian, to have his mind fired up by the gigantic, desert-fitting scale of Egyptian edifices. Besides, he didn't like circenze that much, and when he had to attend a show, he is reported to have read or written or been briefed during the performance. It was he, however, who introduced to the Roman circus the safety net for acrobats.

XIII

Antiquity is above all a visual concept, generated by objects whose age escapes definition. The Latin "anticum" is essentially a more drastic term for "old," deriving from the equally Latin "ante," which means "before," and used to be applied presumably to things Greek. "Beforishness," then. As for the Greeks themselves, their "arche" denotes beginning or genesis, the moment when something occurs for the first time. "Firstness," then? Herein in any case lies a substantial distinction between the Romans and the Greeks — a distinction owing its existence partly to the Greeks' having fewer objects at their disposal to fathom the provenance of, partly to their general predilection for dwelling on origins. The former, in fact, may very well be an explanation for the latter, since next to archeology there is only geology. As for our own version of antiquity, it eagerly swallows both the Greeks and the Romans, yet, worse come to worst, might cite the Latin precedent in its defense. Antiquity to us is a vast chronological jumble, filled with historical, mythical, and divine beings, interrelated among themselves by marble and also because a high percentage of the depicted mortals claimed divine descendence or were deified. This last aspect, resulting in the practically identical scant attire of those marbles and in the confusion on our part of attributing fragments (did this splintered arm belong to a mortal or to a deity?), is worth noticing. The blurring of distinctions between mortals and deities was habitual with the ancients, with the Roman caesars in particular. While the Greeks on the whole were interested in lineage, the Romans were after promotion. The target, however, was the same: Celestial Mansions. Yet vanity or boosting the ruler's authority played a rather small part in this. The whole point of identifying with the gods lies not so much in the notion of their omniscience as in the sense that their extreme carnality is fully matched by the extremes of their detachment. To begin with, a ruler's own margin of detachment would make him identify with a god (carnality, of course, would be Nero or Caligula's shortcut). By acquiring a statue, he'd boost that margin considerably, and it's best if it's done in the course of one's lifetime, since marble reduces both the expectations of the subjects and the model's own willingness to deviate from manifest perfection. It sets one free, as it were, and freedom is the province of deities. Putting it very broadly, the marble and mental vista which we call antiquity is a great repository of shed and shredded skins, a landscape after the departure, if you will; a mask of freedom, a jumble of discarded boosters.

XIV

If Marcus indeed hated anything, and was proscriptive about it, that was gladiatorial shows. Some say it was because he detested blood sports, so vulgar and non-Greek, because siding with a team would, for him, be the beginning of partiality. Others insist that it had to do with his wife, Faustina, who, for all her thirteen children — only six survived — was remarkably promiscuous for an empress. Among her numerous affairs, these others single out a particular gladiator who, they claim, was the real father of Commodus. But nature works in mysterious ways; an apple often rolls far from the tree, especially if that tree grows on a slope. Commodus was both a rotten apple and its slope. Actually, as far as the imperial fortunes were concerned, he was a precipice. And perhaps an inability to grasp nature's mysterious ways was the source of Faustina's reputation (though if Marcus had it against the gladiators because of Faustina, he should have proscribed also against sailors, pantomime actors, generals, and so forth). Marcus himself would make light of this. Once, approached with these rumors and the suggestion that he get rid of her, he retorted: "If we send our wife away, we must give back her dowry, too." The dowry here was the empire itself, since Faustina was the daughter of Antoninus Pius. On the whole, he stood by her unswervingly and, judging by the honors he bestowed upon her when she died, perhaps even loved her. She was, it appears, one of those heavy main courses whose taste you barely sample in the *Meditations*. In general, Caesar's wife is beyond reproach and suspicion. And perhaps precisely in order to uphold this attitude as well as to save Faustina's reputation, Marcus departed from the nearly two-century-old tradition

of selecting an heir to the throne and passed the crown to what
he thus asserted to be his own flesh and blood. At any rate, it was
Faustina's. His reverence for his father-in-law was enormous and
he simply couldn't believe that someone in whose veins ran the
blood of the Antonines could be all that bad. Perhaps he regarded
Faustina as a force of nature; and nature for a Stoic philosopher
was the ultimate authority. If anything, nature taught him indifference and a sense of proportion: otherwise his life would have been
pure hell; *Meditations* strings out solipsism like glacial debris. Toward the wrong and atrocious, Marcus was not so much forgiving
as dismissive. Which is to say that he was impartial rather than just
and that his impartiality was the product not of his mind's fairness
but of his mind's appetite for the infinite; in particular, for impartiality's own limits. This would stun his subjects no less than it does
his historians, for history is the domain of the partial. And as his
subjects chided Marcus for his attitude toward gladiatorial shows,
historians jumped on him for his persecution of Christians. It is
unclear of course how much Marcus was informed about the
Christian creed, but it is easy to imagine him finding its metaphysics myopic and its ethics detestable. From a Stoic point of view, a
God with whom you trade in virtue to obtain eternal favors wouldn't
be worth a prayer. For somebody like Marcus, virtue's value lay
precisely in its being a gamble, not an investment. Intellectually,
to say the least, he had very little reason to favor the Christians;
still less could he do so as a ruler, faced at the time with wars,
plague, uprisings — and a disobedient minority. Besides, he didn't
introduce new laws against the Christians: those of Hadrian, and
those of Trajan before him, were quite enough. It is obvious that,
following his beloved Epictetus, Marcus regarded a philosopher,
i.e., himself, as the missionary of Divine Providence to mankind,
i.e., to his own subjects. You are welcome to quibble with his notion
of it; one thing is quite clear, though: it was far more open-ended
than the Christian version. Blessed are the partial, for they shall
inherit the earth.

XV

Take white, ochre, and blue; add to that a bit of green and a lot
of geometry. You'll get the formula time has picked for its back-

drop in these parts, since it is not without vanity, especially once it assumes the shape of history or of an individual. It does so out of its prurient interest in finality, in its reductive ability, if you will, for which it has numerous guises, including the human brain, or the human eye. So you shouldn't be surprised, especially if you were born here, to find yourself one day surrounded by the white-cum-ochre, trapezoid square with the white-cum-blue trapeze overhead. The former is human-made (actually, by Michelangelo), the latter is heaven-made, and you may recognize it more readily. However, neither is of use to you since you are green: the shade of oxidized bronze. And if the cumulus white in the oxygen blue overhead is still preferable to the balustrade's marble calves and well-tanned tiburtine chests below, it is because clouds remind you of your native antiquity: because they are the future of any architecture. Well, you've been around for nearly two thousand years, and you ought to know. Perhaps they, the clouds, are indeed the only true antiquity there is, if only because among them you are not a bronze.

XVI

Ave, Caesar. How do you feel now, among barbarians? For we are barbarians to you, if only because we speak neither Greek nor Latin. We are also afraid of death far more than you ever were, and our herd instinct is stronger than the one for self-preservation. Sound familiar? Maybe it's our numbers, Caesar, or maybe it's the number of our goods. We sure feel that by dying we stand to lose far more than you ever had, empire or no empire. To you, if I remember correctly, birth was an entrance, death an exit, life a little island in the ocean of particles. To us, you see, it's all a bit more melodramatic. What spooks us, I guess, is that an entrance is always guarded, whereas an exit isn't. We can't conceive of dwindling into particles again: after hoarding so many goods, that's unpalatable. Status's inertia, I guess, or fear of the elemental freedom. Be that as it may, Caesar, you are among barbarians. We are your true Parthians, Marcomanni, and Quadi, because nobody came in your stead, and we inhabit the earth. Some of us go even further, barging into your antiquity, supplying you with definitions. You can't respond, can't bless, can't greet or quell us with your outstretched right hand — the hand whose fingers still remember scribbling your *Meditations*. If that book hasn't civilized us, what will? Perhaps they billed you as the philosopher-king precisely to dodge its spell by underscoring your uniqueness. For theoretically what's unique isn't true, Caesar, and you were unique. Still, you were no philosopher-king — you'd be the first to wince at this label. You were what the mixture of power and inquiry made you: a postscript to both, a uniquely autonomous entity, almost to the point of pathology. Hence your emphasis on ethics, for supreme power exempts one from the moral norm practically by definition, and so does supreme knowledge. You got both for the price of one, Caesar; that's why you had to be so bloody ethical. You wrote an entire book to keep your soul in check, to steel yourself for daily conduct. But was it really ethics that you were after, Caesar? Wasn't it your extraordinary appetite for the infinite that drove you to the most minute self-scrutiny, since you considered yourself a fragment, no matter how tiny, of the Whole, of the Universe — and the Universe, you maintained, changes constantly. So whom were you checking, Marcus? Whose morality did you try and, for all I know, manage to prove? Small wonder, then, that you are not surprised to find yourself now among the barbarians; small wonder that you always were far less afraid of them than of yourself — since you were afraid of yourself far more than of death. "Reflect that the chief source of all evils to man," says Epictetus, "as well as of baseness and cowardice, is not death but the fear of death." But you knew also that no man owns his future — or, for that matter, his past. That all one stands to lose by dying is the day when it happens: the day's remaining part, to be precise, and in time's eye it's still less. The true pupil of Zeno, weren't you? At any rate, you wouldn't allow the prospect of nonbeing to color your being, Universe or no Universe. The eventual dance of particles, you held, should have no bearing upon the animated body, not to mention upon its reason. You were an island, Caesar, or at least your ethics were, an island in the primordial and — pardon the expression — postmordial ocean of free atoms. And your statue just marks the place on the map of the species' history where this island once stood: uninhabited, before submerging. The waves of doctrine and of creed — of the Stoic doctrine and the Christian creed — have closed over your head, claiming you as their own

Atlantis. The truth, though, is that you never were either's. You were simply one of the best men that ever lived, and you were obsessed with your duty because you were obsessed with virtue. Because it's harder to master than the alternative and because, if the universal design had been evil, the world would not exist. Some will point out no doubt that the doctrine and the creed came before and after you, but it's not history that defines the good. To be sure, time, conscious of its monotony, calls forth men to tell its yesterday from its tomorrow. You, Caesar, were good because you didn't.

XVII

I saw him for the last time some six years ago, on a wet winter night, in the company of a stray Dalmatian. I was returning by taxi to my hotel after one of the most disastrous evenings in my entire life; the next morning I was leaving Rome for the States. I was drunk. The traffic moved with the speed one wishes for one's funeral. At the foot of the Capitol I asked the driver to stop, paid, and got out of the car. The hotel was not far away and I guess I intended to continue on foot; instead, I climbed the hill. It was raining, not terribly hard but enough to turn the floodlights of the square, nay! trapeze, into fizzing-off Alka-Seltzer pellets. I hid myself under the conservatory's arcade and looked around. The square was absolutely empty and the rain was taking a crash course in geometry. Presently I discovered I was not alone: a middle-sized Dalmatian appeared out of nowhere and quietly sat down a couple of feet away. Its sudden presence was so oddly comforting that momentarily I felt like offering it one of my cigarettes. I guess this had to do with the pattern of its spots; the dog's hide was the only place in the whole piazza free of human intervention. For a while we both stared at the horseman's statue. "The universal nature out of the universal substance, as if it were wax, now moulds the figure of a horse, then melting this down uses the material for a tree, next for a man, next for something else; and each of these things subsists for a very short time. Yet it is no hardship for a box to be broken up, as it was none for it to be nailed together." This is what a boy memorized at the age of fifteen and remembered thirty-five years later. Still, this horse didn't melt down, nor did this man.

Apparently, the universal nature was satisfied with this version of
its substance and cast it in bronze. And suddenly — presumably
because of the rain and the rhythmic pattern of Michelangelo's
pilasters and arches — all got blurred, and against that blur, the
shining statue, devoid of any geometry, seemed moving. Not at
great speed, and not out of this place; but enough for the Dalmatian to leave my side and follow the bronze progress.

XVIII

As absorbing as Roman antiquity appears to be, perhaps we should
be a bit more careful with our retrospective proclivity. What if
manmade chronology is but a self-fulfilling fallacy, a means of
obscuring the backwardness of one's own intelligence? What if it's
just a way of justifying the snail's pace of the species' evolution?
And what if the very notion of such evolution is a lie? Ultimately,
what if this good old sense of history is just the dormant majority's
self-defense against the alert minority? What if our concept of
antiquity, for example, is but the switching off of an alarm clock?
Let's take this horseman and his book. To begin with, *Meditations*
wasn't written in the second century A.D., if only because its
author wasn't going by the Christian calendar. In fact, the time of
its composition is of no relevance, since its subject is precisely
ethics. Unless, of course, humanity takes a special pride in having
wasted fifteen centuries before Marcus's insights were reiterated
by Spinoza. Maybe we are just better at counting than at thinking,
or else we mistake the former for the latter? Why is it that we are
always so interested in when truth was uttered for the first time?
Isn't this sort of archeology in itself an indication that we are living
a lie? In any case, if *Meditations* is antiquity, it is we who are the
ruins. If only because we believe that ethics has the future. Well,
perhaps our retrospective ability should indeed be reined in somewhat, lest it become all-consuming. For if nothing else, ethics is
the criterion of the present — perhaps the only one there is, since
it turns every yesterday and tomorrow into now. It is precisely that
sort of arrow which at every moment of its flight is immobile.
Meditations is no existential manual and it wasn't written for pos-
terity. Nor should we, for that matter, be interested in the identity
of its author or promote him to the rank of philosopher-king:

ethics is an equalizer; thus the author here is Everyman. His concept of duty cannot be attributed to his royal overdose of it, because he wasn't the only emperor around; neither his resignation
of the imperial origin, because one can empathize with it quite
readily. Nor can we put it down to his philosophic training — and
for the same reasons: there were too many philosophers apart from
Marcus, and on the other hand, most of us are not Stoics. What if
his sense of duty and his resignation were, in the first place,
products of his individual temperament, of the melancholic disposition, if one wants to be precise; combined perhaps with the man's
aging? There are after all only four known humors; so at least the
melancholics among us can take this book to heart and skip the
bit about the historical perspective nobody possesses anyhow. As
for the sanguinics, cholerics, and phlegmatics, they too perhaps
should admit that the melancholic version of ethics is accommo-
dating enough for them to marvel at its pedigree and chronology.
Perhaps short of compulsory Stoic indoctrination, the society may
profit by making a detectable melancholic streak a prerequisite for
anyone aspiring to rule it. To this extent, a democracy can afford
what an empire could. And on top of that, one shouldn't call the
Stoic acceptance of the perceptible reality resignation. Serenity
would be more apt, given the ratio between man and the subjects
of his attention, or — as the case may be — vice versa. A grain of
sand can't resign itself to the desert; and perhaps what's ultimately
good about melancholics is that they seldom get hysterical. By and
large, they are quite reasonable, and "what is reasonable," as Marcus once said, "is consequently social." Did he say this in Greek, to
fit your idea of antiquity?

                              XIX

Of all Roman poets, Marcus knew best and preferred Seneca.
Partly because Seneca too was of Spanish origin, sickly, and a great
statesman; mainly, of course, because he was a Stoic. As for Catul-
lus, Marcus would find him no doubt too hot and choleric. Ovid
for him would be licentious and excessively ingenious, Virgil too
heavy-handed and perhaps even servile, Propertius too obsessive
and passionate. Horace? Horace would seem to be the most congenial author for Marcus, what with his equipoise and attachment

to the Greek monody. Yet perhaps our emperor thought him too quirky, or too diverse and unsteady as well: in short, too much of a poet. In any case, there is almost no trace of Horace in *Meditations,* nor for that matter of the greatest among the Latins, Lucretius — another you would think a natural choice for Marcus. But then perhaps a Stoic didn't want to be depressed by an Epicurean. On the whole, Marcus seems to have been far more fluent in Greek literature, preferring dramatists and philosophers to poets of course, though snatches from Homer, Agathon, and Menander crop up in his book quite frequently. Come to think of it, if anything makes antiquity a coherent concept, it is the volume of its literature. The library of someone like Marcus would contain a hundred or so authors; another hundred perhaps would be hearsay, a rumor. Those were the good old days indeed: antiquity or no antiquity. And even that rumored writing would be limited to two languages: Greek and Latin. If you were he, if you were a Roman emperor, would you in the evening, to take your mind off your cares, read a Latin author if you had a choice? Even if he was Horace? No; too close for comfort. You'd pick up a Greek — because that's what you'll never be. Because a Greek, especially a philosopher, is in your eyes a more genuine item than yourself, since he knew no Latin. If only because of that he was less a relativist than you, who consider yourself practically a mongrel. So if he were a Stoic, you must take heed. You even may go so far as to take up a stylus yourself. Otherwise you might not fit into someone's notion of antiquity.

XX

A stray Dalmatian trotting behind the bronze horseman hears something strange, sounding somewhat familiar but muffled by rain. He accelerates slightly and having overtaken the statue lifts up his muzzle, hoping to grasp what's coming out of the horseman's mouth. In theory it should be easy for him, since his Dalmatia was the birthplace of so many caesars. He recognizes the language but fails to make out the accent:

Take heed not to be transformed into Caesar, not to be dipped in purple dye; for it does happen. Keep yourself therefore simple, go pure, grave, unaffected, the friend of justice, religious, kind, affectionate, strong for your proper work. Wrestle to continue to be the man that Philosophy wished to make you. Reverence the gods, save men . . .

Let not the future trouble you; for you will come to it, if come you must, bearing with you the same reason which you are using now to meet the present.

All things are the same: familiar in experience, transient in time, sordid in their material; all now such as in the days of those whom we have buried.

To leave the company of men is nothing to fear, if gods exist; for they would not involve you in ill . . .

To turn against anything that comes to pass is a separation from nature.

Men have come into the world for the sake of one another. Either instruct them then or bear with them.

The Universe is change, life is opinion.

Run always the short road, and nature's road is short.

As are your repeated imaginations so will your mind be, for the soul is dyed by its imaginations.

Love that to which you go back, and don't return to Philosophy as to a schoolmaster, but as a man to the sponge and slave, as another to a poultice, another to fomentation . . .

The noblest kind of retribution is not to become like your enemy.

The mind of the Whole is social.

What doesn't benefit the hive is no benefit to the bee.

On Pain: what we cannot bear removes us from life; what lasts can be borne. The understanding, too, preserves its own tranquility by abstraction, and the governing self does not grow worse; but it is for the parts which are injured by pain, if they can, to declare it.

There are three relations. One is to what surrounds you. One to the divine cause from which all things come to pass for all. One to those who live at the same time with you.

Accept without pride, relinquish without struggle.

And then there was nothing else, save the sound of rain crashing on Michelangelo's flagstones. The Dalmatian darted across the

JOEL AGEE

Eros at Sea

FROM HARPER'S MAGAZINE

THE YEAR WAS 1962; the city, New York. I was fleeing from the
protracted aftermath of a love affair that had run afoul of a false
pregnancy or a miscarriage or a chemically induced abortion, I
was never able to determine which, but in any case an unhappy
mess for the girl, and painful for me too, since her mother's grief
had elicited what all the inveiglements of her father confessor
hadn't: penitence and a sincere vow of chastity. No crueler joke
could be imagined, because for half a year of almost daily after-
school trysts and occasional getaways to cheap hotels, we had spent
more time in bed than she would kneel at confession for the rest
of her life, I was sure of that. And now all of a sudden she was
telling me in maddeningly "reasonable" tones that it was really best
if we parted, at least for a while, and that she would feel that way
even if nothing had happened — life couldn't just consist of sex,
sex, sex, and besides, I was just too oppressively jealous. And as if
that wasn't enough, she told me her cousin Vince in Albany was
threatening to take me to court: she was a minor, I an adult. Talk
about blind justice.

I went to the Scandinavian Shipping Office on West Forty-second
Street with the plan of putting an ocean between us. But first I
would make love to her one more time. I climbed the fire escape
outside her window, knocked, was let in. She still loved me, she
said, but she wouldn't make love, not until she was at least sixteen,
it would hurt her mother too much. I tried to seduce her. She did
not melt. I whispered my latest suspicion at her: that her mother's
new tenant, that music student who had moved into the upstairs

bedroom, was screwing her, wasn't he, and all this pregnancy stuff was a put-on, just to get rid of me. I think we both knew that I believed only a fraction of what I was saying, but I could not allow such a banal, no, such a mature interloper as common sense to take her away from me, it was too humiliating. This drama had to be played out by the rules of passion. She denied my allegations, I returned to the window. She got out of bed, her face wet with tears, to prevent me from leaving in anger. She had only a T-shirt on. As a sign of her new chastity, she pulled the hem down with one hand while with the other she reached out imploringly: "Stay!" Then the sound of steps in the hallway — her mother? the tenant? her mother! — propelled me down the fire escape. A few days later, I boarded the *Seven Seas,* a Swedish merchant ship bound for Australia, taking with me the memory of Sylvia — that was her name — in that final, ambiguous, ravishing pose.

I can imagine my reader wondering, Who was this nymph, this Lolita, how did she wreak such a spell, what fifteen-year-old girl could drive a man across the oceans and half to distraction? The question is natural, but it misses the mark. I'd met Sylvia when I was twenty, an immigrant, fresh off the boat in an ill-fitting East German suit, a virgin in every sense but the physical (thanks to a hasty transaction with a Mexican whore), and just beginning to ache my way through that awful spiritual dislocation for which "culture shock" would be the right term if it wasn't commonly used to refer to the discomfort of tourists. Once, many years later, I saw five wild-eyed Chinese peasants, men and women, standing terrified plumb in the midst of the New York rush-hour inferno. They clung to the vertical bar of the lurching and screeching subway car with stiff arms like spokes of a hurtling wheel just barely cohering around its hub, and they all had the look of children exposed to a frightening movie and trying not to scream. They couldn't have looked more stunned if a magician had whisked them over here straight from their rice field. The sight of them moved me, and that sympathy, I realized with surprise, came from memory. Berlin is less far from New York than wherever their rural commune had been, so my condition in 1960, fresh off the boat in my ill-fitting East German suit, was different from theirs, but different only in degree. Let's say I was profoundly anxious, not panicked, and carefully masked. Now imagine a tall, clear-skinned, fair-haired girl with a sweet, solemn face stepping into that aching void. She is only fourteen years old, but she looks like one of Botticelli's heralds of spring come to life, and there is a depth in her eyes into which I begin to fall the moment I see her. A beauty, you say, but beauty explains nothing. What spoke to me from that depth was the void itself, but it was ensouled now, it no longer threatened, it had become a well of pure invitation and endless longing. The hellish difficulty in loving her was that she was too young to have any sure sense of what it was that made her so wrenchingly beautiful to me. If I gazed into her eyes long enough, I could reflect it back to her. Invariably she was frightened and turned away. She tried to describe the feeling — a kind of vertigo. What is vertigo but a foretaste of falling? Sometimes the same fear welled up in her when we listened to certain pieces of music together. But there was one plane on which we met without any barrier and on equal terms, and that was her bed. There we invented each other. She was a natural actress. Her sensuality was of the imagination as much as of the body: "Let's be other people!" Her favorite situation was a couple meeting in some forbidden zone of exquisite guilt and enticement. Then, when passion took over and we were ourselves again, it was like meeting anew. *Those* depths she swam with all the assurance of genius. It was my love that bewildered her, because what I loved in her was asleep and protected by fear. And I was always luring her to that edge, I wanted her to take the irretrievable step. She took refuge in brief occasional flings with boys closer to her age, entirely appropriate under normal circumstances, but our circumstances were not normal. She was fifteen and the mistress of a twenty-one-year-old man who had the sixth sense of jealousy, which needs but a hint to set the wheels of torment rolling. And I had more than hints. She was perverse or careless enough to leave evidence in places where I would find it. That is how possessing and repossessing her became the obsession of my days, and why, after losing her, I was pursued by her memory for so long.

Shortly before the *Seven Seas* reached Panama, the third mate, who spoke excellent English, watched me attempting to tidy up the officers' dining room and remarked that I was taking my job title, "messboy," rather literally. He had a point. The officers were enti-

tled to service at mealtimes, and I was feeding them annoyance.
Not a day passed when one of them didn't have to complain that
there was no salt in the shaker, or that the beer I had brought him
was not the one he had ordered. "Ziss horse piss, not beer!"
Halfway across the Pacific, they decided to fire me as soon as we
reached Australia. The chief steward gave me their ultimatum.
"You have one chance," he said. What was that? "No more mistakes." By the slant of his smile and the lift of his eyebrow I saw
that he considered such a feat possible, though not likely. I tried.
God knows I tried! At mealtimes, I observed in the eyes of my
judges two opposing expressions: one a distinctly malevolent, scowl-
ing look, as if waiting for the oversight that would release the catch
on the guillotine; the other, a surprised and gratified look of
pleasure at my unusual efficiency. Then the radio officer's wife
(she had been hired to do the ship's laundry) told me that they
were betting on me, a wager like Satan's with God over Job, to see
if this servant was capable of perfection. I wanted badly to show
them the measure of my contempt, some big gesture, like dumping
the mashed potatoes on the tablecloth, but what good would that
do me? On the other hand, what if they really did fire me? How
would I get home without money? What would I do for work? Cut
brush in the outback? Hunt kangaroos?

The day before we dropped anchor in Adelaide, the *Seven Seas*
was adorned with flags to celebrate the first anniversary of her
launching. The crew ate cardamom-flavored limpa bread, which
was ordinarily served to the officers, and the officers ate cake. The
crew consumed hundreds of gallons of beer, the officers drank
champagne. After lunch, a short, stern, bearded man in a white
uniform with a white visored cap and white gloves came into the
pantry, accompanied by the chief steward, who introduced us in
English: "Captain, this is the officers' messboy. Kalle" — this is the
name, meaning "Charlie," messboys are given on Swedish ships —
"that is the captain." I was ready; the chief steward had forewarned
me. No doubt he was betting on my success. On his prompting, I
had washed each fork, knife, and spoon three times over, checked
the sink for suds and the glasses for thumbprints, the tile floor was
a mirror, I had even scrubbed the outside of the porthole, which
wasn't my job. But the captain did not even glance at this splendor.
He strode through the pantry and stopped in front of the swinging

door to the dining room. Was it clean? Yes, it was. He reached up to the top of the lintel, a surface I had never taken into consideration, stroked it lightly with one white-gloved finger, and showed me: dirt . . . swung open the door, and walked on. The chief steward gulped audibly. I went off to my cabin to pack my duffel bag.

That night a movie was shown outside, on the main deck. For about an hour, it dispelled my worries about what would become of me. The moon was full, the sea was calm. Because of the long distance between the officers' lounge, where the projector was set up, and the crew's cabins, where the screen was suspended, the image was immense. Was the ship's motor turned off? It seems unlikely, but as I remember it, we floated in a wonderful stillness. Every soul on the ship was assembled, from the oilers and deck-hands on up to the officers and the captain — not to forget the radio officer's French wife, Marianne, the only woman on board, whose presence no doubt influenced the choice of films we were shown. After a countdown of squarish numbers ticking down from nine to nothing, the screen lit up with a black-and-white view of a bedroom furnished in the style of the early fifties: next to the bed was a kidney-shaped night table, and above a dresser, in the center of the screen, a mirror framed with pale neon tubes. The door opened, a woman came in, turned around, forbade entry to an obscure male escort in suit and tie, granted him a kiss, closed the door, locked it, put her pocketbook on the dresser, opened a closet, took off her coat, put the coat on a hanger, and proceeded, rather primly, to undress. A few catcalls and whistles rang out, but soon the crew fell silent, as if stunned. Not by any wanton display of sexuality — on the contrary, she was almost ideally proper. No captain would find any dust in her room. The whole purpose of her performance, it seemed, was to document the thrill of knowing herself to be perfectly neat while believing herself to be safely alone. The camera, aroused by the sight of her naked arms and thighs, began a slow zoom, as if wanting to smell her. Unperturbed, she took off her brassiere, pulled off her stockings, stepped out of her underpants, folding each garment and putting it where it belonged. Then she slipped into a flowered nightgown, pulled back the blanket, lay down, covered herself, switched off her bed-side lamp, and, still visible to the camera, emitted a soundless, smiling sigh, and fell asleep. Another succession of numbers, and another woman took off her clothes, this time in a bathing hut by the beach. She, too, was neat. She put on an old-fashioned bathing suit, cupped her breasts in her hands to improve the fit, and scampered out for a swim. The most elaborate and mystifying performance was the third and last one. It began with a woman taking a shower with her hair gathered up in a plastic cap. She soaped herself with great thoroughness and no evident pleasure. Then she toweled herself off, went into her bedroom, took off the plastic cap, and, still naked, brushed her blond hair in front of a mirror, made the bed (which showed off her behind to advantage), got dressed, put on lipstick, strapped a pocketbook over her arm, and left, no doubt on her way to work as a secretary.

The next morning, we docked in Adelaide. Some artist or prankster had painted an enormous white question mark on the mountain that loomed over the shabby little port. It was so large that there probably wasn't a house in the town that didn't have a view of some part of it from at least one of its windows. How dubious could a man feel in a place that conducted its business under such a sign? I almost looked forward to getting fired here. But fate intervened in the person of the radio officer's wife. She pleaded with the captain on my behalf, and he relented. She repeated to me, word for word, what she had said to him, wringing her hands, all but kneeling before him, in her heavy French accent: "*Pleez* don't geev'eem *ze keeck!* He eez a *boy* steel! What *weel* 'eez meuzer *say!*"

Slowly we worked our way through some ten or twelve Australian harbors and slowly wended our way back. The sailors spent all their free time with the sluttish whores who waited for us in the pubs. I wasn't interested. Three weeks earlier, in Panama, in my first effort to forget Sylvia, I had briefly lain on a filthy cot with a young girl whose breasts reminded me of bruised fruit. I felt only pity for her, and the wish to know that she was loved by some boy or young man, not me. Then, instead of leaving her or else taking her as befitted our contract — a dollar slipped into her mother's palm outside the hot clapboard room where we lay under a tin roof — I kissed her, and in that kiss showed her the passion that I felt for Sylvia and no one else, and realized only then, by the startled hurt in her eyes, what a violation that was. I didn't want to repeat that scene or vary it in any way. In Sydney, I stayed away from the brothels whose praises I had been hearing ever since we left New York, and went to the history museum instead. But then a devouring sexual hunger took possession of me. At the poste restante in Brisbane, I had found letters from my mother, my brother, some friends — none from Sylvia. I hadn't written her, either. Her silence was crushing nonetheless. I had to forget her. Discard her, annul her. Dispel her memory with every thrust into whatever soft willing body would offer itself, the more faceless and nameless the better. Oh, I could hardly wait!

But the whores of Brisbane were monuments of unpleasure. Each one had a porch for a pedestal. There, if they were not occupied, they sat in the white-hard glare of a naked bulb, staring, exhausted and brutal, through a square window, showing us what we had come for — limbs, lips, nipples, locks — and, one of them, her gaping cunt like a vertical sneer between fat, blue-veined thighs. Eight men stood in a queue in front of a shack with a curtain drawn over the window, shifting from foot to foot. My crewmates joined the queue. This was the only bitch worth fucking here, they said. They knew her, Marjorie was her name. The man at the front of the line kicked the door several times and threatened to break the teeth, whether of Marjorie or of a client who was taking his time with her I couldn't tell, but presently Marjorie threw open the door, a tall blond woman in a blue bathrobe, and started haranguing "the whole fookin' lot" of us in a voice and with words that shriveled every remnant of desire I had left in me.

My abstinence — then and at future ports — earned me a reputation as an odd, possibly queer bird. My cabinmate was an effeminate homosexual boy from a neighborhood in Brooklyn called Bay Ridge ("Gay Ridge," he called it) who had moved in with me because he could no longer abide the manners of his alcoholic bunk neighbor. We liked each other. This gave rise to rumors about us. And I had other unmanly foibles. I didn't drink like an able-bodied seaman, just a couple of slugs from a bottle now and then, never to the point of stupor. In an argument over a gambling debt, I had absorbed an insult a normal sailor would have answered with blows. Out at sea, on the way to Jamaica, I could be seen on deck in my leisure hours reading a fat book and growing a beard.

But I knew how to compensate. I had an ability that has always been prized by men at sea: I could tell stories. I told war stories and ghost stories, I retold novels by Jack London and episodes from Prescott's *The Conquest of Mexico*. William Beebe's deep-sea exploits in the "bathysphere" were especially popular. These sessions usually took place on deck, at night, with the kitchen staff and a couple of seamen, or, if the weather was bad, with a larger crowd in the crew's messroom, over beer and crackers.

One night the cook asked me in an "out with it" sort of tone whether I really did have a woman waiting for me in New York, as I had claimed. I produced Sylvia's picture for proof, and added a fictitious story about how I had seduced her (it was the other way around), and a true one about a manual for hypnotists that had proved marvelously effective in heightening Sylvia's already more than adequate sexual response. Of this ability my audience demanded an immediate demonstration: could I hypnotize the cook? He was the biggest man on board. I could not refuse this challenge without irreversible loss of face. After about forty minutes I had the cook, all three hundred pounds of him, balancing on one foot and then on the other, and swinging his arms, convinced he was skating on a lake in Uppsala. I gave him the posthypnotic command that he serve me a glass of the captain's wine — which he did, after a bewildered descent to the storage room. That won me the day and regained me my crewmates' acceptance. There was only one thing I wanted more: oblivion in sex or love, an end to the memory of Sylvia, which, far from fading, had rooted itself in the center of my chest as a dull, churning ache.

There was another "Kalle" on the ship, the crew's messboy, a good-natured, wide-hipped Dane who was always grinning as if in memory or anticipation of a joke. Whenever he talked about Kingston, he would wrap his arms around an invisible woman and set his pelvis swinging: "The best! Better than Rio!" Then he would raise a finger and clap a hand over his back pocket: "But careful! Everybody steals in Kingston!"

The whores of Kingston were many in number, and many were pretty, and some even seemed to enjoy their profession. Was this a foretaste of hell? The more tempting a smile or glance or touch, the more savory the sight of a pair of long legs or the swell of a nipple hardening between my fingers, the more sharply Sylvia rose up in revolt against any substitution. I knew what would happen if I went to bed with any of these women: nothing at all, and the crew would hear of it. O thirst of Tantalus! I drank enough rum to drown a whale, but Sylvia, Sylvia just danced in that sea like a buoy, with me clinging to her. What was wrong with me? Was I impotent? How could I murder her in my heart? I walked. I must have walked for miles, turning corners at random, getting lost, coming back to familiar places again, the pain in my chest so deep and wide there were moments when it made me gasp.

The next morning, a crew of dockworkers came aboard. The chief steward told me I could feed them leftovers. One glance at the faces crowding the open pantry window and I could see why. These men were hungry. They pointed at their mouths and held up metal and clay bowls. One of them handed me a tin can. I hesitated. The food was too good to be turned into slop. "Put it in, mahn, put it in," he said. He insisted I give him a little of everything: meat, vegetables, eggs, bread, butter, potatoes, cheese, sausage, gravy, and milk, up to the top. The men had their own spoons. When my supplies ran out, the crew's messboy gave from his.

After washing the dishes, I went to my cabin and found an old man in rags — old by the standards of a twenty-one-year-old: he was probably in his fifties — standing next to my cot with a bundle of outdated magazines he wanted to sell me. I cast a glance around to see if he had stolen anything. He read my suspicion. From a blue zippered pocket sewn onto his dirty white shirt, he drew a plastic folder containing a stained piece of paper bearing the stamp of a Kingston police precinct, a typewritten attestation of his moral probity, a signature, and his photograph affixed with two staples. To get rid of him, I offered to buy his magazines.

"How much?"

"Notting."

"You're not selling them?"

"No, mahn, you can tekkem."

He was hurt. What could I do? I thanked him for the gift and held open the door for him. But he didn't leave. He asked me if I had any currency I needed to change, he would like to take it to the bank for me. Looking into his eyes, I believed him. In view of his rags, the hungry men I had fed, the crew's messboy's warnings about thieves in Jamaica, I didn't trust him one bit. But I was already taking out my wallet, what did it matter, and made a perfunctory count of the bills, and handed them to him. Better to lose my money than insult him.

"Can you change these into dollars?" I asked.

"Yes, sir, tank you, sir," he said, a little hastily, and left, taking the magazines with him. Ten minutes later he knocked on my door.

"Please, sir, if I can leave de magazine? It's raining, I doan wan dem to get wet-up."

Later I learned that the old man had gone from cabin to cabin offering his banking service and using my trust as a reference, telling everyone I had given him forty dollars' worth of Swedish, Australian, and Panamanian bills. No one thought highly of this transaction. Down the drain went my slim account in that precious currency, respect. I was the joke of the ship.

That evening I made the rounds of the harbor again, with my collar turned up against a steady drizzle. Then the sky turned an eerie dark orange shading into purple, a wind started sweeping boxes and baskets about, the clouds cracked open, and the city stood plunged in a thunderous lashing downpour. I hunched my shoulders and tried to skip out of the way of an ankle-deep river of garbage coming my way, and stopped at the sight of a skinny old woman who stood laughing out loud at the sight of me.

"What's so funny?"

"White mahn afraid of de rain!"

And off she went again, howling with laughter and clapping her long hands together. Strangely, it wasn't unpleasant, maybe because there was no malice in it. She just found me very, very funny.

I invited her to come drinking with me. She was from Haiti, she said. I could hear it in her accent, but the melody of her speech was Jamaican. She told me the stories of the harbor — the police raids, the murders: "Lahst week one Feeneesh mahn keel Jamaica girl!" I can still see the cook stooping to look down at us on his way upstairs with one girl straddling him piggyback and another one pushing his enormous rump as if rolling a rock up a hill. He shakes his head in dismay.

The old woman was teaching me how to drum with my hands on the table, or, rather, trying to prove that white men have no rhythm.

Da-doom-da, da-doom.

I repeated it.

"No, no. Not like dis. Like dis!"

"Kalle, Kalle," the cook said, and moved on with his girls. The boy from Bay Ridge was asleep on my left, his arms folded into a pillow on the counter. Other men, other girls descended the steps. Smiles of satiety, gestures of amorous languor.

Da-doom-da, da-doom.

This was getting tedious. I rose to my feet and offered her a dollar. She didn't take it.

"Don't go by self," she said. "Many mahn fight you, cut you, steal you. Come, sit down, I teach you."

And she repeated her beat, which was so simple any child could perform it. Was she taking me for a fool? I sat down and looked into her eyes.

"Do it," she said.

I just kept looking into her eyes. She stared back. Her look was hard at first, then it softened. Her irises were the color of pooled oil, very deep and dark and flecked with small spots of gold. It is an adventure to sit silently face to face with a stranger, and one of the most direct ways I know to persuade oneself of the possibility that there is no such thing as an individual, that each of us is a multitude. My drinking companion's skin, for example, was very dark, but there was a moment when I saw peering through her the features of a ruddy-cheeked white man with twinkling blue eyes. Was this illusion or vision? She, too, seemed startled at moments by what she saw. A couple of times she laughed. After a while, a tear rolled down one of her cheeks. I reached out to dry her face with my hand. She tilted her head, cradling her cheek in my palm, and closed her eyes. We sat like that until my arm got tired. Then I held her hand for a while. She was falling asleep. Several members of the *Seven Seas* crew sat staring at us in complete disbelief. I woke up my cabinmate, said goodnight to my friend, and left.

The next morning, I saw an adolescent boy in tight shorts leave the chief steward's cabin and walk down the gangplank with downcast eyes. Not only I saw him, half the crew did. To this day I don't understand why the chief steward was allowed to live down this incident — a few grinning remarks, and it was forgotten — while I had to endure repeated recitals of what had been perceived as my romance with a hag.

After lunch, the old man's face appeared in the pantry window. He had come back to report to me about my money. The banks did not trust him, he said, despite his police affidavit; the guards

wouldn't even let him near the counter. Would I please write a
note saying that he was my messenger and that I needed his
services? I was touched and repentant for ever having doubted
him. I wrote the note and felt vindicated before the crew. I would
show them my dollars when he came back. And tonight I would
follow the cook's example. No more uptight white man! So many
women! So many styles of allure! I thought of one girl in particular
who had hitched up her dress with an innocent lewdness that
made my heart skip. Why didn't I go for her?

I actually met her again in the evening. She rubbed up against
me: "Mek love to Jamaica girl?" But when I looked into her eyes,
I saw only exhaustion and want. Pity is not an aphrodisiac, and
neither is charity. I drank more liquor than I could hold that night.
Some large men threw me out of their bar for vomiting on the
jukebox. The next thing I remember is finding myself in a fight
with a stocky blond man while my cabinmate screams for help. The
man curses me in a language I don't understand. He punches me
in the chest, I punch the air and fall backward into a puddle, life
is a dream, I am on my feet again, his blows are connecting better
than mine, a swarm of screaming girls surrounds us, they are
pulling at him, "Stop! Stop!," he is flashing a knife — is this possible? is this me? — I am elated, I am amazed, again I fall, something
tells me to accept defeat, I am laughing, I love the world.

I have no memory of how I got home, but my cabinmate told
me what happened. I must have passed out in the ditch. My enemy
walked away with his wrath appeased. Five girls escorted us back
to the ship. I told one of them that I could imagine falling in love
with her. She took down my address.

I overslept the next morning. The chief steward was furious
because, not for the first time, he had to do part of my job. He
needled me about my famous bank messenger. "And where is the
man with your money, Kalle? Are you still hoping?" I was. We were
scheduled to cast off at three-thirty.

At twelve the old man came to tell me the banks had refused to
deal with him even after he brought them my letter. He handed
me my money in a plastic envelope.

"I'm sorry, captain," he said. "Please to tek my apology."

"*I'm* sorry," I said. "You went to so much trouble. Let me pay you
for that."

"No, no!" He held up his hands.

"Please," I said. "You'll make me feel bad."

"I never do notting fe you, so I cahnt tek ye money."

"At least let me pay you for your magazines."

"No no, sir. Are fe you, magazine, I give dem to you." So he hadn't forgotten that.

"But you need the money."

He smiled. "Maybe I do something fe you den. I will buy you a good-good souvenir."

"Like what?"

"You will see. A beauty-full thing. Fe to remember Jamaica."

"How much does it cost?"

He rolled his eyes, calculating: "Twenty dollar?" All my suspicions came back.

"You don't mean to say, sir, you still doan trust me?"

"Oh yes, yes, I do. But twenty dollars is a lot of money."

"It could be less. I doan remember."

"But there's no time. We're leaving very soon."

"Don't worry, sir. I will come back. You trust me now. What I will bring fe you is a beauty-full thing. Fe to give to you' modder, you' sweetheart."

I gave him a twenty-dollar bill.

The worst part of this interaction was that it took place in front of the chief steward, who would not fail to pass it on to the kitchen staff. I gave myself the philosophical consolation that if this was a scam, it was almost a work of art and deserved a reward.

After lunch, I fed the dockworkers, as usual, through the port-hole window, and went on with my cleaning. The cook and the crew's messboy stuck in their heads: "Did your man come yet?" Grin, grin.

"He'll be back," I said, with feigned confidence.

"Kalle, Kalle."

At two-thirty, the chief steward told me to move several hundred pounds of onions from one storage room to another. It was not my job and this was my lunch hour, but I was in no position to object. When I came back up, tired and sweaty, I found my cabin-mate reading on his bunk.

"Have you seen him?"

He shook his head. I had the impression that he pitied me.

"No one's betting on this one," he said.

I lay down on my cot. I was exhausted, but I kept myself awake reading the old man's magazines until three-thirty. Then I fell asleep. A knock on the door woke me up.

"Come in."

It was my man, out of breath, holding in his hand a many-colored glistening object.

"Please, sir, I'm sorry I'm late. But here is de souvenir."

"It's beautiful," I said.

It was perfectly hideous, a pink porcelain conch shell drooling what looked like porcelain water and doubling as a paradise island covered with porcelain fern and porcelain palms, a green porcelain dinosaur, and a miniature pink naked porcelain couple. But I was happy, very happy, that he had come back. Just in time, too. I could hear the clangor of steel plates dropped into place as the hold was being closed on the main deck.

"It was only eleven dollar," he said, handing me the change, "on account of I bargain de mahn down."

"Thank you," I said, "thank you very much. And now let me pay you for all your efforts."

"No, please, I doan want no money," he said, "but if you have a shirt or a trousers that maybe you doan want, I *will* take dat."

I gave him most of my clothes — pants, shirts, underwear, socks, a windbreaker, a pair of sneakers, a pair of shoes, a couple of sweaters. My cabinmate added two T-shirts. We wrapped all these things into a sheet. I would pay for it if the chief steward objected. Let him see it. Let the crew see it. The old man wished me a happy homecoming and left with the bundle slung over his shoulder. I took a shower, changed, and went outside to watch the harbor receding as the ship went out to sea. It would be a while yet. The dockworkers were still on board, waiting for the third mate to approve some papers their foreman had handed him. Some of the men I had fed earlier smiled at me. One of them was wearing my City College T-shirt. Another one had on my paint-spattered jeans. A third one was wearing my sneakers. Another one my shoes. My red socks. My blue sweater. My windbreaker. He had given away all my clothes.

The next day, during my afternoon break, I was leaning on the railing by the bow with the wind in my ears, watching a school of dolphins tumbling alongside the ship, when an impulse came to me, a whim really, but with the weight of a decision confirmed and long past any doubting. I took my wallet from my back pocket and pulled the picture of Sylvia out of its plastic sheath and put the wallet back in my pocket and looked at her for a while. I tried to send her my love. This good resolve met with resistance. I wished her one moment of horrible remorse on my account and a reasonably happy life thereafter. That was more like it. Then I opened my fingers and watched the picture flutter away and spiral down into the sea.

HAROLD BRODKEY

Dying: An Update

FROM THE NEW YORKER

THE AMBULANCE PEOPLE came, and I whispered to them that I could not walk or sit up. Or breathe. They went down for a gurney and for oxygen. Breathing through a tube in my nose and motionless and sheeted on a gurney, I was wheeled through our apartment and into the elevator and across the lobby, past the doorman, onto the sidewalk, into the air briefly, and then into the ambulance. This is how my life ended. And my dying began.

Ellen says I was heroic and completely in charge, and that I surprised her by agreeing *agreeably* to being treated for pneumocystis rather than asking for sedation and being allowed to die. She says she thought then that we would die together, both of us — commit suicide simultaneously — in a few months, when everything was in order. But she didn't want me to leave her now, not this abruptly. Most of us who know Ellen know her as a fine-boned tyrant who looks a bit like a small Garbo. Her hair is gray, and she has never had a face-lift. She is of interest physically still — neatly formed and stylized, like the stopper of an expensive perfume bottle. She is incredibly willful, and she is my human credential. People think she is good-looking and trustworthy and sensible, whatever they think of me. It seems clear from how Barry — my doctor, Barry Hartman — and the harried nurses acted that they saw her that way. They all trusted her judgment and her will, not mine. I remember wanting not to be an exploitative fool in her eyes by asking her to nurse me through a terminal disease, and one with a sexual stigma. I wondered if she would despise me. I knew a woman once who'd had a good marriage, unmistakably so, within limits, and whose husband, a clever banker, fell ill and impressed everyone with how hard he fought to be himself again, to get well again. That woman once said in my hearing, "I wish he would give up." His struggle went on so long, and so dominated everything, that it was killing her. And he was hardly alive except as a will to struggle.

At home, over the weekend, I had got so sick that I could not find a balance point in the gusts of horrendous sensation. It was strange how the sickness kept getting worse by the hour, with a kind of muffled rapidity. I'd never been ill that way. Again and again, it thudded to a level of horrendousness, consolidated that, and then thuddingly sank to a worse level still. Nothing was stopping the progress of strangulation. I had kept putting on a front for Ellen until, in a kind of extreme inward silence, nothing was working.

But when Barry said I had AIDS, I said I didn't believe him. He said, "Believe me." Then Ellen said something, asked him something about what was going to happen, and he said that after the pneumocystis cleared up I had the possibility of a few years of life.

I said, "But it will be embarrassing." The stigma. Incontinence. (Would I have to wear a diaper?) Blindness. He said the good years were quite good, were livable.

I don't want to be defensively middle-class about this, but it was a middle-class decision I made, nothing glorious, to try to go ahead and have AIDS, live with AIDS for a while, and not die with the pneumocystis then.

Ellen says that when we were first told, on a Monday, she sat in the one chair in the hospital room. To prove that she is actually remembering in the Brodkey mode, according to Brodkey theories and method, she says that Barry leaned against the windowsill with his arms folded while he told us I had AIDS. And that the weather was warm. And that I was strangely jovial and reasonable. I remember Barry propping himself with one arm on the sill and then refolding his arms and saying, "You *have* AIDS," and holding his pose and staring at me.

In the confused, muddied velocities of my mind was an editorial sense that this was wrong, that this was an ill-judged element in the story of my life. I felt too conceited to have this death. I was illogical, fevered, but my mind still moved as if it were a rational mind — the mind, everyone's mind, is forever unstill, is a continu-

ous restlessness like light, even in sleep, when the light is inside
and not outside the skull. I took inside me the first stirrings of
acknowledgment of AIDS, not with the arching consciousness with
which I try to write fiction — I didn't feel that isolation — but with
a different sense of aloneness. And maybe I felt the wretchedness
in Ellen. Maybe I was sensitive to what I had, so to speak, done to
her now.

And then I saw it differently: after all, death — and AIDS — are
a commonplace. "Big deal," I said. That didn't lighten anyone's
face. "Jesus Christ," I said. "What a mess." Barry said something
about tranquilizers and counseling to help with the shock and
despair, the natural grief. "I'm O.K.," I said and went on grandly,
"Look, it's only death. It's not like losing your hair or all your
money. I don't have to live with this."

I wanted to make them laugh. I wanted them to admire me, it's
true, but I also wanted Ellen to stop that inward shaking, and I was
afraid to say, "Christ, what have I done?" or "Look what's happened
to me" or "It's all my fault." I have an odd cowardice toward grief.
I would just as soon suffer without it. The two of them were
watching me, ready to sympathize and comfort. Ellen turned to
Barry, who was disapproving. Or worried. "We can help when the
despair hits; we have drugs," he told her.

But, you see, a traumatized child as I was once, long ago, and
one who recovers, as I did, has a wall between him and pain and
despair, between himself and grief, between himself and beshitting
himself. That's the measure for me — handling the whole weight
of my life in relation to polite bowels. The rest is madness, rage,
humiliation.

To be honest, the effort of writing, and then my age, and the
oppressive suffocation of the illness itself, and my sad conviction
of the *important* validity of my ideas (of what my work presents),
and my hapless defense of that work, had so tired me that I was
relieved by the thought of death. But I also wanted to make a
defiant gesture at AIDS. So it became a matter of contrary style.
The disease and its coercions (like all coercions) were contemptible. I figured that later on I would make meek friends with it while
it killed me, but not just yet.

And I felt that if I had AIDS Ellen had the right, perhaps the duty, to leave me; my having that disease suspended all contracts and emotions — it was beyond sacrament and marriage. It represented a new state, in which, in a sense, we did not exist. What we were had been dissolved as if by radiation or the action of an acid. Perhaps the *sacrament* remained, but it was between her and her beliefs now: care wasn't, in my view, owed to me anymore. I wasn't me, for one thing. And she had suffered enough.

I am peculiarly suited to catastrophe, because of my notions and beliefs; I am accustomed to reconstituting myself in the middle of catastrophe. And my ideas, my language, support me in the face of disastrous horror over and over. I am like a cockroach, perhaps — with AIDS, with vanity, with a cowardice much greater than that of Kafka's Samsa. Ellen is not like that. She has an identity, of the real, familied sort. A good many people, including me, care about her. Her children are never alone in the world, and that sometimes irks them. She is gullible toward bad news in a rebelliously saintly way that tends to irritate me. Her rebelliousness extends throughout her existence — it is toward God and death, toward society, toward men. How she reconciles that with the propriety she manifests day in and day out is beyond me. I tell her that we are cowards and artists and are in flight and are and have to be awful people to get our work done. She ignores me when I talk about art or life that way. She does and does not believe what I say or what I believe. "I cannot live like that" is what she says. I mean, I can see, often, the degree of *enlistment* in her being with me.

I have a number of kinds of humility, but I am arrogant. I am semifamous, and I see what I see. I examine everything that is put in front of me — like a jeweler. I am a Jew from the Middle West, not at all like a New York Jew. I am so arrogant that I believe a formulation only if it has the smell or lift of inspiration. I have never, since childhood, really expected to be comforted.

In the twentieth century, the arts have not pictured the reality of actual sex and actual love as they are in life, on actual days, over actual time — they are seen as, oh, socialist bliss, or as paradise before the nightmare strikes, or as nonexistent (Joyce and Beckett, the sexual yet sexless Irishmen), or as obsession and victimization (Freud and Proust), or as some idyll of heat and whatnot. Hemingway was dominated by sexual terror, but how popular he was.

For me, the greatest portrayer of high-art sexlessness was Balanchine, because he captured and beautified so physically the rage and longing and the attempts to escape loneliness. And then there is the sexlessness of Eliot — one should remember that Lawrence was driven out of England while dry Eliot came to be idolized. And perhaps rightly. Love and sex, after all, are unwise: look at me. The foolish nature of sexual love is there in front of you, always. Civic duty, ambition, even personal freedom are opposed to it. We tend to think that popular art is sexual, and perhaps in a way it is — it does indicate that the act takes place, and you can see in it why the inclusion of sexuality and emotion in your life can lead to a horrific response. But it is not as sexual as Jon Vickers' singing, for instance. He caused embarrassment in American audiences as Sinatra never did. He caused embarrassment in the way Billie Holiday did, in nightclubs, from the sheer authenticity of the sexual-emotional event.

What happens in a competitive city, among people who are clever imitators, students, really (more or less sedulous apes), is that the paucity of such authenticity leads to the constant manufacture of what you might call a sore-nerved and sensitive counterfeit sex. Counterfeit sex is a large part of what New York is. People here rebel by means of a jealous promiscuity — a jealously restless sense of the happiness of others.

I will say peevishly that I was never accepted as gay by anyone, including someone who lived with me and claimed to be a lover. I did think that, for me, no decent relations were possible with women back then: the women were rotten with their self-expectation, their notions of femininity, their guilt. And I saw no male role I could play that was acceptable to me. Toward the end of my experience of homosexuality, before I met Ellen, I underwent the most outrageous banishment to a role of sheer, domineering, hated and worshipped masculinity. It was then that I was infected by one person I was interested in. He later left his lover and came to New York to die in my care and Ellen's.

AIDS had never been one of our fears; it was not one of my secret dreads. I am so shaken by what has occurred that I have lost much of the discipline about memory that I had before I was told I had AIDS. Ellen and I were in Berlin in November and December of 1992, and then we went on to Venice, and some people —

everyone, really — said I was too thin. Neither Ellen nor I responded when a blackish spot appeared on my right cheek. We thought it was my macrobiotic diet or the effort of not being overcome by literary politics and leftover sexual jealousies, even while my sexual nature died away, a kind of public modesty. I had written a novel in one year, a novel I liked, that I was proud of, and I had expected such a labor to kill me. During that year, I was slow-moving, easily tired, and subject to small bouts of giddiness. I was underexercised, too thin, and wobbly at times. And I was strained past my level of strength by the difference in reputation and treatment I received in various countries — great artist here, fool there, major writer, minor fake, villain, virtuoso, jerk, hero.

I think it was that the future had vanished for me, had become a soft, deadened wall. In the beginning, when Barry told me flat-out that I had AIDS, I didn't yet feel it, although I also saw that denial was futile. Barry was not even remotely real to me at that point. He was merely a conductor, a sort of lightning rod of medical error. I still didn't believe he was a good doctor — that came a short time later. The framework of the self wasn't changed by the words, the general feeling of its being my body and its having been my body all my life didn't dissolve, as it would in a few days. I had no sense of gestating my death.

Ellen says that she hung back and expected me to be violent, psychically, and to want death immediately once I accepted the diagnosis. Well, that was true. But I was also afraid of death, of my own final silence. And I was ashamed toward her, and angry at her. She does not steadily believe that I love her — it is one of her least endearing traits to expect proof at unreasonable intervals. And what is love? My measure of it is that I should have died to spare her. Her measure is for us to be together longer.

For the next two weeks, the world and all other issues were omitted. We were two people alone in a hospital room. We allowed no visitors, and the interns weren't interested in my case. (Barry explained that AIDS is medically boring now, and I did not have a recondite opportunistic infection, but the most common one.) Ellen and I had two weeks of near-silence with each other and my increasing helplessness. I tended to tangle the IV and misplace the oxygen tube.

As I started to say earlier, one of the first things that becomes distorted and then fades when you learn you're fatally ill is a sensible interest in the future. The moments become extraordinarily dimensionless — not without value but flat and a great deal emptier. Time becomes very confusing, perhaps uninteresting, pedestrian. But my not caring if I lived or died hurt Ellen. And I was grateful that I could indulge my cowardice toward death in terms of living for her.

She got back to the hospital after four horrible hours of night at home in our apartment alone, racked by waking nightmare. She arrived soon after it got light and had a bed for herself moved into my hospital room.

She said, in an averted way, "I want more time with you."

And I said, from within my flattened world, "You're nuts. It isn't that much fun to live. Now. And you know it." I sighed. "But if that's what you want . . ."

"I do," she said.

Optimism. Hopefulness. Our American fondness for advertising and our dependence on it culturally to represent not what works or is worth preserving but what is worth our working *for* — this, in lieu of tradition, is nervously life-giving, a form of freedom. It is also a madness of sorts, a dream-taunted avidity for the future to replace a sense of history.

But it is the basis of America — the forward-looking thing. We-will-create-a-nation, and we will have gardens and swimming pools and corrective surgery. Franklin Roosevelt's speeches — if you compare them with Churchill's, you can see what I'm talking about. You can see it in the rhythms and in the imagery and in the statements. Roosevelt proposed the four freedoms, and Churchill offered blood, toil, sweat, and tears. (Or compare Twain with Wodehouse. Or Groucho Marx with Waugh.) The American sense of tragedy is so diluted by daydream as to seem almost ridiculous. We Americans create symbols helter-skelter, as a form of advertising, an active unreality. Churchill had a quite distinct entity to govern, a well-defined nation to lead, one constituted by its history. America is defined by what it does next: Roosevelt, like Lincoln and Kennedy and others, had to define the United States for us over and over; otherwise it would not have been clear what this nation was that we were actively supporting.

Compare Churchill's cigar with Roosevelt's cigarette holder. Churchill's drinking was overt, but Roosevelt's wheelchair was almost never photographed. The Declaration of Independence and the Constitution and the Bill of Rights are strangely like ad texts, guarantees of the sort that you find in ads. And advertising is to nihilism and the threats of heaven and hell as matter is to antimatter. The foundations of middle-classness in America have nothing to do with social class in the European sense and everything to do with a Utopian attempt.

The American equivalent (which is hardly equivalent) of the landed gentry is a socially wobbly market of consumers who are rich and arrogant as all getout, easily intimidated yet not easily restrained. Here, because the culture is so unsteady (and so new), it is the how-to element that dominates — how to be *happy* or reasonably comfortable and in comfortable circumstances, how to deal with superior sorts of people who have status, who, say, enjoy opera. How to do this next, in the near, improved future. An American daydream, as in Twain (and Hemingway), is about rebuilding after the flood, about being better off than before, about outwitting this or that challenger, up to and including death.

Well, how do you manage to be optimistic *for the moment*? Without hope?

I inherit from my blood father and my blood mother and her father considerable physical strength. One time, when I was seven, I nearly died, because of an allergic reaction to an anesthetic, the ether derivatives then in use. (My mother, who died when I was two, returned in a hallucination, and I found it unbearable.) I went into convulsions, and according to the machines and measurements, I died: my heart stopped, my breathing stopped. Some young doctors and nurses and one old nurse saved me. I can remember their bustling labor, even the nervous smell coming off them. I had been more or less legitimately dead, but I managed to get up and walk partway across the hospital room that evening. My adoptive father called me Rasputin for a while: "Nothing can kill you."

Sick or well, all my life I've had enough strength for whatever I set out to do. But this time, no. That degree of strength was over. I knew how my parents had felt when their strength failed. It is extremely irritating. Certain melodramatic speeches do come to mind: "Kill me and get it over with." They both said that. I said it once or twice myself but with more irony. I would save my strength and then leap — biliously, worm-in-the-muddishly — into speech: "This goddamn hospital bed is so uncomfortable you might as well *kill me and get it over with.*"

I was aware mentally of the threat of death as a rather awful certainty of sensory fact, of physical fact, but only in words. I mean the mind looked on, weakly, and saw the state as a folkish joke, like a newspaper headline: "THREAT OF DEATH FOR HAROLD," or "HAROLD IS GOING TO GET IT THIS TIME," or "H. R. BRODKEY FINDS WHAT IT'S LIKE TO SUCK MUD." With a subheadline: "This Is Rotten, Says Ex-Amateur Athlete." Then the subheads: "The Statistics Look *Bad*," and "Killer-Diller Pneumonia Strikes *New Yorker* Writer."

My parents were ill for most of my childhood, and I was aware of the implacable dissimilarity between people and events in the active world and people and events in the grip of medical reality, the medicines scouring and wrecking, or surgical intervention doing that, or radiation. I was prepared for the loneliness and irritability or even madness of being a patient. I had experienced it already in my life, that time when I was seven years old, and again when I was thirty-one and had hepatitis and felt terrible, and the hepatitis was wrongly diagnosed as advanced liver cancer, and I was told I had only a few months to live.

But I experienced no outburst of emotion, no rage or grief of the sort Joe Brodkey, my adoptive father, had. I realized that I was suffocating, as my blood father, Max Weintrub, had — he suffered from something that was described to me as senile asthma: the asthma starved his heart, and his heart gave out. But he raged and cursed, as did my adoptive mother, Doris, who had cancer and told all those around her that *they were getting on her nerves.*

But, except for the suffocation, none of those things were happening to me. I felt very little of anything, I mean as comment. It was a relief to have the illness unmasked, to have Death be openly present. It was a relief to get away from the tease and rank of imputed greatness and from the denial and attacks and from my own sense of things, of worldly reality and of literary reality — all of it. In the last few years, mental and physical revulsion toward — oh, Lish, Mehta, and Lehmann-Haupt, Hilton Kramer, Barbara Epstein, and Bob Silvers — had grown to the point where hiding and containing it had been a bit like having tumors that cleared up whenever I was upstate in the wilds or in Europe. The inadequacies of the work they did and in the awful work they fostered, the alternate revulsion and pity they aroused, I had had enough of. It was truly a perceptible relief to be out of their reach and into another sort of experience, even if it was terminal. It was a relief to have the future not be my speculative responsibility anymore and to escape from games of superiority and inferiority.

An American idiom is "this fucking intimacy." And the phrase can imply a kind of impatience with it as well as the sexual nature of it: it depends on your voice and on whether you smile when you say it. In Ellen, who echoed with a kind of merciful tenderness my moods and so reconstituted me, the Jewish sense of ancestry and a rebel's sense of enlightenment and escape are both at play. She was hostess in the narrow hospital room to my mothers, my mothers' ghosts or spirits, and the line of fathers, the four millennia of unkillable Jewish males in their conceited stiff-neckedness, then all the dead and dying literary figures, then all the characters who die in the books I most admire — Prince Andrei and Hadji Murad and Proust's narrator's grandmother — and then all the widowed women back to Andromache or Hecuba. And she made room for the nurses and the nurse's aides, for the interns and the residents, and for Barry. I have never seen such intent or such subtle seduction: I cannot even begin to describe the silent promises, the hidden blessings she promised them, she promised them all, the ghosts, too. And the death standing over me and stirring up the muck that refused to be the bottom in the onslaught of the revolting pneumonia.

I lived through her will from time to time during those days: I had her agility and subtlety vicariously. It was like that as long as she was awake, anyway, and as long as her strength held out. I felt a bit cheated, while she was awake, of the mortal solitude that comes at the end, but I had that merciful depth of her female self at my disposal.

Our regular lives, our usual life together, had been reproduced in a truncated form in a hospital room: flowers, fruit, a newspaper, quibbling with each other, a certain seclusion, a habit of judging — the usual things, even at death's door, in death's presence.

But it was a hospital room, and I was dying, and I didn't have many private emotions. The husband in this marital scene was drugged to the teeth with prednisone, a steroid that walls off physical pain and depression by creating a strange pre-craziness of its own. I felt a rather awful clarity of humor, a nauseated comic sense; I was in an odd state. And the wife in the scene was overly gentle, sickroom gentle, terrified, and obstinately hopeful — not her usual self. She was afraid of gloom in this well-intentioned parody-caricature of our former life. The moments of grief I had were immediately contagious — well, the room was very small.

We would hold hands and I would say, "Oh shit" or "This *is* shitty," and we would cry a bit. It seemed like a sufficient amount of poetry. I would say, "Well, who cares?" or "I don't like this mushy stuff. Let's stop."

Equally invasive were the tender moments, Ellen bathing me and turning me, ninety-seven-pound Ellen, or changing the bed. Or her helping me into the bathroom. I had to be propped on her and on the wheeled pole of the IV. I was determined to spare her my excrement. My head lolled. My legs gave way, but only once. I had no strength, but it is true that willpower can do a great deal. It can't halt or cure AIDS, but it can take the place of physical strength and it can mock death and weakness: it can mock those things sometimes. Our bedtime talk or our toilet talk had to avoid sentiment; I had no strength for sentiment. I showed off for Ellen. I talked about business and money, about the information I'd negotiated from the doctor.

But she was the one with hope. She was the one with the sense of drama. She was the one who, with some, ah, degree of untruth, exclaimed on being told that she was HIV-negative, "Oh, I don't want to be clear. I want to have it, too."

An emotional remark. A bit of a marital lie, of marital manipulation. But true enough in that if I decided to kill myself she was still determined, so she said, to kill herself, too.

She wanted to die of what I was going to die of.

"That's bullshit, honey. It isn't what I want. Just can it, O.K.?"

Hospitals have become a mess; they've lost it. The breakdown of the middle-class conspiracy that was urban culture in the West shows in hospitals as a visible and basic and entire decay. Everything is improvisatory and shaky, even cleanliness and the administration of treatment. But perhaps because of obstinate kindness in some people, a determination to embody goodness, or some addiction to the priority of emergency, or because the meaning of rescuing someone from death appeals to the soul or to your sense of importance in the universe, the best nurses and nurse's aides appear and take care of you when you are dying.

Or, I should say, I got that kind of care. I got more of it if Ellen was there. The medicine came on time, the IV was properly adjusted — and the attention, in its smallest details, had in it an element of respectful shoving at the body and the spirit in its fall, a funny kind of summoning, an American summoning, not to glory but to make use of the technology and techniques of treatment, to profit from them. One is expected to make an effort to return to suburbia, to the tennis court, to make an obeisance to life.

I had already browbeaten Barry into saying that there are no miracles, no cures here. No one has been rescued from AIDS so far. The practical limit of survival varies, but one hears a lot about two to five years. Some of that time, you can, with luck and proper treatment, feel quite well. As a prize, as a goal, it is not very *American*. It is not Utopian, although Barry tried to make it that way with amazing generosity; he would raise his voice and smile, and his eyes would brighten; he would look like an inspired pitchman, and he would produce his pitch for *life*.

But it's not life. I rode for a while on my limited breath, on the cadence, the metre of it, in obedience to the muse of immediate survival. I was unable to breathe without oxygen and was racked by my reactions to the huge amounts of medication dripping or pumped into me, or swallowed — fifteen pills at bedtime. I thought I could feel myself being suffocated second by second. But the prednisone did in a way comfort me. What was strange was that all sense of presence, all sense of poetry and style, all sense of idea, left me. It was gone, with not one trace, one flicker remaining. I had a pale sense of the lost strength it would take to think or feel a metaphor, and of how distant it was from me. Everything was suffocation and the sentence of death, the termitelike democracy and chemical gusts of malaise and heat, of twisting fever, and the lazy but busy simmering of the disease in me. Everything outside me was Ellen's breath and the color of the walls in the dim light and was the hospital noises and the television set on its wall mount and a ticking slide of the moments.

And nothing was a phrase or seed of speech, nothing carried illumination in it, nothing spoke of meaning, of anything beyond breath. Attentive to nothing but breath, perhaps in my dying I was alive in a real and complete way, a human way, for the first time after ten or fifteen years of hard work. I lay awake in an almost bright amusement. Did you ever, as a child, play alone in a large cardboard box that a refrigerator came in? Or work alone in a large room? Or at night, when everyone else was asleep? Whatever I say now applies to feelings inside such a box, the box I'm in. No one can possibly know the power of feeling I project inside my carton.

Medical attention, and the horrors of illness and death, great death, amused me in a quiet way. Amused? Well, what do you feel when you're expected to fight against an often fatal pneumonia and you've been sentenced to death already? You are death meat. I don't see how you can cooperate in any ordinary way. You are a foot soldier, cannon fodder. Various functions of the body are endangered routinely. Tediously, you endure. You live in the tidal influx and efflux of medication. You make an attempt to go on as a person in the world. You smile at Barry. You smile at Ellen. You lie very still. But there is the grotesquerie of the patient, the mad person, the electrical flesh; the connection to the ordinary world is broken, yet not entirely. And there is a cartoon aspect: the curses people hurled at you have come true. What do you suggest I do? Be unamused?

And Barry meant to amuse, in the sense that he meant to give me a jolt, a blast of energy and momentum. It was as if he caromed in and set us, like billiard balls, bounding about the narrow room mentally, with animation. At times, he was exhausted and maybe depressed, but he hid it almost rapturously, with medical-business-like adjustments, with watchfulness. He worked in relation to a not yet fully understood disease using clinical experience and analogy. Really, I was grateful that he bothered. His respect for my life verged on the idiotic. He could not win. Literally, he shone and prescribed and analyzed and stole for me a month here, perhaps two years there. He kept studying medications and my face and my eyes while he was handling other patients, studying other faces and other eyes. Barry was moving fast inside a straight line, a medical frame, without much respect for the inevitable medical defeat. He put on a show, put up a fight, and I applauded as best I could. The spirit was cracked in me, but I offered what version of spirit I could to him. I joined the coarseness of struggle: this was my loyalty to the regular world.

To skip ahead for a moment — for the sake of a moment outside the hospital — here is an entry in my journal from two months later:

> Barry was so encouraging after my last visit that yesterday, when we arrived in the country, in the cooler air — with a fine wind and the stodgy trees attempting witty movements in the blowy air, and with the monkshood in bloom, very tall purple panicles next to our stone wall — I went entirely mad, carrying things, charging up and down stairs, and then collapsed, not seriously but totally, for eighteen hours. It was scary. But I went on feeling happy and released.

I couldn't really sleep. I was able on the prednisone only to doze in a kind of shallow unconsciousness. I believe in sleep. In the past, when I was ill, or even just sad, I would sleep it off.

Now, when Ellen slept, I expected to meet, as it were, my own feelings. Toward morning I would doze. I woke each time precariously placed in horizontal stillness, protecting my lungs and heart as I had with my posture when I was awake. I woke aware that I'd dreamed, and there was a fraction's hesitation before it became obvious I would not remember my dreams, that they had been about death, and that my waking self would not reproduce any part of them for me.

In life, I have struck people as being odd, demanding, and evasive. The New York *agreement* among people of my sort is that everything about each other's lives is knowable. You take a few clues, regard them with sophistication, and you know *everything*. In the end, this is a city that acknowledges no mysteries, one that is set on prying, or getting, or revealing. I find New York talk horrendous, the personal conclusions stupid, the idealization of others' experience and the demonization of others' experience hateful and contemptible. And the bottom-lining, the judgments made as if all were known, the lies, the fraud, the infinite oral thuggery here of Jews and Gentiles alike, the cold ambition, is, I repeat, unlivable.

What we really have in this city are able people, competent

people, who as they rise in the world have more and more complicated professional lives. Quite logically, that eats them up, and
the monstrous residue that is left is beyond emotion, but with an
appetite for it, and a terrible and terrified longing and unsuitability
for it. This monstrous residue is beyond friendship, beyond anything.
(It *is* capable of truly marvelous, if ogreish, companionship.)

I have been lectured on this subject, told I am wrong when I say
what dregs they are, what dregs we are, what a creeping madness
our adulthood becomes. The above has been denied to me by
nearly everyone in New York. But surely they must know.

No one can explain what it means to be marked out. The usual
explanations, the traditional ones, have to do with sin — sins of
the fathers and your own sins. But to be American is to be Nietzschean
in half of yourself: you move beyond sin even if part of you still
believes in it. You — or anyone — have to suffer your life or death
under civil law, so to speak.

Part of the self is made of one's work: you get glimpses of
meaning in that. A sense of your crimes can perhaps keep you
alive. Or self-righteous indignation can save you. Doors fly open
as in a farce, and something like Medusa's head swings into the
corridors of illness like the end of a pendulum, turning you to
stone. I kept wanting to cry out as Doris Brodkey had, or take
refuge in rage as Joe Brodkey had. I wanted an inherited death.
But I had, indeed, lost the past. This death seemed entirely mine,
mine and Ellen's, alone.

Death is not soft-mouthed, vague-footed, nearby. It is in the hall.
The weakness does not wash over me and disappear but stays. It
has a stagnant air. It floods me, and the flood is soul-wide. The
casing that my youth and strength and luck came in is empty and
vibrates a bit. A fox cub, a small bird nervous in the shadow, a bag
of tainted blood, a skeletal and stiff figure lying still, is what my
consciousness is. It is like a small bird's being fed to have one's
whispered wishes taken seriously and to be spared predatory sympathy. Barry and Ellen are going to save me for a while.

Do you know the myth of my irresistibility? It isn't easy to talk
about. The Fuck You Dreamed Of, Maybe. What a joke. It was a
matter of rumor — of reputation, all part of the floating aura, the
sharp aroma of New York gossip. I practiced amateurishly and

assiduously, and with some enjoyment and curiosity, but I wasn't up to it. My sexual limits were physically very clear. I failed to be a hero of the 1960s. Or of the 1970s. I wasn't up to the role. I never approached stylishness and acts that Mapplethorpe pictured and made public. I was never in the Casanova range and league of Norman Mailer. What I did and whatever actual events fueled the image — whatever humor or vanity I showed — it was clear that most of the myth was based on the claims and gossip of others. I had a life, but not that one.

Tennessee Williams, who went to my high school long before I got there, and who had some of the same teachers, touched on the subject of male irresistibility in terms of hustlers and handsome strangers passing through town, always in rags, and subject to humiliation. In imitation, a playwright, William Inge, dealt with it more directly, more reportorially, in the play (later a movie) *Picnic.* And such actors as Paul Newman, Marlon Brando, and William Holden for a while embodied this notion in various roles in Hollywood, getting shot and falling into the swimming pool and so on.

The American representation of The Good Fuck (an experience you owe yourself) always dealt with the childishness of such figures and with their failure in the world — handsome orphans, beaten down, beaten back, dependent on aging movie stars or on Anna Magnani as a moneyed storekeeper in a small town or on Kim Novak's depth as a woman; these sexy, bankrupt, Christ-like orphans, these phallus bearers and suppliers, were by definition without power in the world. Brando had trouble playing Napoleon or Marc Antony or any other type but the phallic martyr. And the highly successful writers, the troubled Williams especially, and the successful and power-mad directors could never suppress their contempt for these men in their degrees of failure and lack of power. Billy Wilder's version in *Sunset Boulevard* is the most contemptuous.

I don't know of any British versions of such male irresistibility in the writing of the modern era except for Basil Seal in Waugh's books, and he is a killer at heart. Lermontov and Stendhal and Pushkin are kinder but still cruel. Some of the more ancient versions, such as Joseph or David in the Bible, are treated with less contempt, but then they are pictured in their worldly power, their success; they are said to be blessed.

The American version is always a fool. Well, why not? In my case, it was a stupid thing and a bit hard to believe except in terms of sentimental anecdote, as in tales about my adoption. It is fantastically embarrassing to say that I was adopted illegally and with great difficulty, and the difficulty was accepted because of the infant's, the very young child's — the tales agree even if the photographs don't — extreme beauty.

The supposed beauty of a catatonic toddler as a small-town public "myth" among Jews is the substance of childhood drama — this irresistibility, these looks, these bones and features. From infancy, my life has been, always, always, on the verge of my being eaten alive: *I could just eat you up.*

It seems hardly earthshaking, this crap of *irresistibility,* but in life, in the literal reality this takes, it means gasps and anger at you and people crying because of you and a lot of gossip and various abduction attempts and threats of suicide because of you and your being followed on the street by people who are obsessed with you seriously, ludicrously. It means people hating you for a betrayal that never occurred, for what they feel is your luck, which they then want in their rage to undo. In my childhood, people talked a great deal about me and quarreled over me — and threatened force. And there was violence, some of it directed at me.

I have seen, as an adult, children of such attention become quite violent themselves, and hysterical, and strange. I think of childhood and adolescence as sexual, as filled with the sexual intrusions of others. I was told that Doris Brodkey first tried to buy me from my real mother when I was a year old. I would suspect that the fate of *irresistibility* in the ordinary world is established in infancy as a condition of existence for most of us. But that in my case it has also partly determined my death.

I remember people coming to the house to see me — I remember being brought out after being dressed and combed, and being passed from embrace to embrace. How I hated to be touched. Or even looked at. Sometimes I would kick and scream and not allow my nurse to dress me. I would even climb out the window of my second-floor room and hide on the roof rather than go downstairs. It was commonly said, "That child needs discipline." You'd be surprised how odd — and troubling — a child's "No" was back in the 1930s, and how temperamentally the grownups reacted. Decades later, in New York, in almost any field of endeavor, when a sexual proposition was made to you by anyone, for you to say "No" seemed to mark you as an amateur, as unprofessional, unserious, and to some extent as a fool.

Really, one sees people cursed with *irresistibility* as being finally interesting for how they fail. For how they can be hurt. For how they retreat, become scarred, or obese, or dead. When I am attacked, it reminds me of my childhood. Spite and the desire to humble you combine uncertainly in an angry way to make you laugh with shock and secret recognition. Sanity becomes very pronounced in you, as a defense. Every touch verges on abuse, on recruitment.

Few people will ever see you without an affronted sense of their own *irresistibility* and of themselves as objects of competing emotion. This trait makes others feel that you are taking something large and valuable away from them, and if you believe we know things by comparison or if you believe in democratic (competitive) exhibitionism, then you *are* taking something of value away from them: their projection of themselves as more worth loving than you are.

I was *in fashion* in New York in terms of this *irresistibility* off and on for the last forty years. And it was an insiderish thing to be "in love" with me at those times. Other people won literary prizes or academic honors. *I* discriminated among emotions and suitors — and judged their quality as people, their odors, their intelligence, their powers of comedy and of being thrilling, their emotional intelligence. I had always, explosively, a kind of emotional citizenship, an undeserved welcome. I felt this absurd *irresistibility* as a form of comedy, as a useless joke. I am trying to describe the nature of the temptation offered to the child and by the child, then the adolescent, then the young man in New York who is now the aging man with AIDS.

Another man might "love" me like someone cheating at croquet, but the croquet court had been laid out in *me*, a pleasure ground of a peculiar sort. You play dumb and pretend to be respectable, but you are an old, old hand, an aged whore at this stuff. Outwardly, you perhaps are more distinguished and puritan in your air than that. No one need admit that you are this sort of person. People who become obsessed with you like to tell you that you're nothing special, that you're ugly — a certain amount of high and low melodrama lies in wait for you every day. Ah, the bitter phone calls. I cannot find in memory a day in my life without some erotic drama or other. I probably have never gone a day without it. And the temper with which you bear your history — the erotic slyness or directness — may give you a quality very like beauty, whatever your history is, whatever you actually look like. Perhaps it is a real beauty, the courage to have had a life of some sort, in spite of the difficulty, I mean.

Anyway, the major drama of my adolescence was that my adoptive father, Joe Brodkey, who was ill with heart trouble (a handsome invalid, as one would write in pornography), assailed me every day for two years, sexually — twice a day, every morning and every evening, when I was twelve and thirteen. He had nothing else to do, really. He was ill. We were not the same blood. I am being very shy. He never succeeded in entering me, but it was somewhat scary and sweaty. Except that there was the pathos of his dying. And there was my long history of boring *irresistibility*. And my mind, which was watching all of it. His blood pressure was fragilely high. I was too strong, too frozen, for very much to happen, for the drama to develop.

I am lying. I had to notice that he was heartsick — with feeling, clearly *in love*, in a way. And soon, somehow, when I didn't make a scene about the assaults, or whatever, a great many people knew about "the love story." I suppose my mother talked about it for reasons of her own. My mother said he-can't-live-without-you things and he's-hooked-you-have-him-where-you-want-him-you-talk-to-him-for-me things. Or Dad talked about it — he had rather nineteenth-century ideas of family and of male rights.

I confessed nothing. I complained to no one. My mother, herself ill with cancer and drugged, warned me oracularly, "If I were you, I'd learn to keep my mouth shut." I don't mean to be insulting to her memory, but she was excited, even inspired, by the situation, which — it took no great brains to see — helped keep both her and Dad alive: it interested them, this *love* thing.

Such assaults as Joe's have their aspect of wanting to lower you, but at moments everything was focused, as if in the last line of a story, on a profound concern having to do with the creature in whom my identity was at the moment caught. Either of my parents would have killed the other for me. Sometimes they fought over me, and it seemed to be to the death — this is not uncommon, is it? My mother said advisingly, "You never seem nice if you have to say no." I was a "fine-looking young fella" (which I never actually quite was; I was weirder than that), "a young man with a good smile, if you want my opinion." She said, "You make do with what you're given." It was what she had to play with, to move on the suburban board, in the terminal boredom of her life.

Still, for me, there was the drama, the persecution. And such assaults, such oddities, comic and manic or melancholy or dangerous, occurred everywhere, as if by contagion — with the football guys, with old friends, with the mothers of friends, with strangers. I was even half abducted once, forced into a car, but I fought and talked my way out of it. At school, my God, girls waited for me in the front hall, or in front in good weather. I was often surrounded by kids in the halls, and twice in one year, four times all in all, the mothers of girls whose approaches to me I had ignored complained to the school principal that I had hurt their daughters' feelings, and couldn't I be made to respond? My parents were telephoned, were talked to. Whatever I was, it was not taken to be a private property and mine. I understood my father's actions on this level, in this light.

One of the troubles with the reality of the passage of time is that the past can be lied about. False precedent can be argued. Unexamined realities can be dropped from conscious equations. The thing itself, the sexualized courtship, arose from the boy's comforting and, on occasion, holding and rocking his forty-four-year-old father when his father was racked by death-fever or rage or panic. Life perhaps was defined by one's code of behavior. I would start to laugh and accept an embrace briefly, as in childhood — and then cut it short. It is your own moral judgment that arranges this refusal of your father even though he is dying. Such refusal is arrogant toward Daddy. Or at least it places a positive value on your own life. To ignore the feelings you arouse is indistinguishable from narcissism to someone who wants your attention. I am not complaining. I noticed that the denial of truth was what everyone called *tact*. He accursed me. Now I will die disfigured and in pain.

To tell a little of the story about me and my father less shyly, I would have to change the way I write. In real life, I experimented with homosexuality to break my pride, to open myself to the story.

Medicine and will and luck. Barry and Ellen. I didn't die. I didn't even have to be sent to intensive care. Then, outside the hospital, the light had a perceptible weight, and I blinked and flinched. The outdoor noises, city noises, flew and scratched. I struggled to control my breathing. And it was as Barry had said: I had not really known how sick I was — dying, yes, but not how sick.

I felt myself dissolve into the space spreading around me. In the taxicab, in the streets, I was so crippled by filmy fluctuations of consciousness — on East Seventy-second, on Madison, on West Eighty-sixth, where the walls of brownstones seemed watery and then gauzy — that I was far more imprisoned by weakness than I had been by the hospital and its routines. I was maddened by my silent passing out and coming to in the city stink as the taxi bounded and bounced. I stayed upright. Ellen was stiff-faced and brightly talkative beside me. "I can't respond," I whispered. She held my hand. Halfway home, I was so ill with exhaustion that tears of pain came to my eyes. I had no intention of admitting that I had made a mistake in forcing Barry to let me leave the hospital a few days early. I said, at least half a dozen times, "Boy, is it wonderful to be out of the hospital!" Then I gave that up and asked Ellen if she was managing, if this was too much for her. If she had said yes, I would have turned back. She said she was O.K.

We, I, made it to the apartment, and I climbed into my bed in my clothes. Ellen undressed me, set out the pills and the notebook in which she was going to log my symptoms and the hours at which I took the pills. I dozed and woke, but uncomfortably and without being refreshed by the sleep, which was as truly terrifying as falling off the edge of the world might be — to be so unrefreshed by sleep. I walked, crept, partly crawled to the stereo in my darkened bedroom and played one of Bach's partitas; it sounded harsh to me. I slept, always in an uncurative way, sometimes with music playing. Much of the time, I just listened to the distant sounds of street noises and of Ellen coming and going.

Sick and weak, each day, in the morning, for an hour or more, I stirred myself and worked on the last draft of a book I've written about Venice. Red and covered with spots (allergy to the drugs), I worked, and while I worked I felt nothing apart from a weakness of mind and some nausea. I mean, I had no reaction to the story or to the prose: I had to work with memories of response.

Sometimes I couldn't work at all, couldn't focus, and I would cry, but only a bit, and crawl back to bed, or if I was working in bed I would cover my eyes with my hands and lie still and breathe and doze and then try again to work. I must admit I truly felt accursed. My mother, my real mother, died, according to family accounts, of a curse laid on her by her father, a wonder-working rabbi. When I was barely two, she died painfully, over a period of months, either of peritonitis from a bungled abortion or from cancer, depending on who related the story. Then Doris, my father's cousin, and Joe came for me and, later on, adopted me. I was told that Doris took me once to the hospital to see my mother and that I refused her embrace, clinging instead to the perfumed Doris; the rescued child was apparently without memory of the dying mother. (Perhaps that was the real crime, and not my obduracy with Joe.) So, in between working out when I could most probably have become infected with AIDS, I fell into a mood of being accursed, of being part of an endless family story of woe and horror.

I felt worse each day, almost as if as the emergency faded, so did the mobilized strength. Endless sickness without death is more sickening than I would have imagined. I wanted to make, as a sort of joke, a version of the superhuman effort that Ellen wished for from me. But, you know, as you get older you get worn out in regard to superhuman efforts — you've made them for your child or in your work (superhuman for you) or in sport or love or for someone who is ill. And then the possibility is gone. Ellen was working at a superhuman rate, nursing me, helping me up and to the word processor and back to bed. She shopped, cooked, kept house, took care of pending business, dealt with whatever emergencies came up, answered the phone and lied to people about my illness, fed us and made conversation, and proofread the work I produced. She got us movies for the VCR and lay down with me and kept me company, and brought me ice bags when the fever rose and my head hurt, and kept the medication log and saw to it that I took the medications and my temperature when I was supposed to, and, when I asked her to, she sang to me.

She helped me dress and then undress; she didn't approve of my staying in pajamas all day. Her omnipotence was at full stretch and had a softly shining and rather detached aura to it that enclosed my sense of being accursed and diluted. It was a cousin to that neurotic activity of will in able women which is so often written about with disapproval, and it was crazed, I suppose, that tirelessness, that as if inexhaustible tenderness. Clearly forced, or maybe not, it was far stronger and more unflagging in effect than any courtship intensity that had ever been directed at me.

We called no one. We were still telling the family and anyone else who telephoned that I had pneumonia, nothing more. In a rather transparent isolation, my arrogant deathliness and her burning gentleness were dancing together in a New York light in our apartment. It was like childhood, a form of playing house.

Then she said, "When are we going to tell the children?" She wasn't looking forward to it — it's not just embarrassment, you know: it's preliminary distress in case they're not very nice at first; and, on the other hand, as a parent you are ashamed to inflict this downer on them if they are warm-hearted and do sympathize. The likeliest thing is that you'll have to console them.

"Later. In a few days, we'll start. I can't deal with it yet."

"That's all right."

She was careful, so that I would not blame myself. I felt myself to be thoroughly repellent. I had disowned my body now and was mostly pain and odors, halting speech and a sick man's glances. The truths in such domestic and emotional enclosures tend to go unrecorded. Things drift into the sanctuary from the outer world; the television is a window, and the telephone is a murmurous keyhole. Somewhere in this phantasmagoria, Ellen decided to wake me.

A kiss — how strange her lips felt, and the quality of life in them. Of course, I thought, of course. The sense I had of her, the sensations: the heat of her skin, the heat of her eyes so close to me, everything in her was alive still and full of the silent speeches that life makes. She was warm and full of responsive motion. My lips and feelings had the deadness of a sullen child's.

I accepted her and her affection as truth, as being as much truth along those lines as I was likely to want. This meant that by the second week I was home we both realized that in this limited world of mutual watchfulness and of unselfishness-for-a-while, this period was for us, in awful parody, honeymoon-like, and that this was acceptable to both of us, grief or death at the end or not.

Grief aside, nothing ugly happened at all. Since she didn't mind — or rather didn't show disgust at — my ashenness, I grew more affectionate: the corpse put his arm around her. She noticed and commented on the strength of my heartbeat. "Yes, I've always been especially proud of my heartbeat." She kissed me on the lips with generous marks of interest and amusement. She said to me, "No one would believe that this was one of the happiest times of my life."

I roared with laughter, which hurt my stiff lung and made me choke. And I came alive again, for a little while. Well, why not? When the other things are over and done with, when savagery and silence are the impolite, real thing, you're not alone. You still pass as human among humans. There are things that have to be done, family things, literary stuff, things having to do with AIDS. I do them with her marks of interest and amusement on my face.

Dying, too, has a certain rhythm to it. It slows and quickens. Very little matters, but that little is of commanding importance to me. I feel the silence ahead of me as I have all my life felt the silence of God as a given and a source of reasonable terror. This is something one must bear, beyond the claims of religion, not the idea of one's dying but the reality of one's death. One schools oneself in an acceptance of the terror. It is the shape that life takes toward its end. It is a form of life.

DUDLEY CLENDINEN

When Negative Meets Positive

FROM GQ

AT THE EPISCOPAL CATHEDRAL of St. Philip in Atlanta on a nondescript fall afternoon in 1989, I attended a healing service. I had seen the notice and went on impulse, for Jimmy, I thought, and brotherhood. Jimmy wasn't dead yet, but I had seen him, kept him as a guest for several days, taken him to the doctor, listened to his story. In some ways, he had been ahead of me in the race for identity all our lives, and now it was clear he was going to finish first.

The exterior of the cathedral, like the day outside, was large, suburban, bland. Inside were perhaps sixty quiet men, a few women, in a great dim space splashed with stained glass and saints, banners and candles and embroidered robes. Rituals of ancient times, employed to comfort the sufferers of the modern plague.

It was part of a progression. First you realized that you were gay. Then that there was a disease that stalked people like you. Then that it had touched acquaintances, killed people you knew. Then that someone close, someone you'd grown up with, had it. Someone like you.

Southern boys, puppy WASPs, are trained in the manners of life's occasions. There are christenings, birthday parties, proms, deb balls, rehearsal dinners, weddings, anniversaries, funerals. Most have to do with family. Everyone knows the people at the center of attention. At funerals, those people are dead. Everyone else is more or less alive.

A healing service for AIDS was a different kind of form. No one was dead. No one was really going to get well, either. And those of us attending the service wouldn't be on equal planes. Some would be positive. Some would be sick. I wouldn't know anyone, I thought, and I wasn't positive. Did that matter? Was I presumptuous? Should I go? If I went, would people think I had the virus? Did that matter? Should I go?

I went. There was something familiar, in the crowd or the place, I couldn't tell. Some connection. But I was also a stranger, with that feeling that strangers have, of being separate, being safe. It lasted through the service. And then, turning to withdraw as the crowd went out, I was suddenly looking at this face I had seen before. The words came automatically. "Oh, hi, nice to see you again," I said. He looked a little — what? Self-conscious? Snide? The smile flickered, and he slipped past.

AIDS is a challenge for the absent-minded. I struggled to remember, and suddenly, it dawned on me: maybe *not* nice to see him. Maybe that's not what you say at a healing service. Not if he was there for healing. Maybe I should remember how I knew him. If this was "again," when and what was "then"? And suddenly I remembered him, fair-haired, in his early thirties, in a room full of old things.

He was nice, one of those childless single men who fill the present with the furnishings of family past, anchoring his life in a continuum that will end with him. That is the sadness of some gay men. The dread is of ending life alone. I thought of him as the Antiques Man, there on his grandparents' bed, in a room glinting with warm wood and brass and portrait oils. He said he hadn't been tested since his lover died a year and a half before. He didn't think he had it, but maybe he did.

Yes, maybe he did. None of the manners I was raised with seemed to apply, but if you can go to bed with someone, you can telephone. Maybe I should call and ask about him. Maybe I should reassure him about me, again. He could be worried, too. I did. He wasn't worried about me. He had it.

It is like the beginning of a series of rapids, and suddenly, you're not a spectator on the shore anymore. You're on the river.

The thing to remember about men is that men chase men the way men chase women — aggressively. And with two men involved, usually no one puts on the brakes. That was in the old days, the pre-AIDS years. Gay bars were classless places, and when the attraction was physical, dating amongst men was democracy in action. Plumbers chased lawyers. Psychiatrists fell for cops. Some of us — married, shy, or spoken for — didn't spend much time in bars. But there was all of life outside. Random moments accumulate, and I remember lawyers, doctors, students, dancers, preachers, waiters, producers, artists, teachers, actors, managers, writers, accountants, barbers, professors, nurses, social workers, one masseur, a funeral director, an engineer, a taxi driver, a coast-guard captain, and a railroad man who touched some chord in me at various times. Some proved sexual. Some did not. Life moves on, and the reports filter back. You hear about people you haven't seen. You see people you used to see. They've been tested since you saw them last. They're positive. Or they're sick. Or in the case of the young East Side writer, you hear that the rather beautiful lover he spoke of was Robert Mapplethorpe, and that, like Mapplethorpe, the young writer is dead. Developed what seemed like a bad cold in the country on a Thursday, which turned into a pneumonia they didn't recognize, which killed him by Sunday night. The family buried him without ever being heard to acknowledge the disease or whisper the word "AIDS." That was years ago.

And then there comes a night, the middle of a night, when you are lying quietly, nose to nose with someone you think you could like a lot, and you say, "By the way, you should know I'm negative," because it has just occurred to you that you should tell. You assume he'll like your report. It never occurs to you, because there is such a sincerity about him, such a good-scout quality, that you won't like his. You thought, when you met him at dinner with a bishop and a nun, that he was a priest. But there is no reply. The blue eyes looking back don't blink. Maybe he didn't get it. "I mean, I was the last time I was tested," you say helpfully. "Negative." The blue eyes don't blink.

"Well, I'm not," he says.

And there you are, sandwiched between the experience you've just had and the experiences you'd like to have. But this time you're going to have to choose, knowing that he's positive.

It is the line that each of us who is still negative comes to, staring across into the blue/brown/yellow/hazel/green/gray/black eyes of those in whom the virus has come to live. And it is not just about sex. There are things to do and things to refrain from doing in bed, today. There are condoms and virus-killing lubricants that all people, male or female, heterosexual or homosexual, teenage or grown, should use if they have sex outside of a monogamous relationship. They make sex as safe as sex can be. But there is more. We are looking into the eyes of people we like, people with whom we are intimate, people we might love. What are we to do? If I am to grow in love and humanity, do I decline to take risks, refuse to make myself vulnerable, cut myself off from anyone who threatens me with the possibility of intimacy, love, and death? Isn't that what any investment of real feeling is about? Risk? And don't I risk denying myself love if I deny all who live on that side of the line?

If I took a paint can and a brush and marked that line, how much of life would I cut off? Five percent? One tenth? A quarter? One third? How many people? If the person who might provide the missing part of my daily life stands on the other side of that line, how do I measure that loss? In San Francisco and New York, in conversation and even in print, it is often said now that almost half or more of the homosexual male population may be HIV-positive.

It is hard to comprehend the import of that. It may mean that in those places, we are back to living in the Middle Ages, where the life expectancy of a loved one extended only into his late twenties, thirties, or mid-forties.

I have never lived with such odds. And yet my own experience tells me that the positive no longer live like isolated cells in our culture. We live in theirs. All of us. We all live in the same world, and none of us knows which is who or who is what. We all, from time to time, unless we are monks or in some long-standing pure relationship, embrace the bomb. We may carry it ourselves.

The thing I hate about it is that toxic quality. I don't want to think of people as I now think of cigarettes and alcohol. As toxic. I don't want, having given up tobacco and whiskey and wine, to think that I now have to give up people, too. If we all begin to recoil from one another, it will be not just the protection of our lives that we ensure but also the death of our souls.

And yet the threat of the disease is overpowering. Yes, there is unsafe sex and safer sex. And almost wholly reliable mostly safe sex. But there is not such a provable thing as completely safe sex. And if you want to test the power of your feeling for someone, imagine him as poison behind that smile, those freckles, those nice blue eyes, and then try making love. It is an emotional filter through which, I think, only real feeling can pass.

And that is essentially what I decided in the moment and the weeks after Blue Eyes didn't blink. Not to segregate myself. Not to give him up. If I don't really like him, I thought, I won't really want him. I won't want to risk the virus or the loss. If the feeling is just physical, it will wither. My gut will tell me.

I moved, and time and distance did us in. The virus didn't. But it has with others. And at least I know now what my policy is. And Blue Eyes and I are friends.

Don't you worry about getting involved with somebody you'll lose? he says. Don't you think about being left alone?

Yes. And yes. But alone is what I am now. I just wish I would meet more people who are negative. I don't. It's getting worse. I have a feeling it's going to keep getting worse. And I know it's not easy, when you're positive, to deal with negatives like me.

"You're always wondering what they're thinking and if they're scared. And if they are, it kind of hurts," Blue Eyes says. "You feel like Typhoid Mary." Dating someone like me, even thinking of living with someone like me, may be more responsibility than he could stand. Fear of passing the virus. Fear of being a burden. Guilt about dying and leaving me. So much to think of. So, no, he wasn't, in fact, so glad to hear my announcement of negativity that night.

I made him feel toxic, and he isn't alone in that feeling. "I feel like a diamondback rattler," another man said on another night. I made him what has come to be my speech, which is that I am responsible for me. But he would not come out of his lair, or relent and let me in.

I am not promiscuous, but I am alive, and they kept recurring, these conversations, these moments in the night: negative to positive.

I think it is true for more and more of us.

Person by person, encounter by encounter, each experience reframes our sense of what life is like now. Moment by intimate moment, we recast our expectations and grow older. And each time we throw the dice and they turn up positive, we blink, and there is a sort of pause, in mid-speech, mid-look, mid-feeling, mid-inhalation, a moment, just a shade of time in which the sensory experience of life stops while an exchange is made: a deposit of information to the brain, another subtraction from the soul.

Sometimes, the moment would lengthen, and he would say, "Do you want to talk?" Talk? There was a kind of kaleidoscope going on behind my eyes, a fan of dark blades whirling before an angry red glow.

"Are we going to see each other again?" he would say. And I would breathe, and with what now seems an effort of will say again what I have come to believe I believe. That we all live with the virus now. We all are affected. Some of us have it and some of us don't, and both kinds of us have to decide whether we are going to draw a line between us.

I have decided that I will not, because the person I love could be on the other side. Each person I meet is someone who could matter to me. Each person could have the virus, and almost no one knows for sure, unless he has already tested positive. The rest of us know about our status only as of months ago, because that is all the tests can tell us. And so for those of us who think we're negative, each person is a potential threat, as we are to them.

There are no safe partners anymore, I say. We can't reassure one another, so we have to act as if every person we meet carries the virus of AIDS. I have to be responsible for myself, for being as safe as I can be. And then I have to decide whether there is some future beyond the moment that makes exploring the present seem worthwhile. Yes, I say, I'd like to see you again.

Moment by moment, we get by. Those of us who are careful enough or lucky enough grow older, drawing with excruciating care into deep middle age, and one day we realize another moment. It may be simply that youth is gone, which goes anyway. But there is something else missing that could have stayed, and which I suspect does stay, in lives fully lived.

During the inaugural week in 1993, I was at a ball for which the National Press Club in Washington had been rented on Wednesday night. It was almost two o'clock in the morning. It was a handsome party, a black-tie historic event: men dancing with women, women with women, men with men. I was standing talking with an elegant, thoughtful man who said he was establishing a foundation to grant last wishes to people with AIDS, when it occurred to me that I hadn't danced at this ball, and if I was going to do it, I'd better ask him. It was getting late.

"Would you like to dance?" I said. He smiled. He has had the virus for eight years. He doesn't have the symptoms yet, he said, but he doesn't have the energy either, anymore. His foundation was his own last wish. He was going home.

I didn't dance. That, I thought later, is what's missing. It might just be middle age, but it's the spontaneity that's gone. That's what it is. The promise. The joy.

BERNARD COOPER

Burl's

FROM THE LOS ANGELES TIMES MAGAZINE

I LOVED the restaurant's name, a compact curve of a word. Its sign, five big letters rimmed in neon, hovered above the roof. I almost never saw the sign with its neon lit; my parents took me there for early summer dinners, and even by the time we left — father cleaning his teeth with a toothpick, mother carrying steak bones in a doggie bag — the sky was still bright. Heat rippled off the cars parked along Hollywood Boulevard, the asphalt gummy from hours of sun.

With its sleek architecture, chrome appliances, and arctic temperature, Burl's offered a refuge from the street. We usually sat at one of the booths in front of the plate-glass windows. During our dinner, people came to a halt before the news-vending machine on the corner and burrowed in their pockets and purses for change.

The waitresses at Burl's wore brown uniforms edged in checked gingham. From their breast pockets frothed white lace handkerchiefs. In between reconnaissance missions to the table, they busied themselves behind the counter and shouted "Tuna to travel" or "Scorch that patty" to a harried short-order cook who manned the grill. Miniature pitchers of cream and individual pats of butter were extracted from an industrial refrigerator. Coca-Cola shot from a glinting spigot. Waitresses dodged and bumped one another, frantic as atoms.

My parents usually lingered after the meal, nursing cups of coffee while I played with the beads of condensation on my glass of ice water, tasted Tabasco sauce, or twisted pieces of my paper napkin into mangled animals. One evening, annoyed with my restlessness, my father gave me a dime and asked me to buy him a *Herald Examiner* from the vending machine in front of the restaurant.

Shouldering open the heavy glass door, I was seared by a sudden gust of heat. Traffic roared past me and stirred the air. Walking toward the newspaper machine, I held the dime so tightly it seemed to melt in my palm. Duty made me feel large and important. I inserted the dime and opened the box, yanking a *Herald* from the spring contraption that held it as tight as a mousetrap. When I turned around, paper in hand, I saw two women walking toward me.

Their high heels clicked on the sun-baked pavement. They were tall, broad-shouldered women who moved with a mixture of haste and defiance. They'd teased their hair into nearly identical black beehives. Dangling earrings flashed in the sun, brilliant as prisms. Each of them wore the kind of clinging, strapless outfit my mother referred to as a cocktail dress. The silky fabric — one dress was purple, the other pink — accentuated their breasts and hips and rippled with insolent highlights. The dresses exposed their bare arms, the slope of their shoulders, and the smooth, powdered plane of flesh where their cleavage began.

I owned at the time a book called *Things for Boys and Girls to Do.* There were pages to color, intricate mazes, and connect-the-dots. But another type of puzzle came to mind as I watched those women walking toward me: What's Wrong With This Picture? Say the drawing of a dining room looked normal at first glance; on closer inspection, a chair was missing its leg and the man who sat atop it wore half a pair of glasses.

The women had Adam's apples.

The closer they came, the shallower my breathing was. I blocked the sidewalk, an incredulous child stalled in their path. When they saw me staring, they shifted their purses and linked their arms. There was something sisterly and conspiratorial about their sudden closeness. Though their mouths didn't move, I thought they might have been communicating without moving their lips, so telepathic did they seem as they joined arms and pressed together, synchronizing their heavy steps. The pages of the *Herald* fluttered in the wind. I felt them against my arm, light as batted lashes.

The woman in pink shot me a haughty glance and yet she seemed pleased that I'd taken notice, hungry to be admired by a man, or even an awestruck eight-year-old boy. She tried to stifle a grin, her red lipstick more voluptuous than the lips it painted. Rouge deepened her cheekbones. Eye shadow dusted her lids, a clumsy abundance of blue. Her face was like a page in *Things for Boys and Girls to Do,* colored by a kid who went outside the lines.

At close range, I saw that her wig was slightly askew. I was certain it was a wig because my mother owned several; three Styrofoam heads lined a shelf in my mother's closet; upon them were perched a Page-Boy, an Empress, and a Baby-Doll, all in shades of auburn. The woman in the pink dress wore her wig like a crown of glory.

But it was the woman in the purple dress who passed nearest me, and I saw that her jaw was heavily powdered, a half-successful attempt to disguise the telltale shadow of a beard. Just as I noticed this, her heel caught on a crack in the pavement and she reeled on her stilettos. It was then that I witnessed a rift in her composure, a window through which I could glimpse the shades of maleness that her dress and wig and makeup obscured. She shifted her shoulders and threw out her hands like a surfer riding a curl. The instant she regained her balance, she smoothed her dress, patted her hair, and sauntered onward.

Any woman might be a man. The fact of it clanged through the chambers of my brain. In broad day, in the midst of traffic, with my parents drinking coffee a few feet away, I felt as if everything I understood, everything I had taken for granted up to that moment — the curve of the earth, the heat of the sun, the reliability of my own eyes — had been squeezed out of me. Who were those men? Did they help each other get inside those dresses? How many other people and things were not what they seemed? From the back, the impostors looked like women once again, slinky and curvaceous, purple and pink. I watched them disappear into the distance, their disguises so convincing that other people on the street seemed to take no notice, and for a moment I wondered if I had imagined the whole encounter, a visitation by two unlikely muses.

Frozen in the middle of the sidewalk, I caught my reflection in the window of Burl's, a silhouette floating between his parents. They faced one another across a table. Once the solid embodiments of woman and man, pedestrians and traffic appeared to pass through them.

*

There were some mornings, seconds before my eyes opened and my senses gathered into consciousness, that the child I was seemed to hover above the bed, and I couldn't tell what form my waking would take — the body of a boy or the body of a girl. Finally stirring, I'd blink against the early light and greet each incarnation as a male with mild surprise. My sex, in other words, didn't seem to be an absolute fact so much as a pleasant, recurring accident.

By the age of eight, I'd experienced this groggy phenomenon several times. Those ethereal moments above my bed made waking up in the tangled blankets, a boy steeped in body heat, all the more astonishing. That this might be an unusual experience never occurred to me; it was one among a flood of sensations I could neither name nor ignore.

And so, shocked as I was when those transvestites passed me in front of Burl's, they confirmed something about which I already had an inkling: the hazy border between the sexes. My father, after all, raised his pinky when he drank from a teacup, and my mother looked as faded and plain as my father until she fixed her hair and painted her face.

Like most children, I once thought it possible to divide the world into male and female columns. Blue/Pink. Rooster/Hens. Trousers/Skirts. Such divisions were easy, not to mention comforting, for they simplified matter into compatible pairs. But there also existed a vast range of things that didn't fit neatly into either camp: clocks, milk, telephones, grass. There were nights I fell into a fitful sleep while trying to sex the world correctly.

Nothing typified the realms of male and female as clearly as my parents' walk-in closets. Home alone for any length of time, I always found my way inside them. I could stare at my parents' clothes for hours, grateful for the stillness and silence, haunting the very heart of their privacy.

The overhead light in my father's closet was a bare bulb. Whenever I groped for the chain in the dark, it wagged back and forth and resisted my grasp. Once the light clicked on, I saw dozens of ties hanging like stalactites. A monogrammed silk bathrobe sagged from a hook, a gift my father had received on a long-ago birthday and, thinking it fussy, rarely wore. Shirts were cramped together along the length of an aluminum pole, their starched sleeves sticking out as if in a halfhearted gesture of greeting. The medicinal odor of mothballs permeated the boxer shorts that were folded and stacked in a built-in drawer. Immaculate underwear was proof of a tenderness my mother couldn't otherwise express; she may not have touched my father often, but she laundered his boxers with infinite care. Even back then, I suspected that a sense of duty was the final erotic link between them.

Sitting in a neat row on the closet floor were my father's boots and slippers and dress shoes. I'd try on his wingtips and clomp around, slipping out of them with every step. My wary, unnatural stride made me all the more desperate to effect some authority. I'd whisper orders to imagined lackeys and take my invisible wife in my arms. But no matter how much I wanted them to fit, those shoes were as cold and hard as marble.

My mother's shoes were just as uncomfortable, but a lot more fun. From a brightly colored array of pumps and slingbacks, I'd pick a pair with the glee and deliberation of someone choosing a chocolate. Whatever embarrassment I felt was overwhelmed by the exhilaration of being taller in a pair of high heels. Things will look like this someday, I said to myself, gazing out from my new and improved vantage point as if from a crow's nest. Calves elongated, arms akimbo, I gauged each step so that I didn't fall over and moved with what might have passed for grace had someone seen me, a possibility I scrupulously avoided by locking the door.

Back and forth I went. The longer I wore a pair of heels, the better my balance. In the periphery of my vision, the shelf of wigs looked like a throng of kindly bystanders. Light streamed down from a high window, causing crystal bottles to glitter, the air ripe with perfume. A makeup mirror above the dressing table invited my self-absorption. Sound was muffled. Time slowed. It seemed as if nothing bad could happen as long as I stayed within those walls.

Though I'd never been discovered in my mother's closet, my parents knew that I was drawn toward girlish things — dolls and jump rope and jewelry — as well as to the games and preoccupations that were expected of a boy. I'm not sure now if it was my effeminacy itself that bothered them as much as my ability to slide back and forth, without the slightest warning, between male and female mannerisms. After I'd finished building the model of an F-17 bomber, say, I'd sit back to examine my handiwork, pursing my lips in concentration and crossing my legs at the knee.

One day my mother caught me standing in the middle of my bedroom doing an imitation of Mary Injijikian, a dark, overeager Armenian girl with whom I believed myself to be in love, not only because she was pretty but because I wanted to be like her. Collector of effortless A's, Mary seemed to know all the answers in class. Before the teacher had even finished asking a question, Mary would let out a little grunt and practically levitate out of her seat, as if her hand were filled with helium. "Could we please hear from someone else today besides Miss Injijikian," the teacher would say. *Miss Injijikian.* Those were the words I was repeating over and over to myself when my mother caught me. To utter them was rhythmic, delicious, and under their spell I raised my hand and wiggled like Mary. I heard a cough and spun around. My mother froze in the doorway. She clutched the folded sheets to her stomach and turned without saying a word. My sudden flush of shame confused me. Weren't boys supposed to swoon over girls? Hadn't I seen babbling, heartsick men in a dozen movies?

Shortly after the Injijikian incident, my parents decided to send me to gymnastics class at the Los Angeles Athletic Club, a brick relic of a building on Olive Street. One of the oldest establishments of its kind in Los Angeles, the club prohibited women from the premises. My parents didn't have to say it aloud: they hoped a fraternal atmosphere would toughen me up and tilt me toward the male side of my nature.

My father drove me downtown so I could sign up for the class, meet the instructor, and get a tour of the place. On the way there, he reminisced about sports. Since he'd grown up in a rough Philadelphia neighborhood, sports consisted of kick-the-can or rolling a hoop down the street with a stick. The more he talked about his physical prowess, the more convinced I became that my daydreams and shyness were a disappointment to him.

The hushed lobby of the athletic club was paneled in dark wood. A few solitary figures were hidden in wing chairs. My father and I introduced ourselves to a man at the front desk who seemed unimpressed by our presence. His aloofness unnerved me, which wasn't hard considering that no matter how my parents put it, I knew their sending me here was a form of disapproval, a way of banishing the part of me they didn't care to know.

A call went out over the intercom for someone to show us around. While we waited, I noticed that the sand in the standing

ashtrays had been raked into perfect furrows. The glossy leaves of
the potted plants looked as if they'd been polished by hand. The
place seemed more like a well-tended hotel than an athletic club.
Finally, a stoop-shouldered old man hobbled toward us, his head
shrouded in a cloud of white hair. He wore a T-shirt that said
"Instructor"; his arms were so wrinkled and anemic, I thought I
might have misread it. While we followed him to the elevator, I
readjusted my expectations, which had involved fantasies of a
hulking drill sergeant barking orders at a flock of scrawny boys.

The instructor, mumbling to himself and never turning around
to see if we were behind him, showed us where the gymnastics class
took place. I'm certain the building was big, but the size of the
room must be exaggerated by a trick of memory, because when I
envision it, I picture a vast and windowless warehouse. Mats covered the wooden floor. Here and there, in remote and lonely pools
of light, stood a pommel horse, a balance beam, and parallel bars.
Tiers of bleachers rose into darkness. Unlike the cloistered air of
a closet, the room seemed incomplete without a crowd.

Next we visited the dressing room, empty except for a naked
middle-aged man. He sat on a narrow bench and clipped his
formidable toenails. Moles dotted his back. He glistened like a fish.

We continued to follow the instructor down an aisle lined with
numbered lockers. At the far end, steam billowed from the doorway that led to the showers. Fresh towels stacked on a nearby table
made me think of my mother; I knew she liked to have me at home
with her — I was often her only companion — and I resented her
complicity in the plan to send me here.

The tour ended when the instructor gave me a sign-up sheet.
Only a few names preceded mine. They were signatures, or so I
imagined, of other soft and wayward sons.

When the day of the first gymnastics class arrived, my mother
gave me money and a gym bag and sent me to the corner of
Hollywood and Western to wait for a bus. The sun was bright, the
traffic heavy. While I sat there, an argument raged inside my head,
the familiar, battering debate between the wish to be like other
boys and the wish to be like myself. Why shouldn't I simply get up
and go back home, where I'd be left alone to read and think? On
the other hand, wouldn't life be easier if I liked athletics, or
learned to like them?

No sooner did I steel my resolve to get on the bus than I thought of something better: I could spend the morning wandering through Woolworth's, then tell my parents I'd gone to the class. But would my lie stand up to scrutiny? As I practiced describing phantom gymnastics, I became aware of a car circling the block. It was a large car in whose shaded interior I could barely make out the driver, but I thought it might be the man who owned the local pet store. I'd often gone there on the pretext of looking at the cocker spaniel puppies huddled together in their pen, but I really went to gawk at the owner, whose tan chest, in the V of his shirt, was the place I most wanted to rest my head. Every time the man moved, counting stock or writing a receipt, his shirt parted, my mouth went dry, and I smelled the musk of sawdust and dogs.

I found myself hoping that the driver was the man who ran the pet store. I was thrilled by the unlikely possibility that the sight of me, slumped on a bus bench in my T-shirt and shorts, had caused such a man to circle the block. Up to that point in my life, lovemaking hovered somewhere in the future, an impulse a boy might aspire to but didn't indulge. And there I was, sitting on a bus bench in the middle of the city, dreaming I could seduce an adult. I showered the owner of the pet store with kisses and, as aquariums bubbled, birds sang, and mice raced in a wire wheel, slipped my hand beneath his shirt. The roar of traffic brought me to my senses. I breathed deeply and blinked against the sun. I crossed my legs at the knee in order to hide an erection. My fantasy left me both drained and changed. The continent of sex had drifted closer.

The car made another round. This time the driver leaned across the passenger seat and peered at me through the window. He was a complete stranger, whose gaze filled me with fear. It wasn't the surprise of not recognizing him that frightened me, it was what I did recognize — the unmistakable shame in his expression, and the weary temptation that drove him in circles. Before the car behind him honked, he mouthed "hello" and cocked his head. What now, he seemed to be asking. A bold, unbearable question.

I bolted to my feet, slung the gym bag over my shoulder, and hurried toward home. Now and then I turned around to make sure he wasn't trailing me, both relieved and disappointed when I didn't see his car. Even after I became convinced that he wasn't at my back — my sudden flight had scared him off — I kept turning around to see what was making me so nervous, as if I might spot the source of my discomfort somewhere on the street. I walked faster and faster, trying to outrace myself. Eventually, the bus I was supposed to have taken roared past. Turning the corner, I watched it bob eastward.

Closing the kitchen door behind me, I vowed never to leave home again. I was resolute in this decision without fully understanding why, or what it was I hoped to avoid; I was only aware of the need to hide and a vague notion, fading fast, that my trouble had something to do with sex. Already the mechanism of self-deception was at work. By the time my mother rushed into the kitchen to see why I'd returned so early, the thrill I'd felt while waiting for the bus had given way to indignation.

I poured out the story of the man circling the block and protested, with perhaps too great a passion, my own innocence. "I was just sitting there," I said again and again. I was so determined to deflect suspicion away from myself, and to justify my missing the class, that I portrayed the man as a grizzled pervert who drunkenly veered from lane to lane as he followed me halfway home.

My mother cinched her housecoat. She seemed moved and shocked by what I told her, if a bit incredulous, which prompted me to be more dramatic. "It wouldn't be safe," I insisted, "for me to wait at the bus stop again."

No matter how overwrought my story, I knew my mother wouldn't question it, wouldn't bring the subject up again; sex of any kind, especially sex between a man and a boy, was simply not discussed in our house. The gymnastics class, my parents agreed, was something I could do another time.

And so I spent the remainder of that summer at home with my mother, stirring cake batter, holding the dustpan, helping her fold the sheets. For a while I was proud of myself for engineering a reprieve from the athletic club. But as the days wore on, I began to see that my mother had wanted me with her all along, and forcing that to happen wasn't such a feat. Soon a sense of compromise set in; by expressing disgust for the man in the car, I'd expressed disgust for an aspect of myself. Now I had all the time in the world to sit around and contemplate my desire for men. The days grew long and stifling and hot, an endless sentence of self-examination.

Only trips to the pet store offered any respite. Every time I went there, I was too electrified with longing to think about longing in the abstract. The bell tinkled above the door, animals stirred within their cages, and the handsome owner glanced up from his work.

I handed my father the *Herald*. He opened the paper and disappeared behind it. My mother stirred her coffee and sighed. She gazed at the sweltering passersby and probably thought herself lucky. I slid into the vinyl booth and took my place beside my parents.

For a moment, I considered asking them about what had happened on the street, but they would have reacted with censure and alarm, and I sensed there was more to the story than they'd ever be willing to tell me. Men in dresses were only the tip of the iceberg. Who knew what other wonders existed — a boy, for example, who wanted to kiss a man — exceptions the world did its best to keep hidden.

It would be years before I heard the word "transvestite," so I struggled to find a word for what I'd seen. "He-she" came to mind, as lilting as "Injijikian." "Burl's" would have been perfect, like "boys" and "girls" spliced together, but I can't claim to have thought of this back then.

I must have looked stricken as I tried to figure it all out, because my mother put down her coffee cup and asked if I was O.K. She stopped just short of feeling my forehead. I assured her I was fine, but something within me had shifted, had given way to a heady doubt. When the waitress came and slapped down our check — "Thank You," it read, "Dine out more often" — I wondered if her lofty hairdo or the breasts on which her nametag quaked were real. Wax carnations bloomed at every table. Phony wood paneled the walls. Plastic food sat in a display case: fried eggs, a hamburger sandwich, a sundae topped with a garish cherry.

W. S. DI PIERO

Gots Is What You Got

FROM THE THREEPENNY REVIEW

"I gotta use words when I talk to you."
— "Sweeney Agonistes"

WHAT ARE BEGINNINGS? A constantly melting and recomposing amalgam of images? A sentence we keep writing and revising? A messy album of meanings in which we seek patterns to explain to ourselves the mystery of personality? One of my favorite passages in Ruskin's *Praeterita* describes the soft orchestration of his family's voices:

> I never had heard my father's or mother's voice once raised in any question with each other, nor seen an angry, or even a slightly hurt or offended, glance in the eyes of either. I had never heard a servant scolded; nor even suddenly, passionately, or in any severe manner, blamed.

His household must have been a walled garden of mild manners. This to me is a powerful legend of childhood because it is so mysteriously remote from my own, which was charged with the electricity of blame, of real or presumed or anticipated offense. There were few mild manners in my family or in the immigrant neighborhood where I grew up. Mildness was a liability. In a boy, it attracted predators like a scent. Mildness could not be a chosen mood or humor; it was a flaw in the stone of personality, a symptom of sickness. A diffident, soft-spoken man like my father (who had breakdowns just like a friend of his, the only other mild-mannered man I remember from our circle of friends) was considered weak, inadequate or disabled in spirit, though the nicety people used to conceal this conviction was to say he was (like his shattered friend) "a good man."

The voices of my world were seldom tender and unquestioning. Conversations, especially among members of my mother's family, were choleric eruptions. If by some accident a rational argument took place, defeat was registered not by words or acknowledgment but by a sardonic, defiant sneer. (We became masters as well of the mannered condescension Pope describes in "Epistle to Doctor Arbuthnot": "And without sneering, teach the rest to sneer.") Anger, impatience, and dismissive ridicule of the unfamiliar were the most familiar moods. Everyone around me, it seemed, except for my father's side of the family, spoke in brittle, pugnacious tones that I still hear when my own voice comes snarling out of its vinegary corner. My neighbors, having no servants to scold, scolded one another instead. There were no degrees of criticism or disapproval, only a single absolute pitch of dismissal. I heard it from when I was a child until I was an adolescent, when my friend Joey T., a sweet-hearted boy who sat behind me in home room, enthusiastically offered to shoot a teacher (a priest) who had been tormenting me. A year earlier, he wanted to do the same to a boy who was bullying me: "I'll shoot the son of a bitch in the face!" Later, after I'd left South Philadelphia, I encountered the different sorts of polite, well-bred nastiness and intolerance practiced by other sorts of people, casually genteel Protestant expressions of "displeasure" that made me nostalgic for the operatic candor of my own culture.

A loud disruptive tonality was also the medium for affection or delight, the way a shriek might indicate terror or frivolity. It was, in any case, not an excitability which people directed at one another. I hardly ever heard anyone in my family or neighborhood say they were angry with (or fond of) so-and-so. It was instead an aimless but earnest wrathfulness or rapture, theatrical and mostly purposeless, a kind of roving sparkiness going off constantly in the universe at large, for it also took in God and all His angels and His saints. My people always seemed to be picking a fight with circumstance, with the very fact of circumstance, and in the absence of specific aggravating circumstance the cosmos would do. I did not know how strange or peculiar this was until I left it behind and found outside my culture a broader and more pliable medium for moral feeling. Nor did I realize how deeply its music had settled in my heart until I heard in my poetry the same extremity of unease and rage at circumstance.

The two sides of my family were the hemispheres of my own temperament. My mother's family, which set the dominant tone in our lives, came from a village near Naples whose name no one remembers, though my eldest aunt was born there and my grandparents, Carmela and Simone, lived there until their twenties. The Girone clan had the classic Neapolitan temperament, a volatile compound of hilarity, raucous grief, anger, and consternation over every one of life's details. It's a culture of sublime complaint, of rage or hysteria in the presence of divinely sponsored fate. Grandfather Simone, after immigrating to Philadelphia, worked off and on as a rough carpenter, drinking too much off and on, they say, and often drunkenly whipping his children with a belt strap, as he later menaced us grandchildren. His longest on-the-job stint took place underground, working along with hundreds of immigrant laborers to build the Philadelphia subway system. His wife died after giving birth to their sixth child. My mother, the third of four daughters, became responsible for the family, and when she married my father, Grandfather Simone came to live with them. He lived with us for many years, and when he died at ninety-three, gruffly attributing his age to robust bloodlines, dago red, and blackleaf stogies, he spoke maybe fifty words of English, many of them obscenities that sparked from his mouth whenever Eliot Ness and his archangels killed Italian gangsters on *The Untouchables,* Italian gangsters played by Greeks, Black Irish, and Jews. One night, drunk and in uncharacteristic jolly spirits, he confided to me that in Italy he had once killed a man over an insult and spent time in jail. I never determined the truth of this. None of his children would confirm or deny it. "Oh," they said, "Pop says all sorts of crazy things."

The Di Piero side seemed a different country. In some sense it was a different country, given the distinct geographical identities of Italy's regions. The emotional and intellectual climate of the Di Piero hemisphere was so different that even now, thinking it, I feel it. The Neapolitan Girones were voluble, brash, impetuous, defiant, and proud of their toughness. The Abruzzese Di Pieros were reserved, quiet-spoken, self-contained, and they reflected more complexly on the particulars of experience. The Girones felt that too much thinking would make you crazy, complexity was a kind of sinfulness. Among the Girones I felt I was being watched, among the Di Pieros I was being seen. My father, his younger brother, and his sister took after their mother, Maria, in being gentle reticent souls. I've visited the small hilltop town in Abruzzo called Castel Frentano where my father was born, and I recognize its landscape and the temper of its people from Silone's novels. The Abruzzesi, they say, are *fort' e' gentili,* strong and kind. Regional traits should not fit so snugly as that one fits the Di Pieros. Their laughter was different, small and almost diffident, less assaultive than Girone laughter. Different memory hoards, too. Both families were poor but managed to make decent lives in the New World after much hard work. Grandmother Maria, however, kept a store of knowledge about the old country, the crossing in steerage, her husband Aurelio who died just a few years after arriving in America, her own situation as a young widow speaking no English, three children to support, the years in a sweatshop, and all the rest. It was she who told me, sometimes only vaguely, of our ancestors: the priest who left his property to the prostitute who had given birth to his son; the Di Pieros who left for South America and started new families there without dissolving their first ones in Italy; the collateral masses of Di Pieros in Argentina and Brazil descendent from those ancestors; the gamblers and settlers and plantation tycoons among them.

The Girones were another immigrant mentality: they knew nothing about their past and seemed to prefer it that way. Grandfather Simone was the only one who could tell us anything, but the only story he ever told me was the one about the killing. For the Girones, I think, the New World was a happy oblivion. For the Di Pieros there was some sense of the gleaming shadows of past lives. Even their way with language was worlds apart. Maria spoke real Italian, though with occasional dialect words, the swallowed vowel-endings of immigrant speech and the southernish accent of Abruzzo. Simone spoke only dialect, and dialect is not conventional language spoken with slightly variant vocabulary and syntax, it is a different language. A Bolognese visiting Naples will understand very little, if anything, of a conversation in Neapolitan dialect.

When, in my twenties, I finally learned Italian, I conversed happily with my grandmother and, when she was dying, wrote letters for her in Italian to her nieces and nephews and cousins in Abruzzo. When my grandfather was dying, we tried to communicate, but his dialect was as unintelligible to me as my standard Italian was to him.

In my house, the Girone temper dominated, and so relations were usually tense, disputatious, eroded by suspicion, resentment, and spleen. The sense of the world communicated to me by those voices was that contingency, the fact of living in the world only to die, *disputed* human presence. The most of bird life that I saw in South Philadelphia were starlings, grackles, pigeons, and sparrows hopping around sewer grates. Later on I began to love to watch the varieties of birds, because they are body sustained in a medium of apparent nothingness, at home there. Canada geese barking one fall morning in Vermont. A cardinal flashing in a snowy wood. A cuckoo calling outside a farmhouse in Calabria. The early morning starling screech in South Philadelphia. The lesson I absorbed from the rough vocal music of my childhood was that we cannot be entirely at home in the world because we have a consciousness that dreams of elsewheres, heavens and whatnot. Tenants, not stewards, of the world, and the world carries on like a miserly indifferent landlord.

From when I was very young I was attracted, with the call of what is sensually and intellectually elsewhere, to what Yeats called "sweet sounds together." When I began to read poetry, sheer tonal musicality mattered more than subject matter. I read whatever I happened upon in the public library. Poe, Lindsay, Millay, Sandburg, the Byron of "The Prisoner of Chillon," some anthology pieces by Wordsworth and Whitman. Bits out of Homer and the Arthurian tales appealed to me most for the velocity of the narrative, the tidal progress of surge and arrest, and the pitch of the telling. In good time, I became aware of tonality as event and felt my way into the formal pliability of language. Whatever is authentic in my work is due to the crass commingling of that abstract sense of formal beauty with the given language textures and soul-conditions of my culture, though when I was struggling for postadolescent intellectual and cultural independence, I of course believed I had to refine out the "crudities" of my culture. And yet I never did shed my tribal

legacy of contrariness, the festive abrasiveness and chafing hilarity
that even now I still at once love and cringe at. It took me some
time to realize that abrasiveness, mineral grit, could be the kind
of pumice stone that polishes a surface and gives shapely forms a
chased gleam.

Love poems I've written sound so much like bitter, self-canceling
disputes. (A woman once scolded me that I turn everything into
a chore.) Many of my poems seem to me only half emerged from
mud, or they sound close to breaking apart on their own tonal
irregularities and emotional uncertainty. One can, I suppose, develop tonal range and the protocols of tonal display through study
and imitation and craftiness, but I feel I've become a songbird bred
to a particular register of tones. I have nothing in common with
poets who practice the casual, bland, discursive evenness of the
plain style. My own rhythms, this side of good breeding perhaps,
are in speech and writing so much interrupted sequence, a nervous
anxiety about the possibility of saying something straight and clear.

Sour exasperation, shrill gaiety, raspingly curt affection — these
were the registers most familiar to me. In my childhood, the words
themselves were often not even English. Once I walked into our
corner grocery, operated by a noble, solemn Calabrese named
Gumbo. (Who knows what Italian nickname that comic English
sound violated?) It was a Friday in Lent, baccalà was soaking in a
basin outside, I was the only customer, and Gumbo and his wife
were arguing furiously. The wife grabbed a can from a shelf and
threatened to throw it at Gumbo's head. Though I could understand bits of my grandparents' different languages, I understood
nothing of what Gumbo and his wife were shouting. When I
reported this to my mother — I was seven, I sneaked from the store
without interrupting the quarrel, shaking with fear not only of the
savage feelings displayed but of the unintelligibility of the language
— she explained how Gumbo and his wife weren't a good match
and didn't get along in the first place, and second, they spoke
different dialects and couldn't understand each other. He was
Calabrese, she was from Aldilà. When I asked where Aldilà was,
she said somewhere up north. "Who the hell knows? *Up there.*"
Aldilà, so far as I know, is no place name. Or only in a special sense.
The prepositional phrase *al di là* means "beyond." (*Al di là del fiume*
= the other side of the river.) In Dante, it means the beyond,

heaven, a beatific elsewhere. Where, then, was Gumbo's wife from? "Aldilà!" my mother and her sisters shouted at me, as if to increase my understanding, pointing north.

North of where? Naples? South Philadelphia, which was for us the center of the known world? Who the hell knows? I knew Gumbo and his family well. He was a great lover of horticulture in that rowhouse neighborhood without plants and flowers. He once took me to Bartram's Garden, where I nearly passed out from the powerful fragrances. He spoke halting English. When he quarreled with his wife, who spoke fluent English, the two of them always quarreled in their dialects. In those intensest moments, they became foreigners to each other. To communicate grievance and ferocity they relied entirely on tone, gesture (that can of tomato paste!), and pitch. For most of the people I was raised among, it was ferocity, real or theatrical, that mattered; that defiant energy was our way of meeting the world and pretending we were not subject to its harsh ministrations and unfair judgments. Sense, reason, logic, sequence, sounds strung together intelligibly or coherently or sweetly or gently — these were suspect, untrustworthy, often signs of the power that other forces (bureaucracies, governments, professional agencies, outsiders) exercised to the harm or humiliation of people like us.

In *Praeterita* Ruskin describes himself as a boy:

> I already disliked growing older, — never expected to be wiser, and formed no more plans for the future than a little black silkworm does in the middle of its first mulberry leaf.

In time, we lose the silkworm's constant appetitive present. Expectations grow in us the way language inflects itself into more complex verb tenses, and they become the fungus that corrodes the leaf. One of my soul's conditional tenses ("if only . . .") has always been to live the silkworm's moment, completely in the instant, but even to think that is an act of migratory mind, of the imagination making images of elsewheres. Bunting writes that the poet "lies with one to long for another." The present tense is the stolid, dispassionate judge and minister to the encroachments of the tempter, the "if only" or "what if" or "were it so." I've never felt the urgency of the issue we hear much of in recent years, that of the "marginality" of poetry in American culture. It's usually tied to certain traditional powers which poetry has presumably surrendered to other arts. I believe that the forms of poetry can still express, more completely and complexly than other media, feeling in time and feeling for time. Verb tenses mix, coalesce, bang, and sag. The senses reckoning with their local reality, the heart reckoning with the political relations noded therein and radiating therefrom — poetry makes these a right, fit matter of speech. To turn these energies into mere issues or "crises" is already to concede their incipient powers. It may also be an admission that poetry no longer wants or needs to give voice to the passion of consciousness. The issue is not whether poetry is adequate to the task (though the question figures in harmless after-dinner speeches at poetry banquets) but the ways in which it goes about executing the task. For me, it's not by means of genteel manners and over-refined sensibility but by making the language of poetry a constant viewing or scanning of origins, with ongoing recognitions of reality layered in. Not local idiosyncratic origins, not local-color origins, but the beginnings of species consciousness as they are figured forth in local conditions, local cultures. The migratory passion of imagination, of image-making, burns in the instant.

When I was growing up, my ear trained only a little on the sounds of words in books, and mostly on the cadences and textures of language spoken around me. The idioms I heard, their racy patterns and fiery tonalities, were often only partly released from an Italian bedrock. Since nearly every adult and most of my playmates had at some time spoken some sort of Italian, the English we heard and used was a strangely colored flower sprung from sandy soil. The Neapolitan dialect the Girones spoke sounded eruptive and jabby. English words with Italianate endings tumbled from unintelligible dialect phrases. *Boifrendo* for "boyfriend." *Baccaus* for "back house" or bathroom, because before indoor plumbing the privy was always back of the house. English phrases sometimes translated Italian idioms. Women in my family still say "I'll give you eat" because it translates *ti do mangiare.* I heard a disapproving father threaten his postadolescent son, who was trying to raise a beard, with the hilariously ominous cry: "I'll break your face with that chin!" Italian sounds fused to English ones. English itself was a marshland of strange fogs and apparitions. Esso, Sunoco, rumdumb, rock candy, coalbin. Tootsie pop sounded kin to tootsie brute, which was how people sounded out *Tu sei brutta* (too say BROOT-ah, pronounced instead as tootz ay BROOT), literally "You're ugly" but spoken as an endearment to children, like "Little funny face." The vulgarism *cazzo* (CAHTS-zo, "cock" or "prick," but used like "fuck," e.g. *Ma che cazzo fai* = What the fuck are you doing) was pronounced gahtz. I heard it said a hundred times: You got gots is what you got. You don't have a goddamn thing.

The English I listened to, growing up in the 1950s — I remember it as listening, not hearing or overhearing — was one expression of the unstable, inchoate, poorly bred vernacular which forty years earlier Henry James said would become the emergent language of the immigrant populations flooding American cities. It was a vitally impure, try-it-on language bearing the burrs and toothy surfaces of languages more or less left behind in Europe and eastern Russia, with regional dialects showing up as weird watermarks on those surfaces. The sentences I read in my schoolbooks were, by contrast to my neighborhood music, affectless and imperial. My language for poetry would as a consequence become an English more or less born somewhere else, but where? Its caustic and sometimes comic infusions came from dialects already half forgotten or scrambled by official English. My feeling for idiomatic speech became studied, self-conscious. I feared the embarrassment of misspeaking an idiom or cracking a malapropism. I still have to pay attention when I use catchphrases, commonplaces, idiomatic turns of speech, for fear of getting them wrong and making some heart-rendering error. I still commit to memory and rehearse common turns of phrase I hear on the street. And so I've become a poet who seeks conversational normalcy and vigor in poetry the way one seeks out a distant constellation. My instinct is the still childish one of taking what is given in language and breaking it up into phonetic pieces, syllable amulets, each loaded with some nuance of actual or desired feeling and the pied, scattered clues of sense. The cunning of "Tell all the truth but tell it slant,/Success in circuit lies" is strategic. What happens when your *given* English is in many ways cockeyed or skewed and draws force and complexity from that? The artifice most difficult to sustain is, for me, that of casual normalcy. The amiable knowing style of much contemporary poetry sounds to my ear as phony as the King's English. (Perhaps it is, culturally and politically, the King's English of our time, official and self-assured, but that is a different question.) Working the language of poetry has therefore been for me a struggle to momentarily stabilize what is by nature and culture *off,* unstable, riddled with fabulous obscene errors.

My South Philadelphia language could be brutal, and it was to my heart the purest expression of unreason, awe, gaiety, solemnity, and discontent. But it was also an impoverished instrument for clear reasoning or exact description, it lived in my mind as an enemy of such activities — impatient, stupidly superstitious, intolerant of rational deliberation, suspicious of coherences and consistencies. It blended into its tones and rhythms a sense of the sacred. But *sacre* means both sacred and accursed. We spoke of physical and psychological sickness as if it were the presence of a god among us. This was felt especially with regard to mental disorders, which were carefully separated from other sicknesses. The young bachelor on my block who was epileptic, the woman who moved objects with the power of her mind, the girl who possessed second sight — they were holy presences. But a friend of my father, a workingman who had a nervous breakdown and who wept helplessly for days at the kitchen table before being finally hospitalized, was not sacred or possessed by the god. He was a pollution, shameful and scandalous, as if his disorder were that of blood spilled accidentally in purified precincts. Neighborly expressions of sympathy were ritualized conventions of speech meant to contain the menace, seal off the pollution. The word "sickness" had an aura of mysterious visitation and violation. The phrase "nervous exhaustion" (*esaurimento nervoso:* I learned the phrase in my twenties and I have not forgotten it) signaled some degree of moral expulsion from the community. They should have said, and I would have been better off to hear, that his soul was sick or hurt or fatigued. Physical illness was attributable to divine intent, it was some kind of election and was fingered by deity. Nervous trouble was (and is still) a humiliation, not an affliction, because it was so entirely a human condition, or a sign of having been abandoned by the gods. When I began to find my way as a poet, I wanted to make poetry seem an awareness of the world lived along the nerves but ministered to by the difficult clarities of reason and judgment. The blunt play and immediacy of my local language was given to me. I had to learn the rest.

JOSEPHINE FOO

Endou*

FROM THE AMERICAN VOICE

Boxes

Seems to be mist coming down now, baskets of mist shaken off a steamer. And the pipe hissing, quiet enough here to imagine this is anywhere. It can't fail to be anything but a haven for someone maybe stood on the sidewalk all day with leaflets from a drugstore, or flown in from a distant continent. It has warm and changeable walls. I am here, in this kitchen, like bars *passing the panther in its cage* and a body curled in the shadow slant of a window.

I think about food. Just boiled water for instant ramen noodles, threw out the spice packet and made my own sauce of watered-down tomato ketchup, basil, sesame seeds, and soy sauce. With oil, a drop or two. There're two pork chops in the refrigerator, rib ends at 1.99/lb, and these would be good later, with teriyaki sauce, pepper, and basil again, broiled, with a spray of brown sugar when it's close to done, a spray done with the hand; watercress on the side, that's enough. And perhaps with wine. No potatoes, no night shade. No grains with the meat.

Not so quiet, like I'm swimming and there's a noise undertow, sometimes music, sometimes voices, like a natural current.

I turn around quickly and see things, like I've just now met these pots and pans in the dark part of the kitchen. I don't remember buying them, don't feel like a tenant, feel neither Asian nor American. Natalie, the nine-year-old next door, says she thinks I

*endou: endow

grew up in a box in Times Square, perhaps that's where they think Malaysia is. I've forgotten my mother's maiden name, and search for it in boxes thrown away. Thinking, as always, lonely woman, of a collective story.

There's breeze from somewhere. These buildings are so old that you can lay a cheek on a bearing wall and feel the wind, or feel the wind in a crack in baseboard or molding. The foundation stone of this one says 1906, and people have died here in their rooms, died of futile farming, tarnished silver and stains on porcelain dipped in lye. *All the Strange Hours,* and not a one for bells ringing in beginnings or endings here, in farmland, in blue iron.

Remittance

The men live by a canal where the water is full and high, inches below concrete arms of land; appearing green with vegetation in slow-moving waterfront grays. See the rotund bottom with coffee silt on its tail, and young men kneeling on the lip, reaching out far to break the surface with their fingers, foraging for a second chance. The older ones shelter indoors and dig wells in back rooms; press their ears to the baseboard and hear the canal wiping its eyes on a sleeve through their shut doors; hear it climbing the steps like tired Oo Shak women toward its straight and end.

The men line up by the little folding table of a letter writer. *I feel the canal is a scroll with my words. I see gold-paved streets on the other side of the canal. How do you get by? Do you still play pretend games with the garden wall, make believe that the ants are horses, the flying bugs cranes and swallows? Have you received yet my remittance?*

I play my own pretend game. On the crook on Doyer Street, I sit dreaming of Shen Fu and his wife, of an American daughter riding uptown on the great train for typing work, so simply, as if walking from here to Pell Street. Imagine that. But the drift on the old water has false daughters and fathers and mothers passed on, and meanwhile we've used it for a sewer and drinking water.

I ascend the stairwell to the highest floor where my room is. I tell my neighbors about the treasure in my closet; under the little wind-up toys I sell, the batteries, the blinking telephones, is heaven.

They believe me, once smashed in through the fire escape window
to search for heaven. Did they find it, a scroll with life words. I
moved the toys aside and swept the floor, then unrolled it. Here,
I show you — in the center is my family. Here, surrounding, the
waters I crossed. Here, on the border, is my work, the blacks of my
eyes, the hollow of a bell without its clapper; the soft black berry
put between my fingers; the shape in the mirror.

*Have you received my remittance? The weather is winter now. Use the
money for fuel, warmth, sustenance.*

Uprooting

There isn't much more to do; you count the rooms left behind
and draw them on throw-away slips of paper. The size of one in
relation to another is important, and the time of day the sun shines
in. Where, for instance, books were faded orange. It's difficult
to make inventory of all that's gone, when your parents choose to
say nothing about it; like the Japanese Americans released from
their internment camps, the Jews of Europe liberated from their
death camps. In both began a frenzy of forgetting, a continent
without rules in one, families without direction in another, like
mine.

I draw a figure in the graph of my bedroom, perhaps meant to
be me; or a friendly girl who has it now. Perhaps new owners have
managed to seed the large garden with my mother's favorite car-
pet-grass and planted a high hedge to hide the wire fence. It helps
me trust memory, to decorate my paper garden with begonias,
gardenias, ixoras.

I draw a figure in the garden, perhaps my father surveying what
he'd sold, a priest blessing the house for a new family. I draw in
the TV in the corner, a haunted, abandoned forest, the flimsy
bookshelf over the window my sister made, that would spill on me
sleeping.

I smoke a cigarette in my grandmother's moonlit yard. I walk
lightly on her unfamiliar grass, listening to Tamil music from the
dim light in the gardener's shack. It is South Africa of *A World
Apart.* "You're not Elsie's mother, you're *my* mother," cries the
movie's daughter, and I smile in self-recognition. I've played the

strings at night; walked the plank, mile, ridden the ferry by cigarette glowing. Taken inventory: I am worth — so much — at this
moment in time. Slaves having been auctioned once must have
appraised their worth routinely.

I believe I am a man. At fourteen, I was a slender, sensitive boy;
large-handed, open-handed, self-contained; stepped in a store window to remain there as the world bought and sold itself at wildly
fluctuating prices, beyond a child's understanding.

Endou

If ghosts exist (and they do), when should I see them? The man
dangling in a basket from a pulley high up in the Sierra Nevadas
sees them everywhere in the valleys beneath him. He catches them
scurrying white-headed from his descending shadow and in eagles
pulling blue fabric edges into old, familiar oceans. His tribute to
them scatters over a thousand broken gravestones released from
strings in his hands, while he himself is chained to the wind.

I burn incense for them in my office, thick-scented chinchona
bark. I sense them in the cobwebbed corners, in the farthest point
out the window my eye can focus on: a smokestack on an apartment
building. I believe they linger in our cities with their hands out for
tribute, or wrap their arms around street signs, etching Chinese
names over presidents and "settlers" and the American living.

They are alive, trees, rocks, coats.

The Hmong abandoned their ghosts in their Laotian hills and
are dying in Providence, R.I. "Why don't they adopt Native American hill spirits?" advise whites. In that same logic, I imagine a door
opening to a passage and ending at a booth or elevator, musty with
slow movement, earthbound feet.

Are there ghosts? The scenic elevator carries me to the upper
floors of the Marriott Marquis; the law offices of Paul, Weiss,
Rifkind, Wharton & Garrison look out on Park Avenue. The ghosts
must drift like gases in the middle of the day, I think, dissipating
by night above this traffic noise. I remember Old Lodge Skins in
the movie *Little Big Man*, dressing *to die in [his] own land, where
human beings are buried in the sky.* A wet gold narcissus petal holds
to the heel of my shoe, mile upon mile downtown, carried to

strange lofts like a slip of parachute that flutters, when I release
its string, like wings.

Let Us Reach for Our Hats

Reading Tsvetaeva, how she manages to make each sentence a
shout and her tongue curl around stresses:

> As I love to
>   kiss hands, and
> to name everything, I
>   love to open
> doors!
>   Wide — into the night!

He wishes I would be "more catlike" and I whisper, *I'll try to be, next
time,* thinking of the hemp shirts nuns once wore under their
habits that would chafe their nipples unless they remained entirely
still. Hemmed in, like the oppressive fluorescent light behind the
iron grating left on all hours across the courtyard, revealing the
stark, empty room and boxes pushed to the window without care.
At any moment, I expect to see a battered woman there, perhaps
my mother, in such hollow relief only fluorescent lighting can
scrape on a woman's face.

I've discovered that I nick my cigarette filter with my thumb like
a man. I have a man's stoicism and the capacity to leave my home
and do violence to women out of some strange thoughtless judgment, as my father did. You grow cautious after years of handling
others. I know I have that cruelty and brace myself for such
treatment from lovers; and here it is: don't move, the moment will
gather itself into something to be thrown away.

"Let us reach for our hats in the fire," do you remember it, the Neruda
poem? Yes, I lie (I had not loved it. Tsvetaeva had been too bitter
for Tony, Neruda was for him an epic dancer). Should I tell him
these things? How I would not survey a room like a dancer, nor
enjoy a thing rooted over there out of reach like a thief; how
downstairs, Angel Diaz and his wife keep his gun under their pillow
in their small terrible room, guarding against invasion of their

country by poets with such poems: *I will be glad to reach into the fire.*
I will gladly be catlike.

Danny

There is a nervous calm, as if just after a wreck, without crowds.
One witness walks round and round the site, studying it from all
angles: the limb resting on the sand, the hole punctured in the
side of the vessel; the sense of things built over ten, twenty, thirty
years ending in a moment. But he walks clear from it and forgets
what he's seen in the next hundred feet.

I have been a priest, he thinks, tossing stones into the air, breaking
waves. *In another life, I was surrounded by people murmuring as quietly
as this breeze, facing me; there on the rocks sat a man or woman who would
rise to their feet when they saw me approach.* And there a little girl would
enter, her face marked with the ills of father and mother. Now he
remembers the wreck and turns to glance at it, seeing that child
enter the hole in its side.

He empties his pockets into the froth and walks on to the
marshes and their fermented warm saltwater wine. In the dark
behind him, the ocean touches where he stands, each time felling
a stage wall and revealing its naked catwalks and wires. He has
stood naked here; knows what it's like to be Icarus and rise up
close to the sun and have it melt wax from his wings. Floated tulips
in bathwater for a woman sleeping with her legs spread alone in
a large bed. Cambodia, Bosnia, Angola; Cuba, Burma, Vietnam,
Chile, Argentina, Germany; he adds these to this absurd calm, rolls
them in his pant leg as he wades into the icy, sitting river.

*I've been a prince in my time, been prince and priest and river, and
I've been a dog running on this sacred beach.* With that he wades out
of the water, shakes off his wet, and starts to run, wildly, like the
boy I'd loved, who'd loved me at Vassar, sister with the face of
a prophet.

Father

It is not a cloth, but a million birds; each lifting edges, revealing
my father. He is standing there behind the curtain at the windows,

looking into paths on hills where we bury our dead above our living, unlike westerners, who put their dead lower than the lowest house. Out of sight, powerless to approve of or condemn what the living do. My dead ancestors can see me shitting or peeing through these great windows each time the breeze comes, and the strands and feathers part, the fringes, lace and frayed ends rolled on white tile.

My father walks on the hillside, seeding ground to left and right with his right hand clutched deep in his apron pocket. Moving in rhythm, losing a step, regaining a balance, then sitting on a twisted branch; waiting and listening as if for his name to be called that was missed before, in a room of slightly bowed men. My father seems in shadow as he walks forward in the sun; *the sun don't like some men,* he shakes his head, then nods, kneeling to retrieve some seeds he's sown, weighing them, pressing them to his cheek.

Worries absorbed by bathroom walls and a sheen of tile laid over, hands put flat to walls as a child makes her way downstairs and wonders what to do next; outdoors and indoors no different from closing her eyes. But she smiles when she thinks of her father, of slipping her hand in his landing hand. American men search for their names, like him, on lists tucked away somewhere in the brick without knowing their primary ends, as she's grown used to surrogate fathers on street corners, their earth-colored faces.

I've seen you walking; and when you thought you were alone, I've seen you fold away your clothes, first touching them to your lips and wiping your eyes on them. I've seen you naked, father, doing "naked" things.

The doorway's cold, father. Today's the coldest day in half a decade, and feels like a tomb.

WILLIAM H. GASS

The Art of Self

FROM HARPER'S MAGAZINE

SELF-ABSORPTION, we are told, is the principal preoccupation of our age. It is an odd activity. I imagine a blotter soaking up its own absorbency and disappearing like a Cheshire cat by slow degrees. Still, if the star is more important than the team, the clan closer to our real concerns than the wider community; if minorities are to be promoted to major, and sects gain sole possession of the holy; then perhaps we should embrace the ultimate plurality our selfishness suggests and each perform our person to an empty house.

But what if we really want the world to watch? Look, Ma, I'm breathing. See me take my initial toddle, use the potty, scratch my sister, win spin the bottle. Gee whiz, my first adultery — what a guy! That surely deserves a commemorative marker on the superhighway of my life. So now I'm writing my own sweet history. However, there's a rub. What kind of figure can I count on cutting in another's consciousness or on that most merciless of public stages — the printed page?

The power to see ourselves as others see us is granted only to such disengaged observers as arrive from France by slow sail. Even my mirror puts just that bit of me before my gaze that I permit to fall there. I cannot see all round myself: not anywhere I walk or perch, or if I quickly whirl about to come upon my rear and take it by surprise. I might as well be asleep to such sides of me as disappear out of the corners of my eyes. Nor is the ugliness of my gnarled feet evident anywhere within my skin, where I alone can feel what splendid shape they're in. I think I have a winning smile, but to those on whom my smile is so winsomely conferred, the slightly turned-down corners of its lips convey despair, disgust, disdain — I know not what uninvited attitude in addition — and invariably, if in tears, though I argue my happiness like William Jennings Bryan on behalf of God, the weeping will convict me of a lie, as far as mere onlookers are concerned; because we really believe in no other consciousness than our own, and must infer the contents of another's mind from the perceptions that arrive in ours: from an overheard voice, its screams and groans and heavy breathing; from a body, its weight and posture; from someone's gait, the swagger; and from the face, its signs. And to the groan don't we affix our own ache, to another's risen flesh our yearning, to the sly wink our own conspiratorial designs?

It is safer by far, some say, to rely on behavior to speak by itself. History is something we catch in the act, and only acts have public consequences. Internal states are not even evidence, for pains can be imagined or misplaced, their groaning faked; better to see where the bone is broken or tooth decayed (John Dewey once argued that an aching tooth was not sufficient evidence of something anywhere amiss), and if I promise to give another all my love, it would be wise of the lucky recipient to wait and weigh what the offered love improves, and count what its solicitude will cost.

Feelings are not a dime a dozen, but the price of eggs is eighty cents. Which, do you think then, really hatches chicks in the yard?

Yes, as Aristotle insisted, the Good is what the Good Man does. Does the geologist need to infer an interior to his rock to read its past? Does the botanist really interrogate her plants? Does the zoologist attribute suffering to his frogs as he runs his scalpel round their gizzards? Why, we could weep a world of pain into a thimble and have hollow enough left over for a finger, since consciousness never struts and frets upon the stage or occupies a locker in the dressing room.

Biography, the writing of a life, is a branch of history. It requires quite a lot of labor, and therefore, when such a work is undertaken, one would expect the subject to be of some significance to history as a whole. Yet, except for the encyclopedia of the dead, as Danilo Kiš imagined it, where everybody's obit is already complete or in meticulous construction, the majority of mankind rest, as George

Eliot wrote, in unvisited tombs and have left behind them nothing of their former presence but perhaps a hackneyed scratch upon a stone. Futility is the presiding spirit at every funeral.

Caesar's assassins did not stab him with their souls. In Hades, their shades are not stained by the murdered man's blood. That blood caked, that blood colored, only the blades.

Biography, the writing of a life, is a branch of history, but a broken branch, snapped perhaps heartlessly from the trunk, at the moment when Montesquieu directed the historian's eye to larger themes and toward those general social aspects from which the individual's traits, he believed, had more specifically sprung.

Yet if my tooth aches, it is after all my ache, though you may be better informed than I of the swelling; if my heart is sore, that soreness is unique, though its heaviness does not even tremble the balance bar; if I am afraid, do not complacently say you share my fear and understand my state, for how can you know how I feel? Isn't that our unpleasant complaint? Isn't that how we reject so much sympathy — stale candy on a staler plate? Since, to accomplish our death, there are a thousand similar and similarly scientific ways, but inside that shutting down of the senses there is a dread belonging to no one else even in the same sad medical shape; there is a large dread like an encountered rat, huge, as if fat as an idol, bearded like some ancient northern warrior, yet as indistinct in its corner and as ineffectual as lint. We can't make history out of that.

Knowing has two poles, and they are always poles apart: carnal knowing, the laying on of hands, the hanging of the fact by head or heels, the measurement of mass and motion, the calibration of brutal blows, the counting of supplies; and spiritual knowing, invisibly felt by the inside self, who is but a fought-over field of distraction, a stage where we recite the monotonous monologue that is our life, a knowing governed by internal tides, by intimations, motives, resolutions, by temptations, secrecy, shame, and pride.

Autobiography is a life writing its life. As if over? Or as it proceeds? Biographies are sometimes written with the aid of the biographee, and these few are therefore open-ended too, centrally incomplete, for death normally does the summing up, the bell tolls for the tale beneath whose telling the deceased shall be buried, with the faith that he or she shall rise again on publication day, all ancient acts only pages then, every trait an apt description, every quality of character an anecdote, the mind squeezed within a quip, and the hero's, or heroine's, history headed not for heaven but for the shelf.

If we leap rapidly enough from one side of this insistence to its denial — from the belief that only I can know how I am to the view that only another can see me really — we can quickly persuade ourselves that neither self-knowledge nor any other kind is possible, and, so persuaded, sink dizzily to the floor. Of course, we might, by letting the two positions stretch out alongside each other and observing how these two kinds of information are of equal value and are complementary, conclude that for a full account both the "in" and the "out" are needed. That was Spinoza's solution. It is usually wise to do whatever Spinoza suggests.

How does autobiography begin? With memory. And the consequent division of the self into the-one-who-was and the-one-who-is. The-one-who-is has the advantage of having been the-one-who-was. Once. The-one-who-was is, furthermore, at the present self's mercy, for it may not wish to remember that past, or it may wish the-one-who-was was other than the one it was, and consequently alter its description, since the-one-who-is is writing this history and has the upper hand. Every moment a bit of the self slides away toward its station in the past, where it will be remembered partially, if at all; with distortions, if at all; and then rendered even more incompletely, with graver omissions and twists to the plot by the play of the pen, so that its text will no doubt be subsequently and inaccurately read, systematically misinterpreted and put to use in yet another version, possibly by a biographer bent on revising the customary view of you and surrounding his selected subject with himself, as Sartre surrounded Genet, as a suburb surrounds a town and slowly sucks its center out.

The autobiographer thinks he knows his subject and doesn't need to create a calendar of the kind the biographer feels obliged to compile so she may boast she knows what her subject did on every day of his life beyond kindergarten and his first fistfight. He is likely to treat records with less respect than he should, and he will certainly not investigate himself as if he had committed a crime and ought to be caught and convicted; rather he'll be pleased he's got his defense uttered early, because he understands that the biographer's subjects all end in the pen. No, he will think of himself as having led a life so important it needs celebration, and of himself as sufficiently skilled at rendering as to render it rightly. Certainly, he will not begin his task believing he has led a botched life and will now botch the botch. Unless, of course, there's money in it and people will pay to peer at his mistakes as they pay to enter the hermaphrodite's tent at the fair — ladies to the left, please, then gents, thank you, there to the right, between the chaste screen of canvas. An honest autobiography is as amazing a miracle as a doubled sex, and every bit as big a freak of nature.

The autobiographer tends to do partials, to skip the dull parts and circle the pits of embarrassment. Autobiographers flush before examining their stools. Are there any motives for the enterprise that aren't tainted with conceit or a desire for revenge or a wish for justification? To halo a sinner's head? To puff an ego already inflated past safety? Who is smug enough to find amusement or an important human lesson in former follies? Or aspire to be an emblem for some benighted youngster to follow like the foolish follow the standard borne forward in a fight. To have written an autobiography is already to have made yourself a monster. Some, like Rousseau and Saint Augustine, capitalize on this fact and endeavor to hide deceit behind confession. Of course, as Freud has told us, they always confess to what their soul is convinced is the lesser crime.

How often, in one's second childhood, does one turn back to the first. Nostalgia and grief, self-pity and old scores, then compete to set the stage and energize each scene. Why is it so exciting to say, now that everyone knows it anyway, "I was born . . . I was born . . . I was born"? "I pooped in my pants, I was betrayed, I made straight A's." The chroniclers of childhood are almost always desperate determinists. Here their characters were formed; because of this wound or that blow, some present weakness can be explained. And how often does that modestly self-serving volume wear its author out, or he becomes bored with his own past and forswears his later years. Sometimes, too, Fate cuts the cord, and the autobiographer dies in his bed of love, still high in the saddle of the self.

Since it is considered unwise to wait to write your life till you're entombed and beginning to show your bones, you may choose to do it ahead of time, as Joyce Maynard did, writing her chronicle of growing up in the sixties, *Looking Back,* at age eighteen. Why not? Our criminals are mostly kids; kids make up the largest chunk of our silliest, most easily swayed customers; and much of our culture is created for, controlled by, and consumed by thirteen-year-olds. Willie Morris, having reached at thirty-two what the jacket flap calls "mid-passage," paints, in *North Toward Home,* his cannot-be-called-precocious picture of the South.

Many lives are so empty of interest that their subject must first perform some feat like sailing alone around the world or climbing a hazardous peak in order to elevate himself above mere existence, and then, having created a life, to write about it. As if Satan were to recall his defiance of God, his ejection from Heaven, his year-long fall through the ether, and even his hot landing in a lake of fire for our edification. Still, he didn't defy God just to make the news. Some choose to write of themselves merely as cavers or baseball players or actors or mountaineers, or create the biography of a business. Lives of crime are plentiful, as well as those of derring-dodaddies from the Old West. Others linger, like Boswells, at the edge of events, so that later they can say: "I was there, and there I saw King Lear go mad; I can tell you of a king who cursed, who cried, who called for his fool, who sat slowly down and sadly sighed . . ." Nevertheless, by accident sometimes you will find yourself in an important midst, Saigon falling around your person like a tower of blocks, or, as fortune smiles, have undertaken stale tasks that turned out more wellish than sickly; then an account of them, of how it felt to have grappled with Grendel, or have smelled the Augean stables before Hercules had swept them, or had the blood of an assassinated president sprayed over your shirt as you rode in his cavalcade; yes, then an account might be of value to future travelers who might not wish to go that way.

We have, well before us, the apparently noble example of Bernal Díaz del Castillo, who was a foot soldier in Cortez's army. Annoyed by the incompetence of earlier authors, who spoke the truth "neither in the beginning, nor the middle, nor the end," he wrote his own *True History of the Conquest of New Spain,* and prefaced his honestly unpretentious work with this simple statement:

> That which I have myself seen and the fighting I have gone through, with the help of God, I will describe quite simply, as a fair eye witness, without twisting events one way or another. I am now an old man, over

eighty-four years of age, and I have lost my sight and hearing, and, as luck would have it, I have gained nothing of value to leave to my children and descendants but this my true story, and they will presently find out what a wonderful story it is.

We believe him because what he writes "rings true," but also because, like Cephalus in Plato's *Republic,* he is now nearly free of the world and its ambitions, of the body and its desires. Almost equally wonderful is the account by Apsley Cherry-Garrad of Scott's last Antarctic expedition in *The Worst Journey in the World,* or James Hamilton-Paterson's luminous description of life on a deserted Philippine island, *Playing with Water.*

Nonetheless, these aren't autobiographies yet, for they're deliberately incomplete because no one wants to wade through your parents just to get to the South Face, or read about your marriage in order to enjoy your jungle escapades; furthermore, many of these memories are so completely about a few things seen or endured or somehow accomplished that they are little different than the excited jabber of the journalist who has stumbled on a camp of murderous thugs (you've seen the film) or stood in the square where the martyrs were made, and whose account consequently cannot be called by that uncle-sounding name of Auto, for where is the "I," old "I," sweet "I," the "I"? (Though the so-called new journalism, which Capote and Mailer practiced for a while, made even reporters into pronouns, disgracing the profession.)

Of course, there are a few minds whose every move is momentous, and a few whose character is so complex, complete, and elevated, we wish to know how? and why? and a few whose talent is so extraordinary, their sensibilities so widely and warmly and richly developed, we think naively, oh so naively, that they must have bounced out of bed like a tumbler, cooked morning eggs as if hatted like a chef, and leaped to their work with the grace of a dancer. We think them gods, or Wittgensteins. Just because their off-rhymes did not smell like something spoiled.

But he has a lifeful of private knowledge — our autobiographer. He knows of acts, small and large, that only he witnessed, only he remembers; she recalls a taste from an ancient swallow, or a scent that her lover loved but only she remembers, or a feeling on seeing her first egg cracked or baby beaten; yes, surely Lincoln recollects the rain on the roof when he signed the Proclamation; and don't you remember when you were a burgeoning boy whacking off in the barn before the boredom of the sheep — how the straw stuck to your sweater and a mysterious damp darkened the bowl of your knees? Yet just what use are these sensations to a real biographer, whose interest is in the way you lived solely because of its possible bearing on what you did? And whose interest in what you did exists principally because of the perplexes to which it led.

Between ego and object, we teeter-totter. When the autobiographer says, "I saw," he intends the report of his perception to modify his ego, not merely occupy his eye; he is the prophet who is proud he has talked to God, not the witness who is eager to describe God's garb and what leaves moved when the bush spoke.

But now for a little history of the corruption of a form. Once upon a time, history concerned itself only with what it considered important, along with the agents of these actions, the contrivers of significant events, and the forces that such happenings enlisted or expressed. Historians had difficulty deciding whether history was the result of the remarkable actions of remarkable men or the significant consequences of powerful forces, of climate, custom, and economic consequence, or of social structures, diet, geography, and the secret entelechies of Being, but whatever was the boss, the boss was big, massive, all-powerful, and hogged the center of the stage; however, as machines began to replicate objects, and little people began to multiply faster than wars or famines could reduce their numbers, and democracy arrived to flatter the multitude and tell them they ruled, and commerce flourished, sales grew, and money became the really risen god, then numbers replaced significant individuals, the trivial assumed the throne that was a camp chair on a movie set, and history looked about for gossip, not for laws, preferring lies about secret lives to the intentions of Fate.

As these changes take place, especially in the seventeenth century, the novel arrives to amuse mainly ladies of the middle class and provide them a sense of importance: their manners, their concerns, their daily rounds, their aspirations, their dreams of romance. The novel feasted on the unimportant and mimicked reality like the most cruel clown. Moll Flanders and Clarissa Harlowe replace Medea and Antigone. Instead of actual adventures, made-up ones are fashionable; instead of perilous voyages, Crusoe carries us through his days; instead of biographies of ministers and lords, we get bundles of fake letters recounting seductions and betrayals. Welcome to the extraordinary drama of lied-about ordinary life.

Historians soon had at hand, then, all the devices of exploitation. Amusing anecdote, salacious gossip would now fill their pages too. History was human, personal, full of concrete detail, and had all the suspense of a magazine serial. History and fiction began their vulgar copulation or, if you prefer, their diabolical dance. The techniques of fiction infected history, the materials of history fed the novelist's greed. It is now difficult, sometimes, to tell one from the other. It is now difficult to find anyone who wants to bother.

Nowhere would one find the blend better blended than in autobiography. The novel sprang from the letter, the diary, the report of a journey; it felt itself alive in the form of every record of private life. Subjectivity was soon everybody's subject.

I do not think it should be assumed that history, which had always focused its attention upon wars and revolution, politics and money, strife of every sort (while neglecting most everything that mattered in the evolution of human consciousness, such as the discovery of the syllogism, the creation of the diatonic scale with its inventive notation, or three-legged perspective, to be for centuries the painter's stool), had found its final relevance with the inward turn of its narrative, for it now celebrated the most commonplace and cliché-ridden awareness, and handled the irrelevant with commercial hands and a pious tongue, as if it were selling silk.

Our present stage is divinely dialectical, for we are witnessing now the return of the significant self. Prince — not a reigning prince, of course — Madonna, not a saintly mother, to be sure — stars of stadium, gym, arena, and screen constellate our consciousness, as history becomes a comic book and autobiography the confessions of celluloid whores and boorish noisemakers whose tabloid lives are presented for our titillation by ghosts still undeservedly alive.

If we think about composing our autobiography in any case, where do we turn but to our journals and diaries, our appointment books, our social calendars? We certainly ask for the return of our letters, and review all our interviews to see if we said what we said, if we said it when they say we said it, and whose tape we may have soiled with our indiscretions.

But what are these things, which serve as the sources for so much autobiography? There are differences between diaries, journals, and notebooks, just as there are differences between chronicles and memoirs and travels and testimonies, between half-a-life and slice-of-life and whole-loaf lives, and these differences should be observed, not in order to be docile to genres, to limit types, or to anally oppose any mixing of forms (which will take place in any case), but in order that the mind may keep itself clean of confusion, since to enjoy a redolently blended stew, we are not required to forget the dissimilarity between carrots and onions, or when composing our apologia, the differences between diaries and letters and notes to the maid.

The diary demands to be entered day by day, and it is improper to put down for Tuesday a date who closed your dreary eyes on Saturday. Its pages are as circumscribed as the hours are, and its spaces should be filled with facts, with jots, with jogs to the memory. Diary style is staccato, wirelesslike. "No call from Jill in three days. My God! Have I lost her?" "Saw Parker again. He's still the same. Glad we're divorced." "Finished Proust finally. Champagne." And you are already disobedient to the demands of the form if you guiltily fill in skipped days as if you hadn't skipped them.

The journal still follows the march of the calendar, but its sweep is broader, more circumspect and meditative. Facts diminish in importance and are replaced by emotions, musings, thoughts. If your journal is full of data, it means you have no inner life. And it asks for sentences, although they need not be polished. "I was annoyed with myself today for hanging about the phone, hoping for a call from Jill, who hasn't rung up in three days. She said she would call me, but was she being truthful? Dare I call her, though she expressly forbade it? I don't want to lose a customer who spends money the way she does." "Parker came into the shop, what gall! And ordered a dozen roses! I couldn't believe it! I know he wants me to think he's got another woman. God, he looked gaunt as a fallen soufflé. I think I'm happy we're no longer together. He never bought roses for me. What a bastard!" "Today was a big day, a memorable day, because today I closed the cover on Proust, I really read the last line, and 'time' had the final word, no surprise there. I feel now a great emptiness, some sort of symbolic letdown, as if a soufflé had fallen." You may revise what you have already written in your journal, but if you revise a passage prior to its entry, you are already beginning to fabricate.

Virginia Woolf's *Diaries* are therefore misnamed. We can see, in her case, as in that of Gide, the tyranny of the journal when, like a diary, it wants to have its day-to-day say, and we are led to imagine its keeper hoping from life only something worth writing about, living through the light for the sake of a few evening words and worrying whether her senses will be sensitive, her thoughts worthwhile, and a few fine phrases turned during yet another entry.

With the notebook we break out of chronology. Entries do not require dates. I can put in anything I like, even other people's thoughts. The notebook is a workshop, a tabletop, a file. In one of mine you will find titles for essays I hope one day to write: The Soufflé as a Symbol of Fragile Expectation. *The Notebooks of Malte Laurids Brigge* are misnamed, for the language is far too polished, the episodes too artfully arranged, the perceptions too poetically profound; and there is not nearly enough mess; however, if Rilke's fictive *Notebooks* really resemble journals, Henry James's *Notebooks* are the real thing: a place to plot novels, to ponder problems, to consider strategies and plan attacks.

All three — diary, notebook, journal — are predicated on privacy. They are not meant to be read by anyone else, for here one is emotionally naked and in formal disarray. Unlike the letter, they have no addressee; they do not expect publication; and therefore, presumably, they are more truthful. However, if I already have my eye on history; if I know, when I'm gone, my jottings will be looked over, wondered at, commented on, I may begin to plant redemptive items, rearrange pages, slant stories, plot small revenges, revise, lie, and look good. Then, like Shakespearean soliloquies, they are spoken to the world.

None of these three — diary, journal, notebook — is an autobiography, although the character of each is autobiographical. A memoir is usually the recollection of another place or personality, and its primary focus is outward bound: on the sudden appearance of Ludwig Wittgenstein in Ithaca, New York, for instance, or how Caesar said, "You too," before he fell, or what it was like to go to bed with Gabriele D'Annunzio. Even when the main attention of the memoir is inward, the scope of the memory tends to be limited (how I felt at the first fainting of the queen), and not wide enough to take in a life. Lewis Thomas takes the seventy-year life with which he assumes autobiography concerns itself, and first removes the twenty-five in which he was asleep, and then subtracts from the waking hours all the empty and idle ones to reach a remainder of 4,000 days. When he discounts blurred memories, self-serving reconstitutions, and other fudges, his count comes down a good deal more. The indelible moments left will most likely be found to occupy a thirty-minute burst. Such bits, he says, are the proper subject of the memoir.

What gets left out? That I read the papers. What gets left out? That I ate potatoes. What gets left out? That I saved my snot for several years. What gets left out? My second attempt to circumcise myself. What gets left out? The shops in which I purchased shoes, my fear of the red eyes of rabbits. What gets left out? What demeans me; what does not distinguish me from anyone else: bowel movements, movie favorites, bottles of scotch. What is saved? What makes me unique; no, what makes me universal; what serves my reputation; what does not embarrass the scrutinizing, the recollecting self.

And if we make a collection of such memories, they will remain like unstrung beads, because an autobiography has to rely on what cannot be and is not remembered, as well as on what is: I was born; I had whooping cough before I was three; my parents came to Sunnydale from Syracuse in an old Ford sedan.

Edward Hoagland's piece "Learning to Eat Soup" captures this feature perfectly, composed as it is of paragraphs made mostly of memories: balloons into which the past has been breathed:

> My first overtly sexual memory is of me on my knees in the hallway outside our fifth-grade classroom cleaning the floor, and Lucy Smith in a white blouse and black skirt standing above me, watching me.
>
> My first memory is of being on a train which derailed in a rainstorm in Dakota one night when I was two — and of hearing, as we rode in a hay wagon toward the distant weak lights of a little station, that a boy my age had just choked to death from breathing mud. But maybe my first real memory emerged when my father was dying. I was thirty-five and I dreamed so incredibly vividly of being dandled and rocked and hugged by him, being only a few months old, giggling helplessly and happily.

A good deal of what we remember is remembered from paintings and plays and books, and sometimes these are themselves memories, and sometimes they are memories of books or plays or paintings . . . whose subject is the self.

Testimonies, too, have powerful impersonal intentions. They do not simply wish to say: I was there, I saw enormities, now let me entertain you with my anguished account of them — of how I suffered, how I survived, remembered, yet went on — no no, for they, those witnesses, were there for all of us, were we, standing in that slow-moving naked line, holding our dead baby across our chest to hide the breasts, never staring at others in the row, mumbling a prayer in a vacant way — yes, this is our numb mind, mankind's misery, no single soul should bear it, not even Jesus, though it's said he tried.

It is healthy, even desirable, to mix genres in order to escape the confinements of outworn conventions or to break molds in order to create new shapes; but to introduce fiction into history on purpose (as opposed to being inadvertently mistaken) can only be to circumvent its aim, the truth, either because one wants to lie or now thinks lying doesn't matter and carelessness is a new virtue, or because one scorns scrupulosity as a wasted effort, a futile concern, since everything is inherently corrupt, or because an enlivened life will sell better than a straightforward one so let's have a little decoration, or because "What is truth?" is only a sardonic rhetorical question that regularly precedes the ritual washing of hands.

I know of nothing more difficult than knowing who you are, and then having the courage to share the reasons for the catastrophe of your character with the world. Anyone honestly happy with himself is a fool. (It is not a good idea to be terminally miserable about yourself either.) But an autobiography does not become a fiction just because fabrications will inevitably creep in, or because motives are never pure, or because memory will genuinely fade. It does not become a fiction simply because events or attitudes are deliberately omitted, or maliciously slanted, or blatantly fabricated, because fiction is always honest and does not intend to deceive. It announces itself: I am a fiction; do not rely on my accuracy, not because I am untrustworthy but because I am engaged not in replication but in construction. There will be those who will try to glamorize their shoddy products by pretending they are true and then, when they fail to pass even the briefest inspection, like the movies *JFK* and *Malcolm X,* dodge that responsibility by lamely speaking of "art." Fiction and history are different disciplines, and neither grants licenses to incompetents, opportunists, or mountebanks.

Next, in our travel across this map, we encounter the autobiography disguised as a fiction, presumably to prevent libel suits. For if the disguise cannot be seen through, what is the point of it as autobiography? And if it can, what is the purpose of the disguise? Conrad Aiken, possibly for the sake of objectivity, probably to injure only those who knew the code, put *Ushant* (an analysis of his relationship with Malcolm Lowry) in the third person. Whether confessed to or not, many novels are autobiographies in disguise — so it is often asserted — and the chief advantage of this strategy, apart from the fact that the novelist need only remember what springs most readily to mind and can avoid all the sufferings of scholarship, the burdens of fairness, the goal of truth, is that the narrator of a novel can whine and grumble and play the fool without automatically tarnishing his author's own character, which would otherwise be revealed to be spiteful, small-town, banal, and cheap.

Nevertheless, we should not mistake the adjective for the noun. A fiction does not become an autobiography simply because some of its elements are autobiographical; an autobiography is not a form of fiction merely because a few passages are mistaken, or misleading, or metaphorical. Just as anything properly called philosophy may be assumed to be philosophical without need of remark, so to describe a text as autobiographical is to imply that it is not a biography of the self by the self but is employing somewhat similar data or attitudes or techniques. And normally we would not study the autobiographical in order to decide what autobiography ought to be. That would be putting the quality before the noun. And the quality hasn't the weight of the horse or the bulk of the cargo in the cart.

Perhaps the gravest misuse of the adjective concerns the unconsciously epiphanic text. Any word, any gesture, any act may reveal some bit of the inner nature of its agent, and if we seek concealment, achieving it may seem easiest inside clichés, behind con-

formities, by means of immobility or any of those responses that
are so entirely required by circumstance as to prohibit individual-
ity: running from the bull, answering "hi" to "hi" and "fine" to
"howyadoin'," dying when shot through the heart. But if Kafka puts
a period on a piece of paper, we are shortly trying to lift it to look
on the other side. "Yes, he ran from the bull but in a feminine
way." "His 'fine' was flat as yesterday's soda." "Did you notice? He
wouldn't say 'hi' till I said 'hi,' otherwise he wouldn't have recognized me at all but he would have skated by."

Freud preferred to examine the little ties that accompany more
intentional behavior — our slips, mistakes, our silly errors — on
the ground that these were free to be determined more entirely
by the inner self. So a painting that is wholly abstract might be
more revealing of the painter's nature than a realistically rendered
city street, because on the city street the lamp would have to go
here, the pub's sign there, the leaded glass beneath, and the
narrow sidewalk would have to accompany the stretch of cobbles.

However, autobiography is about a different business: it is an
intentional revelation that may in addition, and by its openness,
conceal; but it is not a fundamental mode of concealment that
then habitually slips up. And the finer the artist, the less likely that
epiphanies will be plentiful, because the requirements of form are
far more demanding than most determining historical causes and
create their own outlines, their own noses, their own internal
relations.

In an autobiography, the self divides, not severally into a record-
ing self, an applauding self, a guilty self, a daydreaming self, but
into a shaping self: it is the consciousness of oneself as a consciousness among all these other minds, an awareness born much later
than the self it studies, and a self whose existence was fitful,
intermittent, for a long time, before it was able to throw a full
beam upon the life already lived and see there a pattern, as a
plowed field seen from a plane reveals the geometry of the tractor's path.

When we remember a life we must remember to remember the
life lived, not the life remembered. For first there is the stunned
child, the oblivious child, the happy child, playing in war-torn
streets, stealing rings from lifeless fingers, pissing down basement
steps, bragging to his friends of the horrors he has seen; and then

there is the old man he will become, looking back, horrified by the horrors the child was a party to, outraged by the awfulness of it all or, conversely, pooh-poohing those few tears once shed over a broken balloon — unimportant to the wise old observer writing down the words "broken balloon," which, when those few tears occurred, stood for total disconsolation and the child's first sense of how fragile the world and its pleasures are. Upon the child the autobiographer must not rest her knowledge of Greek, her memories of deportation, of her father's fascism, of the many untrustworthy men she has had to turn away; yet she cannot look back as if blind to the person she now is, as if unable to think or write, as she now can, just because she is recalling the death of her father and how he sat for several hours in his favorite chair before the fire, growing cold beneath the warmth of its familiar and friendly flames.

So shall we undertake, first, to describe the nature of this historian who picks now at the scab of his history? And to do that, won't we have to split ourselves once more, as Paul Valéry's Monsieur Teste imagines, becoming the observer of our present self, the so-called autobiographer, the self whose life has been no longer than . . . six hours? since it was then we decided to write an account of our life . . . ten days? since it was then our spouse left the family house forever . . . or, eight weeks? since it was then our finances were found to have been fraudulently obtained . . . or, twenty years? Is it that long since we've changed? If we ever have; if we haven't been Sir Walter Scott, the author of *Waverley*, from the day we were born, when the nurse came to our papa and said: You have a bouncing baby boy, sir, the author of *Waverley*, who has arrived at fully half a stone; as if our books were in our genes as well as in our definite descriptions.

That's not an entirely silly suggestion. When, in former philosophies, the existence of a soul or self was argued for, it was always pointed out that our birth name named us as a subject, not as a predicate; that the subject was that enduring and unchanging substance to which life's changes occurred, and if there were none such, and the self altered as a cloud, there'd be no nucleus around which our characteristics might circle like wagons, no title to the text of our doings and days. Autobiography (the noun) was the search for and definition of that central self (which might indeed be genetic), whereas the autobiographical (the adjective) took up the cause of the predicates and was concerned solely with the accidents of time and place, the vicissitudes of the instincts.

Reading, haven't we often encountered a passage that captured — we think perfectly — a moment in our own lives? In language so apt and beyond our contriving? So mightn't we then collect these, arrange them, if it seems right, chronologically, as Walter Abish suggests in his brilliantly constructed book *99: The New Meaning?* We would demonstrate in this way not the differences between lives but their sameness, their commonness, their comforting banality. Three or four or five such compilations might suffice to serve for all personal histories.

And if — as we might imagine — it was the substantive central self that watched us while our outside self shaved (not the mirror); and if it was that same resourceful eye that saw through our daily life's evasions; and if it were timeless, always the same, through defloration, divorce, remarriage; then there is a very good chance it is also the author of any true autobiography; it is the ageless ego that compiles the history of its aging Other, pitiless as it should be, remote, immune to praise; and if so, might not it be the case that we are jointly human instead of merely animals of the same species, because that sleepless watcher, like an eye in the sky, like God was once flattered to be, is, in each of us, pretty much One, unchanging and unchanged, even in Mozart or Mantovani, the saintly Spinoza or the beast of Belsen?

ton's house, in 1954.) After she dried it, she would grease her scalp thoroughly with blue Bergamot hair grease, which came in a short, fat jar with a picture of a beautiful colored lady on it. It's important to grease your scalp real good, my mama would explain, to keep from burning yourself. Of course, her hair would return to its natural kink almost as soon as the hot water and shampoo hit it. To me, it was another miracle how hair so "straight" would so quickly become kinky again the second it even approached some water.

My mama had only a few "clients" whose heads she "did" — did, I think, because she enjoyed it, rather than for the few pennies it brought in. They would sit on one of our red plastic kitchen chairs, the kind with the shiny metal legs, and brace themselves for the process. Mama would stroke that red-hot iron — which by this time had been in the gas fire for half an hour or more — slowly but firmly through their hair, from scalp to strand's end. It made a scorching, crinkly sound, the hot iron did, as it burned its way through kink, leaving in its wake straight strands of hair, standing long and tall but drooping over at the ends, their shape like the top of a heavy willow tree. Slowly, steadily, Mama's hands would transform a round mound of Odetta kink into a darkened swamp of everglades. The Bergamot made the hair shiny; the heat of the hot iron gave it a brownish-red cast. Once all the hair was as straight as God allows kink to get, Mama would take the well-heated curling iron and twirl the straightened strands into more or less loosely wrapped curls. She claimed that she owed her skill as a hairdresser to the strength in her wrists, and as she worked her little finger would poke out, the way it did when she sipped tea. Mama was a southpaw, and wrote upside down and backward to produce the cleanest, roundest letters you've ever seen.

The "kitchen" she would all but remove from sight with a hand-held pair of shears, bought just for this purpose. Now, the kitchen was the room in which we were sitting — the room where Mama did hair and washed clothes, and where we all took a bath in that galvanized tub. But the word has another meaning, and the kitchen that I'm speaking of is the very kinky bit of hair at the back of your head, where your neck meets your shirt collar. If there was ever a part of our African past that resisted assimilation, it was the kitchen. No matter how hot the iron, no matter how powerful the chemical, no matter how stringent the mashed-potatoes-and-lye formula of a man's "process," neither God nor woman nor Sammy Davis, Jr., could straighten the kitchen. The kitchen was permanent, irredeemable, irresistible kink. Unassimilably African. No matter what you did, no matter how hard you tried, you couldn't de-kink a person's kitchen. So you trimmed it off as best you could.

When hair had begun to "turn," as they'd say — to return to its natural kinky glory — it was the kitchen that turned first (the kitchen around the back, and nappy edges at the temples). When the kitchen started creeping up the back of the neck, it was time to get your hair done again.

Sometimes, after dark, a man would come to have his hair done. It was Mr. Charlie Carroll. He was very light-complected and had a ruddy nose — it made me think of Edmund Gwenn, who played Kris Kringle in *Miracle on 34th Street.* At first, Mama did him after my brother, Rocky, and I had gone to sleep. It was only later that we found out that he had come to our house so Mama could iron his hair — not with a hot comb or a curling iron but with our very own Proctor-Silex steam iron. For some reason I never understood, Mr. Charlie would conceal his Frederick Douglass–like mane under a big white Stetson hat. I never saw him take it off except when he came to our house, at night, to have his hair pressed. (Later, Daddy would tell us about Mr. Charlie's most prized piece of knowledge, something that the man would only confide after his hair had been pressed, as a token of intimacy. "Not many people know this," he'd say, in a tone of circumspection, "but George Washington was Abraham Lincoln's daddy." Nodding solemnly, he'd add the clincher: "A white man told me." Though he was in dead earnest, this became a humorous refrain around our house — "a white man told me" — which we used to punctuate especially preposterous assertions.)

My mother examined my daughters' kitchens whenever we went home to visit, in the early eighties. It became a game between us. I had told her not to do it, because I didn't like the politics it suggested — the notion of "good" and "bad" hair. "Good" hair was "straight," "bad" hair kinky. Even in the late sixties, at the height of Black Power, almost nobody could bring themselves to say "bad" for good and "good" for bad. People still said that hair like white people's hair was "good," even if they encapsulated it in a disclaimer, like "what we used to call 'good.'"

Maggie would be seated in her highchair, throwing food this way and that, and Mama would be cooing about how cute it all was, how I used to do just like Maggie was doing, and wondering whether her flinging her food with her left hand meant that she was going to be left-handed like Mama. When my daughter was just about covered with Chef Boyardee Spaghetti-O's, Mama would seize the opportunity: wiping her clean, she would tilt Maggie's head to one side and reach down the back of her neck. Sometimes Mama would even rub a curl between her fingers, just to make sure that her bifocals had not deceived her. Then she'd sigh with satisfaction and relief: no kink . . . yet. Mama! I'd shout, pretending to be angry. Every once in a while, if no one was looking, I'd peek, too.

I say "yet" because most black babies are born with soft, silken hair. But after a few months it begins to turn, as inevitably as do the seasons or the leaves on a tree. People once thought baby oil would stop it. They were wrong.

Everybody I knew as a child wanted to have good hair. You could be as ugly as homemade sin dipped in misery and still be thought attractive if you had good hair. "Jesus moss," the girls at Camp Lee, Virginia, had called Daddy's naturally "good" hair during the war. I know that he played that thick head of hair for all it was worth, too.

My own hair was "not a bad grade," as barbers would tell me when they cut it for the first time. It was like a doctor reporting the results of the first full physical he has given you. Like "You're in good shape" or "Blood pressure's kind of high — better cut down on salt."

I spent most of my childhood and adolescence messing with my hair. I definitely wanted straight hair. Like Pop's. When I was about three, I tried to stick a wad of Bazooka bubble gum to that straight hair of his. I suppose what fixed that memory for me is the spanking I got for doing so: he turned me upside down, holding me by my feet, the better to paddle my behind. Little *nigger*, he had shouted, walloping away. I started to laugh about it two days later, when my behind stopped hurting.

When black people say "straight," of course, they don't usually mean literally straight — they're not describing hair like, say, Peggy Lipton's (she was the white girl on *The Mod Squad*), or like Mary's of Peter, Paul & Mary fame; black people call that "stringy" hair. No, "straight" just means not kinky, no matter what contours the

curl may take. I would have done *anything* to have straight hair —
and I used to try everything, short of getting a process.

Of the wide variety of techniques and methods I came to master
in the challenging prestidigitation of the follicle, almost all had
two things in common: a heavy grease and the application of
pressure. It's not an accident that some of the biggest black-owned
companies in the fifties and sixties made hair products. And I tried
them all, in search of that certain silken touch, the one that would
leave neither the hand nor the pillow sullied by grease.

I always wondered what Frederick Douglass put on *his* hair, or
what Phillis Wheatley put on hers. Or why Wheatley has that rag
on her head in the little engraving in the frontispiece of her book.
One thing is for sure: you can bet that when Phillis Wheatley went
to England and saw the Countess of Huntingdon, she did not stop
by the Queen's coiffeur on her way there. So many black people
still get their hair straightened that it's a wonder we don't have a
national holiday for Madame C. J. Walker, the woman who invented the process of straightening kinky hair. Call it Jheri-Kurled
or call it "relaxed," it's still fried hair.

I used all the greases, from sea-blue Bergamot and creamy
vanilla Duke (in its clear jar with the orange, white, and green
label) to the godfather of grease, the formidable Murray's. Now,
Murray's was some *serious* grease. Whereas Bergamot was like oily
jello and Duke was viscous and sickly sweet, Murray's was light
brown and *hard*. Hard as lard and twice as greasy, Daddy used to
say. Murray's came in an orange can with a press-on top. It was so
hard that some people would put a match to the can, just to soften
the stuff and make it more manageable. Then, in the late sixties,
when Afros came into style, I used Afro Sheen. From Murray's to
Duke to Afro Sheen: that was my progression in black consciousness.

We used to put hot towels or washrags over our Murray-coated
heads, in order to melt the wax into the scalp and the follicles.
Unfortunately, the wax also had the habit of running down your
neck, ears, and forehead. Not to mention your pillowcase. Another
problem was that if you put two palmfuls of Murray's on your head
your hair turned white. (Duke did the same thing.) The challenge
was to get rid of that white color. Because if you got rid of the white
stuff you had a magnificent head of wavy hair. That was the beauty
of it: Murray's was so hard that it froze your hair into the wavy style

you brushed it into. It looked really good if you wore a part. A lot of guys had parts *cut* into their hair by a barber, either with the clippers or with a straightedge razor. Especially if you had kinky hair — then you'd generally wear a short razor cut, or what we called a Quo Vadis.

We tried to be as innovative as possible. Everyone knew about using a stocking cap, because your father or your uncle wore one whenever something really big was about to happen, whether sacred or secular: a funeral or a dance, a wedding or a trip in which you confronted official white people. Any time you were trying to look really sharp, you wore a stocking cap in preparation. And if the event was really a big one, you made a new cap. You asked your mother for a pair of her hose, and cut it with scissors about six inches or so from the open end — the end with the elastic that goes up to the top of the thigh. Then you knotted the cut end, and it became a beehive-shaped hat, with an elastic band that you pulled down low on your forehead and down around your neck in the back. To work well, the cap had to fit tightly and snugly, like a press. And it had to fit that tightly because it *was* a press: it pressed your hair with the force of the hose's elastic. If you greased your hair down real good, and left the stocking cap on long enough, voilà: you got a head of pressed-against-the-scalp waves. (You also got a ring around your forehead when you woke up, but it went away.) And then you could enjoy your concrete do. Swore we were bad, too, with all that grease and those flat heads. My brother and I would brush it out a bit in the mornings, so that it looked — well, "natural." Grown men still wear stocking caps — especially older men, who generally keep their stocking caps in their top drawers, along with their cufflinks and their see-through silk socks, their *Maverick* ties, their silk handkerchiefs, and whatever else they prize the most.

A Murrayed-down stocking cap was the respectable version of the process, which, by contrast, was most definitely not a cool thing to have unless you were an entertainer by trade. Zeke and Keith and Poochie and a few other stars of the high school basketball team all used to get a process once or twice a year. It was expensive, and you had to go somewhere like Pittsburgh or D.C. or Uniontown — somewhere where there were enough colored people to support a trade. The guys would disappear, then reappear a day or two later, strutting like peacocks, their hair burned slightly red from the lye base. They'd also wear "rags" — cloths or handkerchiefs — around their heads when they slept or played basketball. Do-rags, they were called. But the result was straight hair, with just a hint of wave. No curl. Do-it-yourselfers took their chances at home with a concoction of mashed potatoes and lye.

The most famous process of all, however, outside of the process Malcolm X describes in his *Autobiography*, and maybe the process of Sammy Davis, Jr., was Nat King Cole's process. Nat King Cole had patent-leather hair. That man's got the finest process money can buy, or so Daddy said the night we saw Cole's TV show on NBC. It was November 5, 1956. I remember the date because everyone came to our house to watch it and to celebrate one of Daddy's buddies' birthdays. Yeah, Uncle Joe chimed in, they can do shit to his hair that the average Negro can't even *think* about — secret shit.

Nat King Cole was *clean.* I've had an ongoing argument with a Nigerian friend about Nat King Cole for twenty years now. Not about whether he could sing — any fool knows that he could — but about whether or not he was a handkerchief head for wearing that patent-leather process.

Sammy Davis, Jr.'s process was the one I detested. It didn't look good on him. Worse still, he liked to have a fried strand dangling down the middle of his forehead, so he could shake it out from the crown when he sang. But Nat King Cole's hair was a thing unto itself, a beautifully sculpted work of art that he and he alone had the right to wear. The only difference between a process and a stocking cap, really, was taste; but Nat King Cole, unlike, say, Michael Jackson, looked *good* in his. His head looked like Valentino's head in the twenties, and some say it was Valentino the process was imitating. But Nat King Cole wore a process because it suited his face, his demeanor, his name, his style. He was as clean as he wanted to be.

I had forgotten all about that patent-leather look until one day in 1971, when I was sitting in an Arab restaurant on the island of Zanzibar surrounded by men in fezzes and white caftans, trying to learn how to eat curried goat and rice with the fingers of my right

EDWARD HOAGLAND

Strange Perfume

FROM ESQUIRE

IT PAINS ME in retrospect that I didn't give her more fun and a
better time. We were married for a quarter of a century, and she
died the same year, 1993, that our divorce went through. Although
from opposite backgrounds, we were both by temperament conservators, which gave us something in common and lent us an
extra stability. That, with the illuminating presence of our child,
helped us last. Adultery, which by definition is embedded in marriage and is not like a bachelor screwing around, may have, too,
unless you assume we would have been better off wedded to other
spouses, which oddly enough I'm not quite prepared to do.

I was born into the Protestant establishment in 1932, my father
a lawyer for Davis Polk & Wardwell, a white-shoe Wall Street firm,
and was christened at J. P. Morgan's old church, St. George's, on
Stuyvesant Square. But I was sharply and rebelliously disillusioned
by my inside look — the Greenwich, Connecticut, cotillions where
Lester Lanin, the society bandleader, himself used to ask me if I
had forgotten how to smile; the anti-Semitic country clubs, yacht
clubs, and Fifth Avenue clubs my parents belonged to — and ended
up pretty much disinherited by my father when he died. Instead,
at Harvard I enlisted in the retrograde mold represented by John
Dos Passos, John Reed, or Henry Thoreau, going off and rooting
my first novel out of the experience of working for five months in
the Ringling Bros. Circus, then insisting upon being drafted into
the U.S. Army in 1955 in spite of serious asthma and a horrendous
stutter, when many of my classmates were obtaining grad-school
deferments. Later I lived on the Lower East Side while writing a

novel about New York boxing and another one about the Brownian motion of life in a welfare hotel.

Probably because of the vise of my stutter I was a little late in losing my virginity (twenty-three), but in due course married an attractive, idealistic woman, a UN statistician and Bennington graduate — a union that dissolved amicably after four years, with much travel (Sicily, British Columbia) but neither the glory of children nor the specter of infidelity. This was a divorce that came too easily, in the no-fault mode — even our lawyers were partners. It lacked a moral dimension, and I dreamed of her in poignant scenarios for years afterward. Despite my bohemian proclivities, I acquired a distaste for the idea of divorce ever after. Better a folie à deux, stressed and buffeted by time, sociology, and psyche, as my second marriage may have been, than such a bland exit.

In 1968 I remarried. This woman, Marion Magid, was an editor at *Commentary* magazine, a Barnard graduate, thirty-six, dramatically witty, formidably well read, a master of conversational innuendo but never cruel, a high-octane interpreter of what was wrong with Tennessee Williams for *Commentary* and what was hip in London and Amsterdam for *Esquire*. Raised in the Bronx, she had known Yiddish before English and had translated Isaac Bashevis Singer's famous short story "Yentl the Yeshiva Boy" (later a Barbra Streisand movie: Marion quit translating for him only because he groped her). She acted a bit in the Yiddish theater, her name once in lights on a Broadway marquee, and had written two scripts that the avant-garde photographer Robert Frank made films out of. She'd also written and edited for the Zionist literary magazine *Midstream;* had worked for a TV producer at ABC and at Cleveland Amory's *Celebrity Register* and for a New York psychoanalyst, too, for several years.

Marion was compelling, handsome, with a wonderful "whiskey voice" with which to launch her bons mots, good legs, a wide, generous mouth, and shoulder-length reddish brown hair of the coarse, pleasing texture of a fox's pelt. When dressed for success, which was not ordinarily her habit, she wore short leather skirts, net stockings, and what she called Krafft-Ebing fantasy boots, in those salad days. A woman of parts, and I was now marrying into the Jewish establishment; New York's chief judge of the court of appeals performed the ceremony. Though I was not her first WASP nor she my first Russian Jew, we were amused by the contrast when she rattled off the names of her previous admirers: Klaus, Gert, Werner, Baruch, Maier. She hadn't been married before because the love of her life had recently married an Israeli girl, and, like me, Marion was at loose ends. Her mother, meeting me with alarm, confided to her that my Ivy League teeth looked too good to be true, must be bridgework. My mother sailed to Europe the day before our wedding.

Marion and I met at an Upper West Side party, and I called *Commentary*, at the offices of the American Jewish Committee, the next day so we could finger the appeal of our exoticism again. My fragility had not put her off, and I sensed in her a kindred odd duck. Her poli-sci, Nietzsche specialist had recently married the Israeli woman, and Marion was suffering bad bouts of depression, getting by on deli takeouts and already plagued by the writer's block that would become her chief grief for the rest of her life. Postcards from Edmund Wilson could carry you only so far, like the kudos I, on my side, had won. I was more manic, a trifler with tigers and elephants at Ringling Bros. and later in India, as well as with death in its Arctic and later Antarctic guise. I was in a fertile phase, finishing maybe my best book, *Notes from the Century Before*, interviews with frontiersmen, and was living in a new apartment in Greenwich Village that was a good deal less bleak than her digs on Thirty-fourth Street. We needed as well as amused each other and, more important, quickly recognized a rare and basic affinity: that we were each professional conservators. My work consisted of going out on long forays to try to reconstruct the reality of the frontier by talking to old men in shacks alongside great virginal rivers, about old-growth forests and bears and ice. She at her magazine and in the cafés of upper Broadway, because of her elegant, deep-water knowledge of Yiddish, was besieged by lonely, audience-less poets, memoirists, and fiction writers whose only market was the *Jewish Daily Forward*. Our heartstrings were thus tied in parallel fashion to doomed but historic enterprises that remarkably few people cared to pay any attention to in that winter of 1967–1968. Though ignorant of Yiddish, I'd spent hundreds of hours in the same cafeterias, knew countermen with numbers tattooed on their arms, and had lived for two and a half years in Europe without ever setting foot on German soil in reaction to this. Marion, by contrast, had gone directly to Berlin in the mid-1950s on a Fulbright fellowship to study Bertolt Brecht, thereby outraging her immigrant father — that she'd go to Germany so soon after the Holocaust and indeed would even aspire to be an actress — much as my own contrarian acts and wanting to be a novelist had angered my father from the opposite side.

Both complex, feisty souls who lived by our nerves, we had tried to set our own course in life, and after two or three dates she asked, "Do you ever sleep over?" She had funny tales of other artist/intellectuals who would carefully study the books on her shelves instead of making a pass and then try to put her down for authors she didn't have, while mainly of course whining because their own books weren't there. She had not expected to experience motherhood but to burn with a hard, bright thinker's light instead. Yet by and by her pregnancy energized us to marry, as we might have been too dithery to do otherwise. I'd had to be prompted to marry the first time also, this passivity in my relations with women presumably being a legacy from my complicated mother, who I like to say gave me "the fright of my life," as Marion, who knew her, agreed. Suffice it to say, no woman who wears fishnet stockings, short leather skirts, and black leather boots should object if her suitor likes to play the gawky, dominated boy in lovemaking. The skit just gradually came to seem inappropriate to us after we'd got married and had a baby on the way, and she confessed anyhow that her own kinkiness consisted in not being able to make love as freely with somebody she loved as with people who didn't matter — if she loved them her libido shut off.

In the gaiety of being married and seeing my child born, then being up with the baby twice a night and scribbling ideas, the knack I had fashioned in my travel book for speaking to a reader had turned into my first essays. I was scarcely aware of how this happened, but I poured it on, a bookful in just two years — the baby inevitably inventing herself too as we went along.

Yet, reaching forty without ever having broken a marital vow and quite a rara avis in uptown or downtown circles for that, I was restive. Marion used to joke that men ought to have two wives, one for company, one for sex, and she knew virtually no man of mature years who had been sexually faithful. We'd loaned our apartment, in fact, to one of our closest buddies for his assignations. Another went around town showing off nude photos of his ex-wife "to get her married again." But she said what distinguished a tacky man from a decent man was whether he exempted his wife from the messy experience of hearing at second hand that he'd seduced her best friend. Or in another context, powerful editors in the magazine world divided the ingenues they had access to between those they slept with and those they brought home to their parties. It seemed a time of "general copulation," in the phrase from Peter Weiss's exemplary play *Marat/Sade*.

Marion had never had an orgasm and believed herself not good at sex, though I tended to blame myself because I'd never given my first wife an orgasm either — at least not till after we'd split up and she came back to visit me and taught me how the Frenchman and the Hungarian whom she was seeing at the UN did it. And it had required the patient yet peremptory tutoring of a couple of women whom I knew between my marriages to further rid me of the boyish selfishness that had marked my sexuality until I was past thirty. Absorbed nowadays in a different phase of life, helping to find a clever pediatrician, a lively nursery school, moving with Marion and our daughter to a larger apartment, I was less selfish as a person but more tired or perfunctory as a sexual partner.

At *Commentary* parties the mood turned tenser, however, as politics, not literary gossip, became the focus around the time of the 1968 teachers' strike in Brooklyn, when black community boards squared off against Jewish administrators. Neoconservatism was an embryo at these soirees, and an Israeli visitor might stand up before our seated group and describe with visible relish how abjectly a Palestinian prisoner would break under the beatings administered off-street in a police van. Vietnam was an additional issue. Marion and I had our first fights over the invasion of Cambodia by American troops, because for her toughness in Southeast Asia seemed to translate into future support for Israel in the Middle East. The old things whose survival engrossed me — wetlands, wildernesses to be preserved — had no cost to America even if you didn't care about them as a cause, whereas I began to think that neoconservatism, as spearheaded by *Commentary* in championing the South Vietnamese regime, the Argentinian junta, the Salvadoran dictatorship, was warping our foreign policy away from

a Jeffersonian involvement with the Third World, and that her
interest had shifted from Isaac Bashevis Singer to Menachem Begin and Yitzhak Shamir.

From this point on, we felt an undertow in our marriage, and I
suggested, not joking, that we move to New Mexico. So many
friendships were breaking up over politics in this neocon versus
liberal little world that our situation differed only in being marital,
and I was determined that the gravity of divorce not evolve out of
disagreements over the evening news. What happened to us in
particular, however, was that Marion's first love, the Nietzschean
poli-sci professor whom she had fallen for way back in Berlin in
the 1950s, lost his young wife to cancer; and this — as he began
telephoning daily for solace, a man with heart problems but a
roly-poly, untidy vigor, a wispy spade beard, and playful irony —
together with other callers, bachelors who were dependent on her
in Toronto, San Francisco, and elsewhere for company at night on
the phone, doubled the strain. It seemed to me a platonic promiscuity, but since I was out prowling bars two or three evenings a
week, after picking up our daughter at school and taking care of
her during the afternoon, I can't say whose loneliness had precedence. We still sometimes had happy weekends, when she might
bring home the desperate half-English, half-Yiddish manuscript of
a frantic refugee wetly escaped from the Soviet Union, who had
showed up in her office holding the hollowed-out hairbrush in
which he'd concealed the microfilm of his gulag memoirs. Lavish-
ing her free time, she would somehow transmute his anguish to
publishable prose, and after it appeared in the magazine, the guy
would win some kind of book contract or teaching post and be
safely launched.

My twenty essays for *The Village Voice* had gotten me *Sports Illustrated* assignments in the South and trips abroad — to Cairo for
Harper's and on to Cyprus, Jerusalem, later Khartoum, later San'a.
We hadn't moved to New Mexico, though we did buy a cabin in
northern Vermont. But it wasn't distant enough, and the five-year
itch toward promiscuity, which I suspect is built into most men,
was chafing me in any case. I bridled before the wall of the taboo
against adultery, procrastinated, took refuge in my lack of confidence, dodging seductions and making the barriers inconvenient

as well as explicit and thus tougher to scramble across. But at last, down in Texas, I fell in love. It was on a trip to write about red wolves, and Donald Barthelme had given me the number of a friend in his hometown of Houston who had kicked out her husband of umpteen years a few months before. We would meet in the towns of Winnie or Liberty, Texas, or in Cameron, Holly Beach, or Johnsons Bayou, across the state border in Louisiana, and drive the clamshell roads at night listening for wolf howls and admiring the nearly wild Brahman cattle silhouetted against the sunset or dawn, grayish-bluish humped animals that could survive the winds, mosquitoes, drought, heat, rains, and frost.

I hustled another assignment to go out with a number of Cajun trappers in their pirogues while they collected their night's worth of raccoons, mink, nutria, muskrats, otters; it gave me a horror of furs. I went to the annual rat-skinning contests and cross-dressing balls and crabmeat, crawfish, and jambalaya fests of southwest Louisiana, to pepper-sauce factories, egret and stork sanctuaries, and sometimes would show up at midnight at our agreed-upon motel with mud to my knees and eat shrimps, oysters, and chicken-fried steak with my friend. She had a job teaching art and two teenage sons and drove to these Gulf Coast beaches from her Texas-style patioed house. She was slim, lithe, small-faced, and frizzy-haired like my first wife, but less innocent, more socially and professionally ambitious, and her accent was of her birthplace, New Orleans, with hints of the French Caribbean behind that, the ultimate in sultriness for pillow talk. If I wasn't going to New Mexico, maybe I'd move here! My infatuation was so intense that at Houston's airport, going in or out, I groaned.

I wangled other assignments — went to Pilottown at the Mississippi's mouth to watch commercial garfishing and into the freshwater swamps upriver to eat squirrels with bobcat trappers, or visited plantation houses for *Travel & Leisure,* and went to Big Bend on the Rio Grande with a puma hunter. Her name would catch at my heart when I murmured it to myself back in New York, but what held me up was the daily delight of waking up in the same house as my daughter, not as an absentee father two thousand miles away, and the fact that I did love my wife to her dying day. And abruptly the momentum broke when my Houston friend's elder son told his father I was at the house and told his mother that his father was coming with a gun. It was no idle threat. We fled hastily to a motel and I returned to New York, alarmed that she should have been married for so long to somebody who, after their separation, would resort to a gun. It was southern enough but too southern for me, and indeed ten years later, when we met casually, she told me another man she was breaking up with had just threatened her with a gun. The passion of that tongue and that thrilling voice came with a price.

At some point around then, Marion went up to Cornell with our daughter to visit her Nietzschean widower, who was phoning every night with his Germanic Santa Claus voice, inserting himself as a kind of uncle in my daughter's affairs, to see whether Marion wanted to leave me for him. At least so I interpreted the trip. But she came back. I doubt whether she could face leaving the city, and she also said she didn't consider the jumbled household of her friend, with two motherless girls, would be an improvement for Molly upon life in our more focused home, with a decent school.

Like numerous marriages of the era, one could argue with equal cogency that adultery splintered ours or preserved it, enabled it to last or split it into pieces. Adultery, like "adult" books, has little relation to *adultus,* Latin for "grown," because it can be that still-nineteen-year-old sidling down the street, looking into lit windows for a woman alone. Yet it only occurs within the context of a marriage, and may not really be about sex — though I think nature in a schematic sense designed men for polygyny, once each successive child's period of toddlerhood is gone. Men have a sack of seeds to sow, and such a theory does not contradict the adolescent aspects of cheating on your wife, because nature did not construct men with the expectation that they were going to live very long. My wife's telephonic polyandry, as I called it — half a dozen men counting on the intimacy of her wit to buoy their lives daily, or two or three times a week at least — may have been built into her, too. We stuck together by attending school plays, and for wee-hours warmth, and book collecting, and to confront the bureaucracies that everywhere try to make existence as difficult as they can. Her relationship to her mother was exceptionally close — she would converse or cry out to her in her sleep — and that oddity, too, while at first an obstacle, may have become a balancing factor that helped our marriage last.

*

The phone lines hummed; the streets were priapic; the restaurants seemed full of forlorn people whose spouses had recently left them. There was this feeling to the seventies as of a creaking, corniced avalanche in the making. In a deteriorating society conduct tends to be improvised, and the sexual license of the counterculture, as well as Vietnam and Watergate, had wet the underpinnings of the country. Union members who might have sheared a hirsute hippie a decade before looked pretty hairy themselves; traditional loyalties of many sorts were eroding toward the greed-grab that was to follow. Lots of people were getting divorced or having an extramarital affair who didn't need to. A friend of mine, in separate years, found two men she loved dead of heart attacks in her apartment — waking up to discover their corpses on her bed or her couch — and asked me whether orgasms were all that important, that we, and especially men, should search so hard for variety. My fragility or brusqueness prevented me from sleeping with anybody I didn't genuinely like; and probably in order to cut the sin of infidelity in half, I didn't sleep with married women nor with undergraduate students nor with the loves of friends. I regretted the failure of my marriage and yet not many of the specifics of my conduct, just as I wouldn't have regretted writing a novel that ultimately failed.

While teaching a semester at the University of Iowa, I fell into another involvement with a conservator, a woman who headed a social agency that helped the local elderly find housing and shop for food. She had written her master's thesis on a nearby community of Amish farmers, whose Sunday services she used to take me to, and an earlier thesis on the Indians of the Kuskokwim River in interior Alaska. She was interested in old customs, old heroes and adventurers. She was a Texan — willowy yet statuesque, dramatic in gesture yet sympathetic to people who weren't. She lent a comfort and glamour to the Mississippi-midwestern milieu that had attracted me to Iowa City in the first place, and our lovemaking, which was amateur, blundery, and delightful, was like the high school sweetheart I'd never had. She, again, was my age, and an appropriate partner, but I was too New York-ish to uproot myself and she too bound to Iowa by temper and by her career to move.

I may have been a bit like Marion in the quirk she had warned me of early on: that damper that psychologically throttled lovemaking with a loved one. It may have reinforced our original attraction to each other, which was honest and in earnest and which continued at the country place I had acquired. My best writing there was probably done during the years when I was sexually faithful, the directness of a clear conscience matching the springwater. I would meet her sleeper at the Montpelier, Vermont, train station on weekends, when she liked to pretend we were in a Russian novel — "You will find us very dull in the country, Sergei," mimicking a Tolstoyan accent. Her sense of humor redeemed the dullness of being housebound, because she didn't like going far from the house outdoors.

Marion continued her round of editorial lunches and generously painstaking editing of young writers to get their first short stories into print, but at night her retinue of polyandrous callers kept unbosoming themselves in her ear, though sometimes speaking unpleasantly to me if I was the one who picked up the phone. One guy might spin his rotary dial to produce a long-distance Bronx cheer of clicks. Another might mock the latest essay of mine that had appeared; my subjects were "derelicts or animals," he said. I did indeed keep riding tugboats through Kill Van Kull to Newark Bay, or going into the woods with bear scientists, while prowling off-hour haunts such as the Lion's Head bar, which I enjoyed for its tabloid newspapermen with a different take on life from mine, and where I found a buddy who became a friend.

To make love with a woman you must pay some attention to her: in this fin de millennium, that has become heterosexuality's saving grace. Otherwise, the proverbial war between the sexes nearly ensures that you will start scrapping. She will remember her callous ex-husband or oafish dad or the last chump who tried to manipulate her or just plain everyday feminist exhortations. In part we resent the opposite sex because of the helplessness with which we lay for years in some big person's arms, without having had the later satisfaction of growing up to replicate them; and thus the wholesale anonymity of bathhouse same-sex promiscuity that pervaded Greenwich Village would not have worked between men and women even in those years.

My friend was a photographer's model who was finding modeling hard going as she aged. I was hobbling around with a hernia and parathyroid problems and whatnot and was touched. Women who make their living with their bodies have always reminded me of athletes, such as the boxers I'd written a book about in the 1950s and the baseball players I'd admired in the 1940s, with the mortality question telescoped. Her black flare of hair was turning crisper, her figure thicker, and she discovered with alarm that she was descending from glossy pages to newsprint, from top-of-the-line airport magazines to bottom-shelf "skin rags." The brisk professional photographers who paid a decent wage and made a game of it were calling younger models — she showed me her portfolio to test my sexuality through my breathing — and she was left with the Brooklyn shutterbug clubs, where ten or twenty cheapskates got their kicks from ogling her for a few bucks in "dues." Or a solo operator would put aside his camera and try to corner and paw her, having hired her presence for an hour, then in "revenge" trade her phone number to a scary deviant who phoned at midnight to ask her measurements, discuss poses, and threaten and revile her. She did do poses for a comic-strip artist in dominatrix costumes that he supplied, but his wife watched, joking about it, and it was an excuse for ordering in lunch.

Frightened — because where would it end? — she liked men more than women, nevertheless, and understood that her livelihood was grounded in their vulnerabilities. What she wanted from me, apart from the bookish talk and chat about trips to Africa that she didn't get from her dinner dates, who were mostly businessmen or professional men, was the simple reversal. "Kiss the queen. Kneel to the queen," she'd whisper as I licked her and she came six or seven times, purging those humiliations of the camera for the time being. Nobody should ever enter her again, she promised herself, without first doing the same — while I, for my part, sought spellbound to climb headfirst into the primal womb in our deep-swimming, almost pelagic, sessions. Then she'd do Air Force exercises while I unwound by watching Johnny Carson.

Trotting home through the sweet, funky Village streets with the lights of New Jersey glistering on the wide Hudson at the end of our block, hinting of trips west or to other rivers that were the inspiration of so many writers I loved — Cather, Twain, Faulkner, Anderson — I felt I was sideslipping trouble like a quick coyote and doing the possible, assembling a doable life. But when I actually entered our cozy apartment, dodging into the bathroom to scrub myself in the shower, I felt guiltier than a rat — trying to

figure out if the perfume was finally off, if the soap's scent would
mask it, before sneaking into our bed and trying to lie on the far
side so Marion wouldn't smell my body if she awoke. Unless, on
the other hand, I heard her purring and blowing into the phone
in the next room to one of her polyandrous crew. Then I didn't
feel like a bad husband. She was "the darling of our hearts" (as
the phrase came to be) to so many men, each half in love with
her, that I was merely sad.

Infidelity can be a cliché like trying to flee death or sexual inse-
curity, or the more casual hoist-a-beer cheer that you only "go
around" once. It may seem to alchemize lies into white lies by
siphoning off the poisons that might otherwise lay low a marriage.
I prefer to think ours didn't fit any truism but was unique. Would
we have found monogamy in New Mexico if we had moved?
Instead we stayed put and provided a stable framework for our
daughter to go to school and for us to work hard for twenty years,
turning out two or three hundred issues of her magazine and my
own set of books of the period. We played our word games, read
classy novelists, ate good meals, passed our doctors' exams, and
shared a mostly comfortable bed.

   If you teach college students, as I do, you see the results of
pell-mell divorce and concupiscence — homes that have fractured
into shards; kids whose parents are no more than a ready credit
card, who have lost track of where their titular paterfamilias actually is; kids who are sleeping together not for sex but only for
company. I've met the father of a student of mine at a New York
party who didn't know what his son was majoring in. An honest-
to-goodness sea change has occurred, and Generation X is a name
they accept for themselves because almost every basic remains an
uncertainty. The torque applied to marriages now is unprece-
dented: the speed of travel, of electronic stimulation, the cultural
crosshatch, the diverse titillation and rudderless liberation, the
no-fault method of reckoning everything. Jobs are changed like a
suit of clothes. Adultery is not biblical, but "acting out." Nothing
is binding or even binary, not sexuality or ethics.

   What can happen — to choose a painful, down-to-earth example
— is that through the miracle of TV, you can see people dying as
you sit in your living room. You can see children shot in the West

Bank by Israeli soldiers for the crime of stone throwing, and remember meeting, on a visit to Israel with your wife, the man now responsible for the aggressive new policy of shooting more children — sharing a Shabbat dinner with his family, in fact. The intifada, when it burst out in Israel's Occupied Territories in 1987, was like the Tet offensive in Vietnam. It proved the conquering power's assumptions were wrong. In my weeks in Israel and a hundred New York discussions, one of those assumptions, at least at the leadership level, had been that Palestinians weren't quite human beings. Their grief, pride, courage, and feeling for home weren't real, and reprisals could grind them down. For some of my acquaintances, Arabs were a kind of unsleeping preoccupation, equivalent to the worst bigotry I had ever seen in the WASP neighborhoods in the Northeast, where I had grown up, though with the distinction that the deeds of the Nazis were rung in to justify any oppressive measure visited upon the Arabs. I came to believe that the reason I'd hear Gandhi and Martin Luther King, Jr., spoken of so slightingly was because of an unease with the reality of how a King or a Gandhi would have fared in the Occupied Territories.

Marion, meeting friends of mine, expressed a corresponding disparagement of their intellectual integrity and the character of their books on nature or the Middle East. I was enduringly touched by the angry slump to her shoulders, her disappointment and irony when I would come home sneezing because my allergy to cat fur had been triggered (most single women keep a cat): "Have you caught cold?" But our alliance gradually tore, despite the empathy we felt for each other. I remember a specific moment when it registered on me that I was traveling with the wrong crowd. We were driving to the Upper East Side with a man who, with his deep tan and good car, had done pretty well, like so many of her friends, riding the neocon wave. We were passing the Martinique Hotel, a welfare dumping ground at Thirty-second Street whose haggard beggars this lunchtime had spilled over the curb at the stoplight. They weren't blacks on this particular day, so the crux was poverty, not race. They were Appalachian-looking whites — bony, vitamin-starved, despairing kids of ten or twelve with faces out of Walker Evans or Dorothea Lange, the product of some social cataclysm in coal country. This man's father, if I recall, had had a horse and wagon hauling junk in Winnipeg fifty years ago, but when these hungry-looking, country-looking children asked for change for groceries at his window, he was exasperated, rolling it up — that he hadn't clear sailing all the way uptown. It was of a piece with the neocon idea that the problem of homelessness was being exaggerated by liberals, and I made up my mind that I had better cut and run.

I was in love with Alaska, and in Alaska, at this point with a person who had shown up at 6:30 A.M. at my door in Fairbanks, where I was teaching for a week. We'd talked, and after a side trip I flew down to Juneau, where she lived, and, wildly, we did more than talk. She was a public-health nurse who had been flying out alone to half a dozen Tlingit villages on the islands of the Alexander Archipelago on a schedule of troubleshooter visits for total health care, from prenatal to easing old people into a gentle grave. Like me, she loved hearing old lore and pristine stories, loved seeing wildlife and sizing up individuals who had rarely encountered a bureaucracy or perhaps even piped-in electricity before. On a ferryboat we went visiting some of her clientele, now that she was preparing to take up a new job in Anchorage directing the nursing care for all the tuberculosis patients in the state. Our curiosity, our enthusiasms, our sexual personalities jibed, though she was much younger and more radical politically than me. She was a woman of salient mercy, constantly fighting for the best she could get for her patients — doctor visits, medevac flights, operations, preventive measures. She was the kindest person I've ever known and as intrepid as any. Our sorties to Eskimo hamlets and trappers' cabins, traveling all over Alaska together checking on Athabascan or Inupiat people who had caught TB, would imbalance this essay if I put them in. We stood on the ice of the Yukon River in January and the Arctic Ocean in February, and flew in tiny ski planes, seated on the floor, clasping each other in tandem, to see how a child on the Koyukuk River or the Holitna River was doing. Crooked Creek, Sleetmute, Red Devil, Point Hope, Kotzebue, Tanana, Angoon: we saw them all. She left nursing and eventually became an anthropologist, working with other Indians, preferring the single life to do that.

Not surprisingly, my marriage broke up by and by, though years after some of my friends had expected it to. ("We thought you liked being unhappy," one said.) Our daughter was at Harvard and heading for graduate school, but because it had been a full decade since more than a couple of my friends had been welcome visitors in our home, she knew almost none of them, only Marion's circle, an exclusion I'd come to resent. I felt quarantined, with Marion beginning to jeer generically at WASPs — distressed to the brink of wanting to jump out a window when I left.

I'd expected that my wife's first love would at last move in. But he didn't, and so it was I who shared with my daughter watchman's duty at Marion's deathbed in the hospital several years later. I was not an inappropriate presence, because I still cared for her and respected her as a brave partisan for what she believed in. I admired her passionate motherhood and her faithful affection for her many friends, and was present to the last, when the morphine the doctor had prescribed very peacefully suppressed, first her fierce, ebullient wit, and then her breathing, high over 168th Street of the city she loved.

My father would not have approved of our marriage because Marion was Jewish but would have disapproved of our getting divorced more. He once told me the only excuse for indulging even in infidelity was if you were married to a person who was mentally ill, without specifying whether my mother's spates of hysteria had made him do so. I've said she gave me the fright of my life but have never been able to define it through a series of incidents that connect like dots. In the warp and woof of our marriage my mother and Marion's father were heavy bettors, although both of them were spirits from a world eclipsed. Yet I think our failures and betrayals were mutual and common to our era, driven by our era, and that our stopgap solutions were improvised in a fervor of stubborn conservatism. I don't think anybody should enter a marriage they later regret. And I never have.

DIANA KAPPEL-SMITH

Salt

FROM ORION

THE FIRST SPRING I spent in Utah there was too much rain in the Wasach Range. Not having been west of Ohio before, I didn't know those mountains one way or the other, though I knew that the West was supposed to be dry, but not how dry, or how changeable, or how much in the end it would change me.

I was going out there to work with sheep, and weather is the number-one item of conversation for sheepherders anywhere. The old man I worked for said that the whole winter had been wet — it was the first thing he told me when he picked me up at the airport in Salt Lake, just like that, not even "Hi" first. He was a fine, kind man, and good to work for, but like most people whose lives are made from the land he was obsessed. He needed to be. He had eight thousand ewes lambing in the hills above Spanish Fork. It was my job to solve obstetric problems and to bring any orphaned "dogies" into the compound for bottle feeding, and to carry a loaded rifle in case I got a shot at a coyote.

There were a lot of coyote problems, as usual. Lambing time is always the worst. In my first week there I saw enough eviscerated sheep and dead lambs and hind ends of coyotes escaping clean across the country to do me for life.

Even with the old man's sons and their wives working, we were short-handed. As the weeks passed exhaustion set in and my vision narrowed (or expanded, depends how you think of it) to the world of the animals. Everything hung on them and I ceased to matter. Any shepherd will recognize this as the way it always is at lambing time, and I was familiar with it, certainly, but not like this.

I knew a lot about sheep in those days, but my understanding of other things was primitive. I still saw myself as the center of the world with nature as a kind of backdrop, a beautiful backdrop in which I spent as much time as possible. It was also the raw heart-breaking place in which I worked. I had not begun to put these things together.

That spring I would be jolted out of these old notions. My ideas of what I was, and what the world was, just gradually . . . ceased; collapsed, emptied, ended by default. It wasn't just the drama of the animals, it was the landscape. To begin with it was the Wasach front and the Manti-La Sals, high white sugarcones gleaming rosily at dawn, streaked with impenetrable darkness. I breathed their breath. There they rose, always above the grubby fray. The distance between us was a lens of air, round and terrifying, like the palpable weight of distance one sees looking down from a height, sus-pended, miraculous. And all this landscape began to dictate, to sing in its own mineral voice, until any ideas I might have had about the primacy of People or the prettiness of Nature no longer held together by even as much as a thread of self-delusion or popular myth. It was rebirth; I was pushed, slithering and ex-hausted by emotion, by the wide open question of the desert itself. I began a kind of journey in which my life would become more insignificant and more wonderful than I could have ever imagined. And — this was the odd thing — every step of the way would taste of salt. Salt came in through my skin and my mouth, left its mark on my hatband. It was part of the earth that moved through me. Gradually, not looking for it, looking for coyotes, salt became my teacher.

One day early that spring, before the lambing got too busy, the old man took me with him when he went to Nevada to look at the state of the winter range. It was a kind of holiday. We tooled along in the pickup with the windows open and sunglasses on against the blare of light. He took pleasure in pointing things out to me, the greenhorn, and today it was the wonders of all this water. Water is different in the desert than it is in other places. Here there are no rivers, only washes; there are no lakes, only basins. Water in the desert is temporary, yet can be destructive just when you want it most.

Parts of the Great Salt Lake were levied with walls of sandbags so the flood wouldn't inundate the highway. The sandbags were sloppy looking, like melted bricks. After we'd passed miles and miles of them I began to wonder if anything in the world stayed put, if all our works were bound to be crudely kicked apart and beaten down by the forces of nature. Rain or coyotes; both seemed inhabited by the same pixie will. We stopped once and walked to the sandbag wall and looked over at an expanse of filthy fluid that stretched away to the rim of the universe.

The Great Salt Lake is a place where you can question the rightness of preconceived ideas. The water has the smell and color of a pickle, the surrounding hills are red. There are salt mines — mechanical giants surrounded by piles of white that sear the eyes. "Salt mines" is an archetypal image of banishment, imprisonment, the opposite of what my own life was, riding green hills under snow-decked mountains, surrounded by life — and death, too — but death is part of life and any country person accepts this and rolls with this as instinctively as he or she obeys the circular nature of the year. Mines are something else again: they go down into darkness and out of nature, like a kind of hell. They made me shiver.

Southwest of the Great Salt Lake are the Bonneville Salt Flats, a hundred square miles of them as level all the way as the surface of water. Water brought the salt there, laid it down, vanished. Time is visible in the salt, as it is visible in the hands of a clock that seem motionless.

We crossed the Great Salt Desert south of the flats and on past Sevier Lake, heading for Nevada. The old man said that most of the time Sevier Lake was dry, but now it was a great wet mirror laid between the mountains. It was shallow and turbid and was filled with migrating waterbirds that rose as we passed with a massed roar of wings.

Even before the Nevada border the earth settled into basin and range, the sun grew hot, the land shrank down into itself, and the sky grew more immense. The old man pointed out the rocks where he'd seen a lion, a canyon where he sheltered the flock when a blizzard came, and another where he'd corralled mustangs to get himself a riding horse. Out here on the desert you never needed to give salt to the sheep. All grazing animals — and humans too if their diet is mostly grain — need salt as a necessary nutrient.

Usually you have to give it to sheep by the hundred-pound sack —
loose salt, not blocks, because they need so much of it in order
to thrive.

But here all the minerals were in the feed. The old man gave
me a leaf to chew and it was salt and bitter. He told me this was
the best winter range that one could imagine. I believed him. The
ewes I cared for had all wintered here. Their chunky lambs were
the pure product of this Nevada brush. Now the range was re-
bounding: "Look at this here, look at that, well, well . . . ," he'd
say, again and again. He would pluck a leaf here and there and
chew it and then spit it out, nodding his head, pleased.

The red mountains thrusting up, the basins between them flat
as glass, salt everywhere; it made me wonder what had happened
here. I was new to the desert and to its nakedness and to how the
earth is not hidden under anything, its history open to the air. I
wanted to know everything about it at once. So on the way home
I asked the old man about the salt. A Mormon, he stopped the
truck and gave me an answer that had to do with God. This was
not what I was after. It was the only time his Mormon-ness made
me impatient, but I should have listened to him.

Since then I've found other answers to the questions of salt — the
what of it, the how, the where, the how come — different answers
from the one the old man gave me. I'm not sure they're any better,
just different. And since that spring I've traveled all over the
deserts: from the Wasach to the Sierras, from the valleys of eastern
Oregon to the Owyhee hills of Idaho and south clear to the
Mexican border, and across that into Sonora and Chihuahua. If
anything, these dry landscapes grow more powerful with time and
increased acquaintance. The answers to things get shorter, with more
room for the unknown built into them, and the unknowable. They
get more like the old man's answer, if you want to know the truth.

In the desert there aren't many people to get in the way of the
earth's own mineral music, so one can hear it, after a while,
without any mortal agendas in the way. Which is a fancy way of
saying that I go to the desert for happiness, as other people go to
concerts, or plays, or markets. Or churches.

I still go around tasting and smelling things the way I did when
I was assaying the palatability of sheep feed; a handy skill, it turns

out. There's the funky tang of sage — like rotted lavender — beautiful or foul depending; and the tarry marvel of creosote bush in the summer after a rain, in the darkness, thunder still drumming the air, while the snakes are emerging, and the spadefoot toads come out to ring and blurt from transient pools. A thousand scents: the sweet headiness of desert mistletoe in dry Mojave canyons in January, the piss smell of the tiny white night-blooming flower called desert snow, the cactus blooms that have a tang of tangerine or horehound, the mucilaginous beany taste of young *nopales,* and the scent of a salt spring, which is a little like death.

All that salt: vast white plains of it, cracked like ice floes. All through southern California the center of every valley is a pan of saline silt, flatter than any other place on earth, and dun colored, and cracked. If there's still a little water, then it's a salt marsh, with water so saturated it's caustic. Up around Pahrump and the Amargosa there are plenty of salt springs in which one can soak naked and by moonlight, and everyone seems to have their favorite. There's a brittle whitish horn I carry in a plastic bag in my pack; I crush and sprinkle it as a sacrament on everything I eat when I'm living out there. I stole it from Badwater in Death Valley. One isn't supposed to do this. Robbery of anything from any National Monument is forbidden, but that salt has all the crunch and flavor of scofflaw freedom.

I'm eating what I love: the unendurable places, the bone-stuff, the ground. The same electrolytes that dance their vital dance in my blood — sodium, calcium, potassium, carbonate, chloride — are there in the evaporites at the fringe of desert marshes and ephemeral lakes: sulfates, carbonates, and chlorides crystallized on basin rims as white residues as though a pot had boiled dry. The chemistries of the planet and of our bodies are similar enough (why should we be amazed?). Our body fluids contain 0.9 percent salt, nowadays, very likely the exact salinity of whatever ancient sea we managed to crawl out of, a sea we could leave because we had learned, first of all, to contain it.

This is a marvel: that we still contain what once contained us. What is more marvelous is that we maintain it with exactitude. The concentration of electrolytes in our blood is regulated by the kidney, the kidney is in turn regulated by adrenal and pituitary hormones. Regulatory feedback loops operate constantly so that we run through natural cycles of ion concentration every eighteen days or so, our water content, and body weight, fluctuating, too, in tidal ripples of which we are largely unconscious. Emotional stress increases adrenal activity, and severe hormonal upsets or kidney disease can lead to edema: to swelling out of control, our cells drowning in a tidal wave of body fluids. When body salts are depleted below critical levels we get diarrhea, we vomit, we sweat, our blood pressure drops, we faint, our kidneys fail. Doctors have learned to treat the deadly phenomenon of shock with heavy doses of Ringer's solution: sodium chloride, potassium chloride, calcium chloride, and sodium bicarbonate, in the same concentration as blood plasma. When we are at the brink we can be pulled back into life by the renewal of our internal sea.

So I crush the white horn of Death Valley salt and sprinkle it on my food, and partake, of life, of my own life in which this salt moves, as it has moved through infinite numbers of others. The next day it will leave itself on my hat brim or dry on my shirt or sink with my urine into the soil in another place, attracting butterflies, who need the salts too. Until then it will dance in the most intimate machinery of my being.

It has been suggested that our almost universal religious concern with salvation, in one form or another, comes from our consciousness of time. The idea seems to be that if we understand the notion of *time,* then we are confronted slam-bang with the fact of our own mortality. Animals do not have time consciousness (so far as we know), so they don't suffer from the same need to be delivered from the *now* to the *eternal.* Knowing that we're mortal, we yearn for salvation, for release from the finitude of life and death.

That is one explanation, perhaps not the only one, but when you are in the desert it seems that one thinks of these things as easily as breathing. The grandeur of that space draws the mind beyond the present and beyond the self. The salt says this: our life is at one even with the stones. So after a few days in that country it becomes clear that one does live in the eternal all the time.

If there is good reason to preserve some desert untrammeled and unchanged, it is this: what the desert has to teach us is almost impossible to learn when we are surrounded by people. And if one scrawls all over those landscapes with the graffiti of dams and developments and mines and wells, then the sense of it and the singing of it vanish, chopped into a senseless confetti, sad little fragments of blowing paper, meaning nothing.

What becomes clear is that the world is tied together in wonderful ways, most of which are mysterious. For instance, when a wave breaks in the ocean it makes millions of bubbles and when the bubbles pop tiny droplets fly into the air, and they are carried up where the water itself is sucked away — leaving fragments of salt to whirl in the dry jet streams of the upper atmosphere. Later, encountering cloud, these become the nuclei of drops of rain.

In the desert in a wet year the runoff from winter storms may flow as far as the basins, the bolsones, the playa lakes, all names for the same things: the bowls of desert air surrounded by mountains, the place where all flow ends. There, spread shallow as if on a plate, water dries away.

Or, invisibly, it enters an underground river. A river no swifter than the seepage between pores of Jurassic sandstone. A subterranean seep as long and brachiated as a system of nerves. The water may surface hundreds of miles and thousands of years away.

In the Mojave just east of the Sierras, where the crust of the earth has been crazed by active faults, there are lots of springs. Many of them are hot and most of them are saline. These oases are furred with crisp saltgrass and are surrounded by fan palms. Where a pool overflows the salt makes a crust on the sand, a fragile glazing, like ice.

Nearby there is almost always a rock or two with petroglyphs of bighorn sheep: rams with immense headgear, flocks of ewes cavorting over the rock with their tails in the air and their bellies as round as bowls. People's passions and obsessions have not changed much.

The springs welling up in the drought of the Mojave are a way to see that the earth has a three-dimensional body, too, has creaking bones, secret fluids. What I've also learned is that layers of salt buried deep in it do strange things. Under pressure of gravity or tectonics, salt becomes plastic and moves. Under pressure it can flow and coalesce into a reverse-teardrop shape that punches upward like an immense fist: a *salt dome*. These domes come up from as deep as 50,000 feet, piercing all the rock over themselves. They can be as much as ten kilometers high and fifty kilometers long.

These domes are of astounding purity, so that when they're near the surface they are often mined — for salt — and the surrounding rock layers are wonderful sources of oil. The dome acts like an impervious plug. Oil migrating through rock layers reaches it and stops.

Then near the Zuni Mountains in western New Mexico there is a single cindercone filled with salt; this is one of the strangest things I've ever seen. No geologist I've talked to knows where the salt has come from — there's none of it anywhere near, not for hundreds of miles. What must have happened is something like this: on its way up from wherever volcanoes come from, this one tapped into some very deep saline plumbing, and there was a gush, like the bursting of a water main. After the cindercone blew, its crater was filled by this spring of highly concentrated brine. Add a few millennia of evaporation, and now the cindercone is filled with a plug of pure lovely salt topped by a few feet of briny slush. The salt spring still springs, as heartily as ever. This white circular lake with its steep dark walls — strange place! — is called the Zuni Salt Lake. This is a sacred place to the Zuni people, the home of their Salt Mother, the place of their emergence from the previous World.

All life came from the sea, once, and this is one of the great mysteries, like the mystery of having been born once from the inside of one's mother. We were elsewhere, and in emerging we have been transformed. This is the truth of history, of biology, of myth, and of the spirit.

Nowadays I live by the sea, which is like the desert in many ways. It's spacious, and changeable, and dangerous, which means that when one travels on it one has to be keenly aware — of weather, tides, things that one cannot control.

One recent summer I was sailing with friends off New England when the wind picked up and blew a steady twenty-five, then thirty, and then thirty-five. By mid-afternoon everything was double-reefed and straining and still we clawed our way to windward, screaming at each other to be heard, wearing safety lines, our knuckles white where we gripped the wheel or the rails. The waves grew or we shrank — it was hard to tell — the sea became a landscape of wicked unpredictable hills.

I was at the helm when one wave came that was larger than the others. It rose up from the dark of the sea and turned green and finally silver as the tip of it came over the rail and flicked drops of water in my face. Then it went down, under the boat. The boat leapt up and slewed and hung a moment leaning in the air, then it plunged, and we were rudderless and beyond hope as we fell down the wave . . . until the wheel was solid again in my hands and the bows lifted, reluctant, toward the wind. Then the wave growled out under the leeward rail and ran away like an animal. I licked its salt from my mouth.

Then I understood something. Perhaps it's a matter of semantics, but to me the word "understand" means to possess physical knowledge; it means to have a corporeal grasp, a surety that the body owns. A purely cerebral construct is "not understanding." And — going back the other way — something that one has truly understood is so personal and visceral that it's almost impossible to express in words. But this happened: the taste and feel of that wave left me with something like terror but more like awe, an inhabiting whole-body awe.

The spring in Utah was my first taste of that. Though almost certainly not the very first. A saline flavor must have been on my tongue when I was born, and before; the flavor of the eternal and internal sea, from before we were conscious, before we were separate, before we emerged.

During those weeks above Spanish Fork I remember coming back to the ranch house many mornings with half a dozen orphan lambs hog-tied and draped over my saddlehorn. Some of the little ones just got tucked into my jacket and zipped in and I would forget about them for hours, until they moved. Their mothers had been half eaten by coyotes as they labored to give birth, or they had cast themselves in a hollow, or had succumbed to one of those diseases to do with birthing that can happen to any animal: mastitis or milk fever. For the most part the coyotes scorned the sickened sheep and chose as prey the youngest and best fleshed. Or they took lambs. And there were so many of these that they did not bother to eat more of them than the liver. Every morning when I came in with my harvest of dogies I left behind me frantically bellowing ewes, calling for life, ignoring what life had become: those punctured deflated scraps of gray hide.

Scenes of this nature are not pretty, but they are common. They happen with the hyenas and the wild dogs and the wildebeest on the Serengeti, with wolves and caribou on the North Slope, and they have always happened. It can be said that predator and prey are opposite halves of a single unity, a unity we belong to and always have. Here I had mixed myself into an ancient rite of birth and death, and the mixing had the flavor of salt, so I began to believe that this was the coin of the realm, the medium of life's exchange.

I rode over the hills twelve hours a day, circling and circling again. It was often raining. I wore a trash bag over my hat until the old man took pity on me and gave me a plastic hat cover. Either way the hat would dump gouts of water into my saddle at intervals. Sometimes there was a difficult birth or an impossible one and I would dismount and lie flat in the grass to turn the lamb or find the front feet, which are supposed to be tucked under the nose as if the lamb were diving or praying. If they are swept back, the lamb gets jammed. Women seem to be better at sheep obstetrics than men; perhaps it's just because their hands are smaller. In any case, shepherds have noticed that when women do the work, more animals tend to survive. I would lie down and join the struggle. The birth mucus would mix with my streaming nose and the blood on my hands would mix — I couldn't help it — with tears, that were from rage or helplessness or finally relief. Sometimes when the birth took a long time the grass under me would turn to mud and the ewe would kick it up over me as we fought to do the thing. Afterward the ewe would lick mud and wet from its lamb with a frantic whickering delight and I would stand and wipe my face on my sleeve, which was salty with I don't know what. Pressing my face against my horse's neck, I tasted horse and horse sweat and rain. All things had become inextricably mixed. The medium of our common life began with this sea that flowed over us.

MAXINE KUMIN

Jicama, Without Expectation

FROM PRAIRIE SCHOONER

> There never blows so red the rose,
> So sound the round tomato
> As March's catalogues disclose
> And yearly I fall prey to.

THIS, MY FIRST published poem, appeared on the Home Forum page of the *Christian Science Monitor* in March of 1953. Forty years ago, in a handkerchief-size suburban back yard dominated by a huge maple tree that admitted very little sunlight, I raised half a dozen spindly tomato plants and first made the acquaintance of the fearsome zucchini. Burpee's was my catalogue of choice back then; indeed, I doubt that I knew any others existed. The prolixity and seductive lure of today's catalogues almost exceed my desire to leaf through them. It is not roses I seek; I am in search of the perfect vegetable. Open-pollinated, disease-free, all-season producer, easy to harvest, fun to cook, and heaven to eat. What cultivar is this, as yet unborn?

I have lived long enough to see the sugar snap pea survive its trials and move into the glossy pages of Harris, Stokes, Shepherds, et al. I have seen the great viney winter squashes shrink into manageable bush types. A white eggplant has swum into my ken, as have seed potatoes, and giant onions that spring up from seed in a single season. The red brussels sprout has arrived. There is an ongoing revolution in the pepper world: orange, red, yellow, chocolate, and now white peppers are all said to be possible.

Lettuces of every hue and configuration have all but obliterated the boring iceberg head, and Japanese vegetables are so numerous that they now command their own category in the catalogue. Central and South American varieties are not far behind, although I have only this winter tried to jump-start jicama, a delightfully crunchy root I first met on an hors d'oeuvres platter in Texas ten years ago. To my surprise, it has a vining habit and will want something comforting to twine itself on.

Climbers of the leguminous persuasion, from heirloom shelling-out beans to a strain of leafless peas, all do well in our soil. Frankly, I am deficient in the pepper department. *Capsicum's* podlike fruit mostly just sit and sulk in my central New Hampshire garden, although the long green Buddhas, which I haven't deliberately planted in a decade, continue to volunteer in all the wrong places. As do Oriental poppies, broadcast by unseen birds. These refuse to be transplanted into some other location but dot themselves among the carrots and beets at will.

For just shy of twenty years now I have been gardening in the same spot abutting the forest, out of which emerge such menacing outlaws as raccoons and woodchucks, skunk, deer, and black bear. I long to have my garden closer to the house, where it would be less subject to depredations. The dogs could keep an eye on it there. But our hilly farm yields only this distant tabletop for garden, a hundred yards above the house and barn, and it must serve. The earth dries out slowly there, backed by our pond. But it stands open to full sun and yields eight hundred pounds of produce in a decent season.

Substantial credit for this prodigious yield goes to the *New York Times,* which arrives Monday through Saturday in the mailbox at the foot of the hill, courtesy of the RFD mailperson and her jeep. On Mondays or Tuesdays the *New York Times Book Review* comes via the same route. I don't subscribe to the Sunday edition, partly because it weighs too much to carry half a mile north, and partly because I fear it would usurp every Monday to work my way through it.

It makes no difference that the news is a day late when I carry it up the hill, usually on a horse, sometimes on foot. For breadth and depth of coverage, the *Times* has no peer. Certainly no other newspaper can match, inch for inch, its thick accretion of words, stacked and ready at all seasons in the mud room.

In March, when I start seedlings in flats on top of the refrigerator and dryer, little cutouts of wet newspaper line the trays and help hold in the moisture. New York City's ten best Szechuan restaurants underlie Johnny's new hybrid pepper seeds, which seem to take forever to wake up and grow. My almost-antique celery seeds that have not failed in four years lie atop Charles Schwab's ad for how to open an IRA account. Germination rates may exceed interest again this year.

A little later in the growing season such directly sown vegetables as beets and green beans are also mulched with "All the News That's Fit to Print." Once the individual plants are well organized with their second set of true leaves showing, I enclose them, tearing slits in three or four thicknesses of paper to fit around the whole plant.

This is tedious and time-consuming, but pays off mightily in shutting out weeds and preserving the soil temperature that suits each variety. Green beans, for example, like warm soil, but want to be mulched before summer's full heat strikes. While kneeling to put paper around them, I can catch up on an enormous range of topics that eluded me when they were current events. If it's windy, though, I have to hurry and weight down the papers with mulch.

A vegetable garden just below a pond, just inside a field bordered by hundreds of acres of forests, clearly needs to be fenced and refenced. To keep down weeds that take tenacious hold in, around, and through the original buried chicken wire fence and the later additions of hardware cloth, screening, and other exotica thrown into the breach when emergencies arise, fat sections of the *Times* are stuffed into the gaps and pleats, then mulched for appearances' sake.

All around the outer perimeter, whole sections of the newspaper lie flat, weighted and stained with handy rocks. Before I climb over a stile of poplar chunks and into my garden, I sometimes stop to marvel at the Roche Bobois furniture ads, the gorgeous lofts in Chelsea, the halogen lights and sunken marble baths of the back pages. Here where tomatoes overgrow their cages and Kentucky Wonders climb chaotic tepees of sumac branches, I admire engineered closets and beds that fold up into walls.

My corn is not sown here, but in an inviolate space facing south in the uppermost and hottest pasture. A year's worth of book reviews, exactly the correct width when opened out, serves as carpet between the rows. And an opened-out page folded into thirds slips between individual plants, once they're six inches high. It's an Augean labor, but only needs to be performed once. Hay and/or sawdust mulch covers the paper, and nothing further is required except to eat the ears when they're of a size. No, I misspoke. Just before the corn really sets ears, I need to energize the two strands of electric fence that keep raccoons at bay.

Next April, when a general thaw makes it possible to turn the garden once again, nothing much is left of the *New York Times*. A few tatters with mysterious pieces of words on them are in evidence, but thanks to thousands of literate earthworms, not enough remains to construct even a minimalist story.

Cultivating a garden satisfies at least some of my deep yearnings for order. Everything else has a ragged sort of shape to it. In an old farmhouse, cobwebs cling to exposed beams. Pawprints muddy the floor. Doors have to be propped open with stones, the stair risers constructed two hundred years ago are amateurishly uneven. Wisps of hay ride indoors on our sweaters. It's a comfortably down-at-the-heels atmosphere. Sometimes, guiltily, I think of my mother, who would never have tolerated this welter. But the garden is composed of orderly rows and blocks of raised beds. Weeds do not penetrate the deep mulch. Serenely, plants grow, blossom, set fruit. All is as workable as Latin grammar: *Amo, amas, amat* among the brassicas; *hic haec, hoc* in a raised bed lively with parsnip foliage.

You cannot justify a garden to nonbelievers. You cannot explain to the unconverted the desire, the ravishing need, to get your hands into the soil again, to plant, thin, train up on stakes, trellis onto pea fence, hill up to blanch, just plain admonish to grow. From Pliny to Voltaire, from Thomas Jefferson to Saint-Exupéry, gardening has been an emblem of integrity in an increasingly incomprehensible world.

There is an intimacy to the act of planting as tantalizing as possessing a secret. Every seed you sow has passed through your fingers on its way from dormancy to hoped-for fruition. "Trailing clouds of glory do we come," Wordsworth wrote. Thus come the little cobbles of beet seeds that separate when rolled between your fingers, the flat, feathery parsnip ones that want to drift on air en route to the furrow, the round black dots that will be Kelsae onions, fat and sweet by September, the exasperatingly tiny lettuce flecks that descend in a cluster, and the even harder-to-channel carrot seeds.

Some of my seed packets are a decade old, but they've lost little vigor. Stored out of season in an unheated closet, they have amazing keeping qualities. But consider the lotus seeds found under an ancient lake bed in Manchuria. Carbon-dated at eight hundred years old, they grew into lotus plants of a sort that had never been seen in that particular area. Such extravagant longevity makes me hopeful that we humans too will ever so gradually advance into new forms, a higher level of lotus, as it were.

A few years ago, early in May, while upending a wheelbarrow load of horse manure onto the pile, I noticed some splayed green leaves emerging along the midriff of this sizable mountain. They were not poke or burdock. They had a cultivated look. By tacit agreement my husband and I began to deposit our barrow loads on the north face of the pile.

By mid-June the south slope was covered with a dense network of what were now, clearly, squash leaves. Male blossoms, visible on their skinny-necked stems, were popping up and a few bees were already working the territory. *Let this not be zucchini,* I prayed to Mother Nature.

Around the Fourth of July, green swellings could be seen at the bases of the female blossoms. The solo plant had overrun the manure pile and was now racing along our dirt road, uphill and down. Every few days I policed the road's edge and nipped back each of the brash tendrils that thought, like turtles, to cross the right-of-way. Thwarted in this direction, the heroic squash began to loop upward, mounting a huge stand of jewelweed in its eagerness to get at a telephone pole.

Well before Labor Day we knew what we had: Sweet Mamas of an especially vigorous persuasion. About ten of these pumpkin-shaped winter squashes were visible from the mountaintop. Several looked table-ready.

We watched and waited, despite several frost warnings, secure in the knowledge that the warmth of the pile would protect this crop from an early demise. A two-day downpour flattened some of the luxuriant foliage; we could see that the plant was still setting fruit, heedless of the calendar. After several sunny days, when things had dried out a bit, I poked around a few of the giants at the top of the mountain. They had orange streaks and some of the stems were cracking.

Harvest time was at hand. I began yanking the vines hand over hand, as if coiling the ropes of a seagoing vessel. In all we garnered thirty-five beauteous volunteers. Not a single squash bug anywhere. No chipmunk toothmarks, no tiny gnawings of mice or voles. It seems that even the lowliest creature disdains a manure pile.

We compost all our garden and table scraps, from elderly broccoli plants to orange peels to onion skins. The simplest method is just to dig a hole anywhere in the brown mountain, deposit the leavings, and backfill with a few shovelfuls of the usual. Leftovers disintegrate in a few days; sometimes I catch a glimpse of grapefruit rind or eggshell not fully digested. I reinter them without a backward glance.

Late November is manure pile demolition time on the farm. As much of the mountain as can be moved manually or by machine is returned to the gardens, pastures, and riding ring. In the course of upending and hauling, some ancient Sweet Mama cotyledon must have been stirred to germinate. I like to think of the seed lying there through several seasons before the right combination of sun and warmth, moon and rain awakened it.

Early in October, in Geese Go South Moon, leaves rain down with a muffled sideslipping sound. Dust motes spin in sunlight like flour sifting in puffs onto the beginnings of batter. For the horses this season is heavenly. We haven't had a killing frost yet. All of our fields are open to them, and they wander like sleepwalkers from one area to another, grazing intermittently, sometimes standing for long thoughtful moments silhouetted against the backdrop of forest or granite outcropping.

This is the season when tails at last become superfluous. The biting insects have fled, migrated, died off, or entered hibernation. Except for the usual small ectoplasms of gnats that still hover in quiet air, all is benign and salving in the ether. Gone the vicious little trapezoidal deerflies that draw blood from animal and human. Vanished too the horn and face flies, bots and horseflies. The ubiquitous blackflies, that penance of the north country, never quite disappear, but they are greatly diminished. And this summer's long tenure of mosquitoes appears to be over.

We are in the briefest and most beautiful moment of stasis. Along the perimeter of the pastures, fall-flowering asters, tiny blue florets with yellow centers, flourish. A few late blackberries go on ripening, daintily pursued by the greedy broodmare, who rolls back her lips in order to nip them off, one or two at a time, without getting pricked by thorns. The Jerusalem artichokes, harbingers of frost, are in bud and threaten to open in today's sunlight. Toads in the vegetable garden, deprived of their prey now, have begun retreating to the woods after a long and profitable summer. Mushrooms appear everywhere — two brain puffballs in the dressage ring, little pear-shaped lycoperdons dotting the pine duff like misplaced miniature golf balls, smoky hygrophorus clustering in the dark corners of the pine grove, and in the rocky acre allotted the ewes, brickies — *Hypholoma sublateritium* — spring up, breaking their gray cobwebby films. The chanterelles we prized and ate all summer are gone, but clusters of honey mushrooms at the base of decaying oaks are now ready. Sometimes, traversing the woods on horseback, we spot a full bloom of oyster mushrooms swelling on the trunk of a dying tree. Foraging for mushrooms has its own visceral pleasures: we reap where we did not sow, paper, mulch, or water.

The war against the thistles continues. Day three of eradication, extirpation, elimination, waged by me with a large serrated bread knife and by my helper with a presharpened posthole shovel. I bobble along on my knees, repositioning the kneeling pad that was a birthday present, scraping my knuckles against the inside of these thistle-proof deerhide gloves. I infer from what I see that the thistle is a biennial plant. The great green overlapping swords I am digging up — though seldom does the entire taproot come with the plant — will be the stalk and flower of next summer. The dried vicious pickets we can pull out, thereby scattering ten thousand new seeds for the future, are no threat for the immediate season. While we're about it, we yank any surviving nettle plants, which ovines will eat if desperate.

Nothing on this farm ever reaches the desperation stage. The several ewes who summer here, leaving their home pasture to the newly weaned lambs, make little single-file trails, over to the pond, behind the pond to the woodlot, thence along the fence line back to the rockpile, and in the heat of the day, into the run-in shed where they lie on green pine sawdust in a flaccid heap like dirty laundry. We are their sabbatical. They arrive sheared and anxious in May and go home in October wooly, plump, and totally at ease, to be bred once again.

In the garden broccoli continues to bud, the Kentucky Wonders still put up beans, and the cauliflower plants left unpulled have, to my wonderment, made multiple tiny new heads. We've pulled and dried and braided our onions. Carrots too cannot stay in the ground, as voles and mice begin to nibble them. Two years ago I left parsnips in their bed to winter over and found not a trace of them by spring; last winter I pulled and scrubbed them, dried them off, and froze them, on the theory that they sweeten in the frozen earth if undisturbed. My theory proved itself, for we ate them with relish all last winter in soups and stews.

Kale, brussels sprouts, leeks, celery root, and three purple cabbages remain. Two five-gallon pails of tomatoes, last of the line, are ripening on the porch. A small group of gargantuan zucchini, somehow overlooked, have already been converted into zucchini bread and/or grated, salted, squeezed dry, and frozen to be sneaked into next winter's recipes a little at a time. They blend unnoticed in winter soups and are barely discernible when spread on pizza dough before the sauce and toppings are added. The freezer is packed with the summer's haul of strawberries, raspberries, peas, corn, green beans, and aye the rest. Part of me — the weary part — longs for frost. The other, frugal self is happy to receive each day's reduced provender.

November 15. Now I am removed by a thousand miles from my farm and garden. A wet snow is falling in central Illinois, locus day and night of mournful diesel whistles at grade crossings. Here, the campus grounds are littered with crabapples and I find myself mourning that no one cared enough to gather the harvest and make jelly. I think of my own shelves full of blueberry, strawberry, elderberry, and grape jams, and the fifteen gallons of blackberries waiting in the freezer for a January nor'easter so they can be cooked into "that tar-thick boil love cannot stir down."

There are still brussels sprouts to be picked and half a dozen daikons to be pulled, but otherwise the garden is done for. And with it the unremitting labor. Dilled green beans and bread-and-butter pickles crowd the storage shelves, abutting bottles of decorative purple-pink chive blossom vinegar. Mint, tarragon, and dill plants are drying in paper bags hung from the porch rafters.

Visitors to the farm fall into two categories: the urban admirers, nostalgists who long, but only in their imaginations, for gardens to tend, and the Others, who see this as madness. It's not cost-effective, they remind you. Look at the money you spend for seed, blood meal, Dipel, whatever. Look at the fencing (which is now deplorable and needs to be redone). On the other hand, nothing we eat has been drenched with pesticides or fertilized with chemicals. There's also the deeply Calvinist satisfaction of knowing you have earned by the sweat of your brow this delicious feast of fresh asparagus, new spinach, sweet corn, either harvested in situ or now, at this season, brought up from the capacious freezer in the cellar.

"The poet," Thoreau wrote in *A Week on the Concord and Merrimack Rivers*, "is he that hath fat enough, like bears and marmots, to suck his claws all winter. He hibernates in this world, and feeds on his own marrow."

December. Home again, to bountiful snow. Such good cover we can open the fields again, as soon as hunting season passes, to the horses to wander at will. This is the Moon That Parts Her Hair Right Square in the Middle, so styled because of the shortest day of the year and the welcome beginning of longer days. December and the arctic months that follow belong to the writer in a leisurely way, to read, think, scribble, declaim aloud, and develop a dozen fantasies of fulfillment. In January's Help Eat Moon — stay inside; too cold to do anything else, so eat more — and February's Moon of the Eagle and Hatching Time of the Owl I will suck my claws.

Ruminating in February, I read through a stack of old *Smithsonian* and *Natural History* magazines, my favorite provender. When I lift my eyes to the hills that surround us, all visible activity is suspended. This could be a glacial prehistoric era but for the two woodstoves radiating a hospitable warmth indoors and the two domesticated wolves several times removed dozing on the hearth. As I muse on the tenacity of the life force — the mice and voles unseen, running along their narrow tunnels under the snow, deer bedded in a hemlock grove far from any road — I come upon an article about suspended animation. The technical term is cryptobiosis. Brine shrimp, which flourish in brackish water that other plankton cannot tolerate, manage to survive even after the ponds dry up. They stop consuming any oxygen at all and simply encyst their embryos until conditions improve. Researchers have carbon-dated some cysts they retrieved from sediment found to be ten thousand years old. Amazingly, several of these hatched when placed back in water. I am comforted, and it is not a cold comfort; it cheers me to learn that certain kinds of brine shrimp reproduce by parthenogenesis and have persisted without male assistance for millions of years. This is less a feminist statement than an affirmation of reproductive forces.

Now we have arrived at Groundhog Day, an increasingly trivialized ceremony in this epoch of electric lights and central heating. Once, it was an event that pledged the faith of human beings in the approach of the vernal equinox. Early Slavic peoples celebrated a holiday that translates as "butter week," when, as an act of sun-worship, they devoured mountains of the pancakes we know as blini or blintzes, slathered with melted butter. Preparing, chewing, and swallowing were meant to ensure halcyon days to come with abundant crops, golden marriages, and sturdy offspring to till the fields. I like this story much better than Pennsylvania's Punxsutawney Phil, dragged out of hibernation and paraded before the television cameras to make the feature page of every newspaper in the East.

We have forgotten that we celebrate the coming of the growing season. Most of us are so far removed from the acts of cultivation that we would be unable to recognize a tepee of horticultural beans at twenty paces. But we are evolved from East African hominids that once subsisted on a totally vegetarian diet. This line of herbivorous prehumans possessed incredibly powerful chewing teeth about five million years ago, but the species did not last. Our molars and premolars have shrunk, our craniums have enlarged, and we are less robust omnivores, and what has it profited us?

It's fascinating to realize that the formal notion of agriculture, of actually sowing, weeding, and reaping plants from the soil for human uses, is only about ten thousand years old, a mere blip on the screen of human/prehuman history. We seem to have evolved in response to varying temperatures; "successive cooling plunges," anthropologist Elisabeth Vrba calls them. Wet forests gradually shrank into dry grasslands and then climatic upheavals probably reversed this action several times. Rainfall amounts and geographical boundaries tend to isolate animal populations, limiting the exchange of gene pools. These smaller groups may then diverge to permit the development of new species or they may simply die

out — more's the pity — as did our very early vegetarian ancestors.
I read that the biosphere is "a living layer, stretched thinly over
the globe, responding rhythmically to the beat of the earth," and
I think of the holes we are poking in this thin curtain that sus-
tains us. What new species will evolve once we have destroyed
the atmosphere we require in order to breathe? What new brine
shrimp will we become?

This past winter I've had a sleigh at my disposal, a little two-
seater built by the Excelsior Sleigh Co. of Watertown, New York,
around the turn of the century. At some time in the past hundred
years an importunate horse's hoof has kicked a crescent-shaped
hole in one side of it, but this in no way limits its serviceability.
With new shafts and a few mended braces, it's sturdy enough to
drive across the fields and, before the plow arrives, down the road
as well. Twice we sojourned with it to Vermont to attend festive
sleigh rallies that looked like events recorded by Currier and Ives.

When conditions are optimal — about six inches of snow over
hardpack — going sleighing is as exhilarating as the daredevil
belly-flopping runs of my childhood. Down the steep of our back
yard that connected with the Kellys' driveway, around Devil's Elbow, and out onto Pelham Road we flew, perilously side by side,
in Germantown, Pennsylvania, long ago.

My half Arab, half Standardbred gelding loves to pull. Once he
overcomes inertia and the sleigh begins to glide, he finds it all but
effortless to keep it skimming. I have to hang on tight; I drive him
with the reins on the lowest (most severe) slot of his Liverpool bit.
In summer with the two-wheel phaeton, I can trust him with just
a snaffle. The term "mercurial" accurately reflects changes in
equine temperament according to the vagaries of weather. When
the mercury plunges, their exuberance rises proportionately, and
vice versa. In winter our horses are very shaggy, volatile, round-bel-
lied from free-choice good hay. By midsummer, freed of those
heavy coats and in regular work, they are sleek, supple, almost
obedient.

There's a place we love to go, on horseback or by phaeton and
now by sleigh; it's a protected stretch of wetlands under federal
jurisdiction, crisscrossed by a network of driveable trails. Weekdays
we are usually the only travelers. The dogs go with us, sprinting
into the woods to follow some elusive scent, bounding back to
catch up with us around the next bend. In winter we cross-country

ski here, too, along paths that weave through managed stands of red and white pine, hemlock and some few larches. Only an occasional patch of sunlight makes its way here. The prevailing northerly wind is deflected by the abundant growth. The stillness is so palpable I would risk calling it holy.

Rhythmic hoofbeats and arrhythmic sneeze-snorts echo like gunshot in these vasty rooms. Although I have never seen the taiga, I think it must look like this, with a three-abreast hitch of caribou flying over the tundra, outstripping their wolves. We seldom raise any wild creatures here, as there is very little understory for browsing, but once, around a bend in the trail, we came upon a magnificent coyote, well nourished, tall at the shoulder. There was barely enough time to admire him before he was gone. Oddly, our dogs never picked up his scent but continued their dilettantish feints around the bases of trees up which a few sparse squirrels had scampered.

These are the best of days. At noon when the temperature peaks in the twenties the fresh powder of last night's little snow squalls squeaks under our skis or runners. My horse is shod with borium caulks on all four feet. In front he wears snowball poppers, pads designed to keep the snow from balling up in the concavity of his hoof, known as the frog. He is sure-footed and a little too eager! We fly along in an extended trot until he wears down the edge of his enthusiasm and will come back into my hand.

Is it dangerous? Of course. A spill in cart or sleigh is far more fraught with peril than an unceremonious dumping from the saddle. The horse's life, too, is at risk when he's in the traces and upsets. But I mind the trail, squint in a sudden stretch of sunlight, settle into a long easy trot on the flat, and ask him to walk the last mile back so he can cool out without chilling.

In March the lambs — singles, twins, and triplets — begin to be born to various small-farm and hobby-farm breeders. The professionals who raise lamb in quantity for the market breed early, risking losing some newborns in order to have table lamb, as they call it, in time for the Easter trade. It's baby chick and rabbit time, too, most of them destined for oblivion in eight to ten weeks. Goat farmers are happy to have infant bucks on hand for the Greek Orthodox Easter market in Boston, where roast kid is considered a delicacy.

I can't blink these facts, but I'm grateful I don't have to participate in them. By and large, the small breeders raise their animals for slaughter in a far more humane fashion than the animal factories of agribusiness. Around here, veal calves are not confined in slatted cages in the dark, chickens scratch in capacious barnyards and are not debeaked, sows farrow in full-size pens or in the open. Does it matter how they live, since they are all going to die to feed us? I think it matters mightily, not only because these uncrowded creatures need not be shot full of antibiotics to survive to marketable size, but because how we treat the animals in our keeping defines us as human beings.

April is punctuated by the geese going over, baying like beagles in the dawn sky. Our hundred maple taps run grudgingly around midday, then seal up tight until the next day's warmth releases them again for a few hours. Traditionally, George Washington's birthday is the first acceptable date to go out with brace and bit and bore holes in preselected trees. This year, blizzards and relentless cold delayed the start a good three or four weeks. Sugaring-off time depends on the freeze-thaw cycle of March and early April. This hasn't been a good run compared to last year, but the deep snow cover is prolonging it clear to the end of the month, which is unusual. Things have a way of balancing out, a fact it has taken us thirty years here to accept. Drought one season, monsoon the next.

For the first time in our long tenure here, the spring peepers have been all but inaudible. True, we've had a slow, cold spring, but except for a few tentative pipings, no evidence of *Hyla crucifer,* whose high, shrill whistle ordinarily raises a deafening chorus every night during mating season. Some nights I've even closed the bedroom window on the lower-pond side to reduce the noise pollution. Now I find myself straining to hear that high-pitched stridulation.

Reflecting back on last summer, the population of bullfrogs in our upper pond, normally abundant enough to keep our dogs busy startling them off their sunbathing perches, seemed to have diminished. There were sporadic late-afternoon jug-a-rums announcing the locations of various kings, but the usual clumps of tadpoles in the shallows sprouting forelegs and gradually absorbing their tails were greatly reduced.

The salamander density seemed undisturbed, especially in the red stage on dry land, when they are known as efts, a useful Scrabble word. The salamander is voiceless, so far as I know, but consider this lyrical outburst from my sobersides bible, the *Complete Field Guide to American Wildlife, East, Central and North,* by Henry Hill Collins, Jr.: "The cries of the ancient frogs may well have been the first voices in the springtime of the Age of Land Vertebrates. For millions of years before the coming of the songbirds, the calls of various frogs and toads must have been the most musical sounds on earth."

Another mystery is the absence of great blue herons from the rookery in our secret beaver pond a few miles away. For years we've gone on horseback every few days beginning at the end of April to keep tabs on this enormous nursery, where a dozen or more nests decorate the tops of dead pine trees still rising from their flooded bases. So far this year, no activity is evident. No crying and flapping, no ack-ack-ack of hungry fledglings, not even any tardy parent brooding over her eggs. Are we simply in a new cycle of birth and decay, have the herons relocated to a better, even more remote pond, or is the culprit manmade: acid rain?

Still, the geese go over barking in formation, the rusty-hinge sound of the red-winged blackbirds announces that insects are once again abroad. Tongues of snow retreat in the woods, the ubiquitous mud ebbs, pastures begin to green around the margins, fiddlehead ferns poke their spokes up through the woodland wet, and the first harbingers of spring, wake-robin trilliums, which will send up their distinctive burgundy blooms, announce the tidings with their earliest leaves.

Everything resurrects in May. Nettles first, followed by wild mustard, then dandelions and clover and tender grasses. The hardwoods flush faintly red with new buds, prelude to leaves. The willows sprout catkins, then laces of yellow strings. Wake-robin is followed by bloodlilies, violets, lady's slippers, and the whole procession of miniature blossoms that dot the grudgingly greening pastures.

In the bird department, phoebes are the first to return after the blackbirds; I worry what they will find to eat before the air fills with insects. Robins next, then all smothered in a brief snowstorm. (I put out raisins and hope for the best.) Finches, both purple and gold, hung around all winter, as did the evening grosbeaks, but here come the song sparrows with their old-john-peabody, pea-

body, pea refrain, and finally the rose-breasted grosbeaks, spectacu-
larly jousting at the feeders.

How joyous the first light is now, with all this territorial music!
How lucky I feel to come awake to the overlapping trills and calls,
a symphony of screes, caws, and warbles, many of them distinctive
and recognizable, some tantalizingly elusive, even unknown. It is
deliciously noisy at 5 A.M. Everyone is staking a claim. But what
falls so happily on human ears actually reflects a tense struggle to
survive and procreate. Life is not harmonious for the insectivores,
it seems to me, who must sieve the air from dawn to full dark for
enough protein to sustain a clutch of nestlings. Prodigal nature
dictates their stern routine: two, even three batches of babies in a
season to guarantee the future of the race. In much the same way,
nature sends down a deluge of volunteer dill into my vegetable
garden, along with torrents of sprouting jewelweed, chickweed,
lamb's quarters, and half a dozen extra-prolific others to bedevil
the deliberately planted cultivars.

It's a penance of sorts to rise extra early and get the horses out
on grass for a few hours before the wings of midges and blackflies
have dried. By 9 A.M. you cannot inhale outside without ingesting
blackflies. Even with face masks in place, the horses are driven wild
by them and prefer to be in their stalls. We will endure blackflies
until the mosquitoes overtake them, but even this plague is self-
limiting. In a few weeks, once the richest flush of growth has passed
and with it the danger of founder from too much grazing, the
horses will be out on grass all night. The cruelest pests — deerflies,
horseflies, bots — are diurnal. Admittedly, mosquitoes raise welts
on equines as well as humans, but they are more easily deterred
with repellents and oily lotions.

One dawn's reward: a pair of loons crying their thrillingly de-
mented cry overhead. That same week, wood ducks overnighting
on the lower pond. The next morning a great showy splashing on
the big upper pond. Two pairs of mallards, and later, one hooded
merganser. What can you do with these treats? Like the winter's
wild turkeys parading across the back lawn, the daily visitations by
pileated woodpeckers, the late-summer fawn still speckled with
camouflage who bounded out of the tall grass like an enormous
rabbit, these are honoraria to share with like-minded friends. We
commingle our passions with a small band of other beast-bird-and-

flower fanatics, like a secret cell of communists. Some of them have snapshots of moose, blurry because the photographer's hand was shaking with excitement, some have up-close black bear sightings, one has even come into the presence of a bobcat. Such events make us celebrities of a sort.

A Montana visitor in May, however, complained that the world of New England was far too verdant for her eyes. She could not differentiate the variations; all was a huge humid sea of green vegetation in her parched sight. Her retina longed to record the yellow and brown vistas of her native heath, the open plains and craggy mountains, canyons, and draws that comforted her.

Especially you know what not to rhapsodize about. Nothing rhapsodic about the enormous male raccoon who seems to have taken up permanent lodgings in the grain room of the barn. He sprawls over the cats' feeding shelf while they wait respectfully on the back sill, and it takes a snap of the lunge whip to drive him off. I am a bit leery, given the recent rash of reports of rabies in New Hampshire. All our animals have been vaccinated, but we humans are certainly vulnerable. Now I remove the cat dishes every evening, hoping to deprive our adoptee of the easy pickings he seems to have come to expect. Bad enough to feed a flock of forty aggressive evening grosbeaks year-round. Am I destined to deliver cat kibble to the multitudes of masked bandits?

One afternoon our raccoon arrived just as I was feeding the cats. Abra growled, a sound I have never heard her utter before, and instantly decamped. I looked up into the coon's handsome feral face; he paid no attention to my shouts. I snapped the lunge whip at him, but he stood his ground. The next crack caught him across the shoulders but hardly dislodged him. He retreated twenty paces into the broodmare's stall, where she totally ignored his presence and went on eating. A raccoon that bold by daylight? We called the town's animal officer, who offered us the loan of a Havahart trap.

"Take him at least ten miles from here, or you'll have him back next morning," he said. "Course, last time I did this, I got a skunk in the trap. If you catch a skunk instead, throw an old blanket over the cage before you pick it up so he won't spray." (Do I believe this will work? Not for one moment.) "Try peanut butter, and if that don't get him, tuna fish."

Peanut butter didn't work, but the trap was sprung. We continue to reset it with various baits, but this fellow is apparently a graduate of Havaharts. He gets the goods and goes free. The cats and he seem to have agreed on a nonaggression pact. The dogs, too, have grown quite used to him; the horses treat him with total indifference. His hideout lies between the double walls that separate the broodmare's stall from the sawdust bin. He materializes and fades away as soundlessly as the Cheshire Cat. Often now I find him resting comfortably on the top ledge of that divider, eyeing the general proceedings. He is extremely handsome, with his narrow feline face and foxy ears. I count five rings on his great tail.

Now I look over my shoulder before I open the grain bin, expecting the marauder to leap in unannounced. And as if raccoons weren't enough, Rilke, our mostly German shepherd, came home from a trail ride today with ten porcupine quills in his face. Luckily, we were able to yank them out with needlenose pliers while distracting him with dog biscuits. Dozens of other times with our other dogs, particularly with the handsome but ineducable Dalmatians we used to raise, we had to make emergency runs to the expensive open-all-night city vet to have forty or fifty quills removed under total anesthesia. "The reason we don't learn from history," my poet friend Howard Nemerov once said, "is because we are not the same people who learned last time." Dogs, it seems, are never the same dogs who learned last time. Every porcupine, every skunk is newly imprinted on the brainpan, which then reverts to tabula rasa.

After a week of imprisoning one barn cat after the other in the Havahart — each seemed perfectly content there, having polished off a plate of tuna fish — our raccoon took the original bait of peanut butter. He slept most of the way to Mount Sunapee State Park, lulled into slumber by the gentle motion of the automobile, leading me to suspect that he has made this journey before, but came awake at once when the trap door was opened. He snarled, leapt out, and shot up a tree. We hope we are permanently delivered of raccoon.

In mid-June we take our first delivery of next winter's hay, a hundred bales of first-cut timothy, insurance in case the second cutting, which we prefer for its better keeping properties, comes late or, heaven forfend, not at all. (There is always Canadian hay in an emergency, but the bales are wire-tied and the contents are coarser.) The farmer who supplies us is an old friend by now. He takes a proprietary interest in the well-being of our horses, especially my driving horse, who took him for a few fast passes in the cart one day, and he is a source of rich anecdotes about the past in this corner of New England. His family has been here since, as he puts it, the back of the beyond. Steer are his specialty, but he also raises up a fine crop of local boys who hire on with him for summer jobs as soon as they are tall enough and strong enough. His work ethic is stringent but kind. Graduates of his school go on with better biceps and enlarged self-respect.

And so we grope our way into high summer again, into the time of strawberry-picking, followed by the first peas. If rain is bountiful there will be hundreds of coprinus mushrooms, our first available fungus, to make into soup. The green beans will ripen all at once, there will be too much broccoli, and when the yellow squash and zucchini begin to set fruit, there will be no sane way to cope with their overabundance. We will wait on the cusp of August for our first vine-ripened tomato. Turn around twice and they will be too many.

Just as we ate asparagus every night for three weeks when the crop gushed magically forth in May, so will we devour corn on the cob every night for those few weeks — if we're lucky! — at the end of August and into early September. A little melancholy will creep in when the corn is done. I know I will grieve as I stand there feeding the succulent shucks to the horses, as one does when a wonderful novel draws to its close. "What do I want of my life?" Stanley Kunitz asked in a poem. "More!"

Another year, please. Another year of the same. Hay in the barn, heavy snows, ten cords of dry firewood, split and stacked. Send in the blackflies, let a new crop of nettles emerge, may the broodmare bring forth a healthy foal. Next year I promise to plant a smaller and thriftier garden. If I get another summer like this one, I vow to spend an hour every afternoon sitting by the pond or swimming in it. I will cultivate leisure as tenderly as jicama, which, by the way, made splendid vines and never cared to develop edible roots. I will grow jicama again, without expectation, simply to cherish it, along with the dogs and horses, the cats, even the raccoon, if he returns to raise a family, a not unlikely prospect.

For I too plan to stay.

JAMES A. MCPHERSON

Saturday Night, and Sunday Morning

FROM WITNESS

> "One of these days I'm go'n show you how nice a man can be
> One of these days I'm go'n show you how nice a man can be
> I'ma buy you a brand new Cadillac.
> After, always speak some good words about me."
>
> — Muddy Waters

PEOPLE SAY it is always cold in Chicago.

Once in the dining room of the Hyde Park Hilton, I saw a father and son arguing over Sunday dinner. The father wore a dark blue gabardine suit with shoulder pads, a colored shirt, and a striped tie. The son's three-piece suit linked him with the commercial life of the city. The father's tentative manner, in that upscale hotel, defined him as self-consciously lower class. The son's manner was smooth, manicured, consciously geared to the decor of the dining room. The father did not "belong" in the dining room of the Hyde Park Hilton. The son did. The son kept saying, "But Dad, can't you see?" The father could not see. The father kept insisting on what the Bible says. The son kept making exceptions. They were discussing the son's responsibility toward a woman who was bearing his child. Each seemed determined to pull the other into an alien world.

The winter of 1985 is bitterly cold. It is the coldest day on record, and people have been warned to stay indoors. It is Saturday. At the entrance to the El station, at State and Randolph, two frostbitten boys try to sell at half-price the Sunday edition of the *Tribune*. Down on the platform, the man selling newspapers behind the concession stand is Asian. Along the platform a young black man, in a formal black suit and white shirt and black bow tie and black gloves and black sunshades, is tap-dancing. People waiting for the El, mostly white, applaud and toss coins into his top hat, upturned on the cement platform. Still another black man, hand-cuffed, is being led away by two Chicago policemen. One police-man also leads a lean German shepherd on a leash. The second officer, escorting an enraged white female, follows behind. The polished handcuffs on the young man's wrists catch the cold yellow light. He seems to be crying without sound.

People pretend they do not see.

During the 1980s, as traditionally, *money* best defined what Chi-cago runs on. People come to this city because they want to do well. Its traditions are rooted in fur trading, riverboats, railroads, stockyards, banks, commodity futures, and in buildings so tall they almost swagger in the wind off Lake Michigan. This city is un-abashed in its commitment to material values, ruggedly honest about its areas of corruption. But it is also a city of great contra-dictions. Its downtown skyline competes with New York, Atlanta, Houston, San Francisco; its neighborhoods are rigidly ethnic and provincial. It is a city always in the process of reforming; it never seems able to get away from the same old gang. Its overt allegiances are to material values; its covert allegiances, the texture of its soul, are extremely complicated. There are probably more active places of worship in Chicago — Protestant, Catholic, and Jewish — than in any other city in the country. Chicago has contributed more to the arts than any other city; it is still self-conscious in comparing itself to New York. It is one of the most racially polarized of American cities; it is a city still capable of profound human gestures.

Perhaps Chicago is all that can be expected of America.

During the 1930s, the young Richard Wright, in search of values to replace those he thought he had left behind in Mississippi, expressed personal contempt for the public values of Chicago. "Perhaps it would be possible for the Negro to become reconciled to his plight," he wrote in *American Hunger*, "if he could be made to believe that his sufferings were for some remote, high, sacrificial end; but sharing the culture that condemns him, and seeing that a lust for trash is what blinds the nation to his claims, is what set storms to rolling in his soul."

> "Precious Lord, take my hand, lead me on, let me stand,
> I am tired, I am weak, I am worn . . ."
> — Thomas Dorsey

During the same time Wright lived there, Mahalia Jackson, Thomas Dorsey, and Muddy Waters came to Chicago. Like many thousands of other Mississippians, they brought with them an idiom, a technique for transcending personal storms, that Wright had somehow bypassed. They used aspects of this idiom to confront, and then to transcend, the hard facts of life. From within their roles as entertainers, from behind the various masks that provided safety, they provided Chicago's material culture with a spiritual optimism. It was Studs Terkel who, back in the 1940s, recognized the value of Mahalia Jackson's music and helped it reach a wider audience. And it was a white Chicago promoter who brought Muddy Waters from the small clubs of the South Side of Chicago to the folk festival at Newport, Rhode Island, in 1960.

Several decades later, these two giants still define the blues idiom.

Saturday Night

During his last set that evening at the Checkerboard, Buddy Guy said to his audience, "I would like your support in helping to make it possible for part of Forty-second Street to be named for Muddy Waters. He did the most to make this street famous, and I think the city should honor him." Buddy Guy was a young blues artist with a rising reputation. Small clubs like the Checkerboard, and Theresa's further down Forty-second Street, supported him. Only those who value authenticity of feeling, the "real" blues, come to these clubs. They are mostly black people, middle-aged or older, whose roots are close to the rural South. For them, the music is not entertainment. It is an organic part of a settled way of life. Groups of white students from the University of Chicago come here, especially on the weekends, but they are not really in the idiom, the felt experience. Still, they brave the cold, and the warnings of black cab drivers ("Don't flash any money. They'll knock you in the head!"), to get a feel for the authentic blues. The armed black policemen, or guards, at the doors of the clubs are there to ensure the safety of the white patrons. But still the mostly black audience sets the musical standard. Next to the front door, beside the armed black guard, a sad-faced, middle-aged black woman sits alone, playing her nightly game of solitaire. Next to the bandstand, an old black man, probably a laborer, does a slow grind to the music. Two women, one toothless and wrinkled and the other young, wearing a red headrag, embrace closely as they dance together. They seem to be supporting each other's souls. Behind my table a man is singing to himself. Suddenly he gets up, walks around the room, and says, "I got the blues! I got the blues!" He stops at my table and makes a statement: "My daughter died last week from heroin. Went out to Michael Reece Hospital, she was layin' up in bed, needle holes swole up in her neck big as a basketball. She was the baddest one of my kids. Monday, I'm takin' her ass down to Clarksdale, Mississippi, and put her six feet under. I'm go'n bury her right. I ain't go'n bury her wrong."

He asks for a contribution for the funeral and I give it to him. Then he goes up onto the small stage and sings.

I try to hear his feelings for his daughter *beneath* the words of his song. But the electrified guitars, in their mocking commentary, seem much too loud and playful. The singer seems to be crying from within his song. I find myself remembering another blues artist, a much older man named John Jackson — a gravedigger by profession and a musician by necessity — of Rappahannock, Virginia. I remember the night he was told, during a gig, that his second son was dying, this one of cancer. To outpourings of sympathy from friends, John Jackson said, "Yes, ma'am. Yes suh. I thank y'all." Then he continued with his music, making very joyful sounds on his blues banjo. John Jackson confirmed for me my suspicion that inside the best musicians is a very delicate mechanism, one guarded at all costs, trained by hard experience to transform deep pain into a kind of beauty. This mechanism, or perhaps it might be called a style, is completely integrated into the fabric of the musician's personal life. The best of them would be incapable of crying. The best of audiences would not allow it.

The blues singer steps down from the platform while the audience applauds politely. He is introduced, to all newcomers, as

Muddy Waters, Jr. He passes my table as he moves back to his own. "My *main* man," he whispers to me. "My daughter has some children and I'm tryin' to do the best I can for them."

I give him more money.

While leaving the Checkerboard I observe to the guard how well Muddy is holding up under his tragic loss.

"What loss?" the guard asks.

I detail the circumstances of his daughter's death.

The guard laughs. "Man," he says, "Muddy ain't got no daughter. You give him money? He told that same shit about his mama last week, right in this club, and she was alive and well up in her own house."

It came to me that I was only a tourist from Iowa, someone who lives apart from the current uses of the blues idiom. It also came to me that the idiom had gone desperately commercial. The narrative statement had become detached from its ritual base, and survives now as a form of folklore. There was now *crying* in it.

Sunday Morning

Chicago is an urban center that is receptive to black folk art in all its forms. The many blues and jazz clubs, and the hundreds of churches, are expressions of a rural cultural tradition. How peasant traditions have been able to survive within a highly technological and commercial culture is a profound mystery. Perhaps it has to do with the midwestern lack of pretension, or with a predisposition toward democratic values, or even with Chicago's unofficial policy of ethnic segregation. Whatever has sustained its vitality, it was the cohesive power of this core culture that was the basis of Harold Washington's election as mayor. His sagging campaign finally came together on the coattails of one song, "Move On Up a Little Higher," sung at a rally by Curtis Mayfield.

The core culture is part of the city and at the same time is apart from it. To see the complex simplicity of the connection, one only has to sit on the rear seat in the last car on the El, the one going south, and watch the downtown skyscrapers become toylike and small. One can actually feel the hold of hierarchy diminishing. And, briefly, it becomes clear that Chicago is still a prairie town,

one whose various outlying sections have a loose relationship with
the controlling powers in the skyscrapers. This arrangement en-
courages a closeness with one's own ethnic roots.

> "I can't say one thing and then do another,
> Be a saint by day and a devil under cover,
> I got to live the life I sing about in my song . . ."
> — Mahalia Jackson

The purest expression of the blues idiom was once found in the
black Baptist churches. Hundreds of them thrive on the south and
west sides of the city: First Baptist, Christian Tabernacle, Greater
Salem Baptist. It was at Greater Salem that Mahalia Jackson reached
a national and international audience. She was the greatest of
gospel singers, and her aristocratic presence still dominates this
expression of the idiom. Each January 28, the anniversary of her
death in 1972, Studs Terkel plays a retrospective in her honor. He
had great love for her. Now, several decades later, in the hums and
phrasings of individual singers, one can hear the style she imposed
on a folk form. Inside the churches, on Sunday mornings, one can
feel that her definition of gospel music ("Having faith with a little
bounce added") still holds true.

Inside Shiloh Baptist, on Forty-ninth Street, one feels a sense of
redemption and renewal. For almost half an hour, a slender young
girl leads a two-hundred-voice choir in urging a full congregation
to "Don't Give Up." Although the organ is electrified, and although the choir is being "conducted" as if it were a symphony,
the spirit *is* there, among the people. The call and response between the girl and the choir is hypnotic. Time stops, and she is a
priestess performing an ancient ritual function. People shout,
dance, wave hands, shake tambourines, are "possessed," transcend
private selves and are redeemed into a common spiritual body.
They become a collective soul, all essentially equal, before God.
The minister comes, now that the preparatory work is over, and
begins what soon becomes a jazzlike riff on one line in the Book
of Matthew. The message is unimportant. His sole function is to
keep the spirit active among his people. Trained nurses in white
uniforms rush back and forth, reviving those whose souls have
been released from tremendous burdens. For a while, it seems
absolutely evident that "Jesus Is on the Main Line," and that one

only has to tell Him what one wants. Feeling the collective faith and spirit of the people, it becomes clearer why Christianity is the most radical of religions, why the bedrock and basic values of American society cannot erode. The resilience, the optimistic dream of a foundation in the future, are rooted in churches such as these. It is no accident that gospel music is an essential idiom in evangelical Christianity. It speaks directly to the soul.

"When you get a song in your heart," Mahalia Jackson said, "and you just sing it, it makes you forget about everything. It's good when we can be on one accord. It's good to be on one accord . . ." The serenity and eloquent economy, the personal dignity, that characterized Mahalia's rendition of gospel can still be heard in the voices of some singers. But like the blues, the basic form has become somewhat standardized. In many of the churches, the idiom has shifted back toward its roots in dance music, threatening to deprive the individual singer of her ritual significance. It is difficult to appreciate the vocabulary of a moan when it is heard against a background of electrified music. The orchestration of the choir, the incorporation of electrified organs and guitars, the almost predictable up-tempo — these are concessions to trends that have become a part of *most* American music. One consequence is that the same arrangements of sounds flow out of a variety of different churches in Chicago each Sunday morning. It is almost as if the technological bias in the outside culture has begun to impose its own highest value, the interchangeability of all parts, on the spiritual values basic to the transcendent ambitions of the idiom. One has the sense, after listening to the music for a while, of human souls encased in metal cages struggling to rise above them. One misses the feel of a *single* human soul speaking out of its own inner calm to the collective soul. One misses the *silence* of the spirit as it descends, or is made manifest, among the congregants. As one misses the simple lyrical compassion that a single human voice and a piano once had for each other. Perhaps I miss only certain people — Mahalia Jackson, Thomas Dorsey — whose personal sounds said that they had gone through the fires and had come out *redeemed.* The purifying work of the fire was in their voices.

In Chicago, the sacred and the secular are inextricably linked. It is a sophisticated commercial city, but it respects artistic integrity.

It is ethnically segregated, but it allows each group to preserve its own culture. It is a cold city, but it preserves many islands of human warmth. It has provided a home for the blues idiom, and it has nurtured a few giants. Their influence and the standards they set still dominate the popular culture of the city. The names of developing musicians in the idiom suggest a continuing stance of apprenticeship: Muddy Waters, Jr., Buddy Guy, Sons of Blues. They perform at the Checkerboard and at Theresa's, against the old standard. But they also perform on the North Side, before ethnically mixed, middle-class audiences, at the Kingston Mines, the Blues, the Wise Fool. They seem to know that their roots go back to the South Side, and from there to the rural towns of Mississippi and Alabama, to the tough experiences of *life* that went into the making of the idiom. Many of the current singers seem to have not yet settled the philosophical distinction between the requirements of folk art and the requirements of entertainment. Some of them guide their audiences from one set into another with a certain promise. "We go'n play some Muddy Waters for you. We go'n be right back and play some Muddy Waters for you . . ."

One expects that in time, and through the hard lessons of the *life* behind the expressions of the idiom, some of them eventually will.

On that trip nine years ago, I went into Chicago looking for something much better than what I saw. Perhaps I expected to see areas of "purity" in my own ethnic community, some kind of muscular resolve, derived from the traditions of the blues idiom, to forego participation in the general cannibalizing of basic values which characterized that bleak time. Instead I saw what was there: human beings trying to make it as best they could.

It has become an easy cliché by now to say that corruption, public as well as personal, became normative during those years. The stance I took, while trying to explore the cultural life of the city, was bemused disbelief. I did not want to believe that those people who were hit the hardest by Reagan's policies would actually participate in the corruption of the very aesthetic forms created by their ancestors to fortify their souls against oppression. I suppose I nursed a romantic expectation that the mere fact of physical segregation would insulate black people, and our values, from the basic corruption of that time. But the cities, as everyone knew except me, had been written off. Poverty and homelessness had been placed on the back burners of national consciousness.

The word "decadence" is now gaining currency as a way of defining, in 1994, the state of the American soul. I would sharpen it to mean a debilitated, spiritless level of existence, such as what I saw in Chicago, and was defined by Ortega y Gassett in *The Dehumanization of Art:*

> The acute dissociation between past and present is the sign of our times, a generic factor of the epoch, and with it arises a suspicion, more or less vague, which engenders the restlessness peculiar to life in our times. Present day man feels alone on the face of the earth, and suspects that the dead did not die "in jest but in earnest," not ritually but factually, and can no longer help us. The remnants of the traditional spirit have evaporated. Norms, models, standards are of no further use. We must resolve our problems without the active collaboration of the past, totally confined to the present — whether our problems be in art, science, or politics. Modern man finds himself alone, without any living shadow at his side . . . That is what always happens at high noon . . .

I saw in Chicago nine years ago a period just before "high noon." It is now some time past that hour and little has changed to help renew the vitality of the blues idiom or the Chicago landscape against which it once thrived. The cities have been abandoned as a total loss. Yet there are some hopeful signs. The jazz musician Wynton Marsalis, in his ongoing attempt to renew the blues idiom, has taken it back to its ritual beginnings in the African American church. His recent "In This House on This Morning" is the most "pure" and ritually based sound that I have heard in the idiom since Pharoah Sander's "Journey to the One" just at the beginning of the madness that was the 1980s. Perhaps the black American community will reclaim through its musicians, after all, its old enclaves of artistic purity.

EDNA O'BRIEN

Waiting

FROM THE LOS ANGELES TIMES MAGAZINE

"JUST YOU WAIT, Henry Higgins, just you wait," Eliza Doolittle says, advancing the threat of equality, or maybe even superiority, over her cranky mentor, Professor Higgins. Everyone I know is waiting, and almost everyone I know would like to rebut it, since it is slightly demeaning, reeks of helplessness, and shows we are not fully in command of ourselves. Of course, we are not. In his book on Jean Genet, Sartre says, "To Be is to belong to someone." He was speaking in particular about Genet the orphan child, who felt he had never belonged and therefore never was. Orphans or not, the pain and seeming endlessness of waiting begins at the cradle, goes through many permutations, assumes various disguises, but is as native to us as our breathing. Some do it discreetly, some do it actively, some keep so abreast of things that their determination not to wait is in itself a kind of fidgety waiting. One thing is sure, nobody is proud of it except perhaps Job.

There is the angry waiting, the plaintive waiting, the almost cheerful waiting in which we believe for certain that the phone call or the revelation will occur presently. All these states, of course, overlap and can bafflingly succeed and re-succeed each other in a matter of minutes. For sheer brutality, the telephone waiting, in my opinion, takes precedence, insofar as it can (and does) ring at any moment. I think with no small degree of apprehension of the promised future when, thanks to the optic fiber in our computers, we will be able to see and, worse, be seen by the recalcitrant caller, and imagine how hard it will be to explain away the puffy eyes, the umbrage, the piled-up dishes, in short, the depression and inertia that attends waiting.

Is there anything good about it? Well, there are some fine moments of literature founded on excruciation. There is, toward the end of *Godot,* that wonderful exchange between the two characters:

"He didn't come?"
"No."
"And now it's too late."
"Yes, now it's night."

And there are hordes of fictional heroines — I am thinking at this moment of those of Patrick White and Karen Blixen in outbacks waiting for the arrival of the promised one, and there is a scene in Zola's *Nana* that to my mind surpasses all others in its depiction of that malady. A philandering count who suspects his wife of adultery stations himself outside the paramour's window at two in the morning to watch the room, a room he has once visited so he knows every detail: furniture, hangings, the water jug, and so on. With what tension Zola depicts it — the man waiting for a shadow to appear keeps thinking of the couple in bed, determining that at the first sight of a clue he will ring the bell, go upstairs despite the concierge's protest, break down the door, and strangle them. Then, in his musing, he sees a silhouette spring to life in the dimly lit room and wonders if it is his wife's neck or a slightly thicker neck but cannot tell. Darkness again. Two o'clock, three o'clock, four o'clock, and guess what happens. In the end he grows weary and decides to go home and sleep for a while and, in fact, misses the moment of verification that he had so achingly and so ardently longed for. We mortals weary of our vigils, unlike the animals who wait in the most concentrated and flexed way until the prey is caught. They seem unperturbed, possibly because they know they are going to succeed, and therein lies the secret of the sickness or the nonsickness of waiting — the wait that is founded on hope and the wait that is founded on despair.

Do women wait more than men? I think women wait for men more than men wait for women and this despite the sisterly enjoinders that suppose that you can suppress instinct with statement. You cannot. We learn a few things as we go along, but we do not learn to love, to hate, or to quarrel very differently. Men wait, too: they wait for the promotion, they wait for the kill, they wait for the prize, and one has only to watch the antics in Parliament or in the

Senate to see with what libido each is waiting for his moment to rise and strike a blow that will vanquish his opponent. Very often this seems to me more impassioned than the very principle about which they are debating. Men wait for women, too, once they have decided this one is the one, but they wait more busily, and so the little atoms of dread are likely to be diffused and tossed up and down so that they scatter. Activity always leavens waiting, but now, of course, with a beeper connecting us to our own abodes, we can in some restaurant or gymnasium, as longing strikes, call our own number to discover whether or not our prayer has been answered.

Prayer itself is a form of waiting but fortified with a glimmer of faith — or do I mean hope? For those who pray or chant with great perseverance, there is the suggestion that their waiting has been converted into purposefulness.

Of course, we do not just wait for love; we wait for money, we wait for the weather to get warmer, colder, we wait for the plumber to come and fix the washing machine (he doesn't), we wait for a friend to give us the name of another plumber (she doesn't), we wait for our hair to grow, we wait for our children outside school, we wait for their exam results, we wait for the letter that will undo all desolation, we wait for Sunday, when we sleep in or have the extra piece of toast, we wait for the crocuses to come up, then the daffodils, we wait for the estranged friend to ring or write and say, "I have forgiven you," we wait for our parents to love us even though they may be long since dead, we wait for the result of this or that medical test, we wait for the pain in the shoulder to ease, we wait for that sense of excitement that has gone underground but is not quite quenched, we wait for the novel that enthralls the way it happened when we first read *Jane Eyre* or *War and Peace,* we wait for the invitation to the country, and often when we are there, we wait for the bus or the car that will ferry us home to the city and our props, our own chairs, our own bed, our own habits. We wait for the parties we once gave and that somehow had a luster that parties we now give completely lack. We wait (at least I do) for new potatoes, failing to concede that there are new potatoes all the time, but the ones I am waiting for were the ones dug on the twenty-ninth of June in Ireland that tasted (or was it imagination?) like no others. We wait to go to sleep and maybe fog ourselves with pills or soothing tapes to lull us thither. We wait for dreams, then we wait to be hauled out of our dreams and wait for dawn, the postman, tea, coffee, the first ring of the telephone, the advancing day.

Waiting in a theater bar in a London interval to secure a drink is galling, convinced as I am that the ladies behind the counter are congenital teetotalers. Waiting in the post office in any city large or small sends me into a tizz. Waiting in one's place in the hairdresser's is another scenario devised to oust any semblance of grace or good manners, and hairdressers, if they are good at all, tend to cultivate suspense. How many times has one not sat on a stool along with other enraged victims fuming while the stylist lingered over a long head of hair as if discovering its aura?

While indoors, waiting has a touch of masochism, outdoors it takes on a martial turn. Out in the street we join the army of waiting people, to cross the road or not to cross the road, to catch the bus, to skewer some obstreperous mortal with the ferrule of an umbrella! Waiting for a taxi shows us in splendid pugilistic style. In New York one evening lately, I waited and waited — it was that fallow hour between five and six — and eventually sighted a free taxi and hopped in, only to find three gentlemen had got in by the other door, claiming they were first, refusing to get out, giving me, as it seemed, threatening Gallic looks — they were Spanish — while a driver with a vexing combination of ennui and insolence asked where it was we wished him to go. I refused to leave the taxi, they refused, and as we set out for a destinationless spot, it occurred to me that this somewhat risk to my person was preferable to having to get out onto the street and wait again.

Logic and waiting, at least to our Western sensibilities, are not great bedfellows. It ended happily; they dropped me on East Sixty-fourth Street, refused money, and even suggested a drink later on.

To wait for a taxi is one thing, but to wait for a friend is quite another, and as we know, there are those friends who are always late, because they cannot help it, or because they are so busy, or because time is not a factor that matters to them. One wonders what does matter. I used to endure it, but I no longer can. Ten minutes and I feel the implosion, twenty minutes and it's an explosion. One thinks of things that one could do. Knitting. Crocheting. One can neither knit nor crochet in the street. Tai-chi. Except that I have not learned tai-chi. Memorizing a poem or passage from Shakespeare. Except that I have not brought Shakespeare with me. No. The exasperation mounts, and by the time the friend arrives, the lurking umbrage for each and every wrong is unleashed and a happy evening kiboshed.

It may be my race or my trade or it may be my childhood, but I seem to think that writers are worse at waiting than other breeds. As an aside, I think that fishermen are best. You see them on riverbanks, perched on their little stools, rod and line apparently motionless in the water, and they have the contemplativeness of cows chewing the cud. Not so writers, who, from their diaries, their confessions, their essays about their crackups, have less aptitude for it than others, which seems a contradiction, since to write and rewrite requires infinite patience. I think it may be that unlike actors, brain surgeons, or animal tamers, writers never really feel that they matter. The book is finished, it is sent away, the publication day is nine months hence, and on publication day one may or one may not receive a telegram or a bunch of flowers. Reviews trickle in, but there is no palpable connection between the doer and the doing. The writer in that sense is a kind of perpetual exile from himself or herself.

To train myself in the art of waiting, I sometimes think of insufferable situations — I think of people in prison having to fill up the hours, I think of people in hospitals or in asylums. I think of the Portuguese nun writing her dirges or that other nun, Heloise, who, after her lover, Peter Abelard, was castrated, went to a convent, where, indeed, she still hoped that he might come for her, and I think of the last empress of China as described by Sterling Seagrave in *Dragon Lady*, this woman who had been chosen as a concubine at a very young age, left a widow, still at a very young age, spending the rest of her life inside the walls of the Forbidden City, her day starting with her toilet and then being dressed, flowers put in her hair, her breakfast of porridge and lotus leaves, gift baskets arriving, bolts of silks sent by courtiers, playing with her dogs, twisting blades of grass into the shapes of rabbits or birds, tending her flowers, a eunuch reading perhaps a piece of history or lore to her, playing a board game or painting onto silk, meals, the tiny dishes on little saucers that she mostly declined, and thinking of it I thank my stars that I was born in the west of Ireland in relative hardship and not in imperial China.

This brings me to either the value or the futility of waiting, and I think one must distinguish between the two. The telephone waiting, the waiting for the miracle — these seem in their way to be both crushing and ridiculous, because we all know that things do not happen when we wait too keenly. They happen when we least expect it. There is, however, a fertile kind of waiting that was brought to my attention by a piece written by Václav Havel that was called "Planting Watering and Waiting." He spoke of his own impatience while he was president of Czechoslovakia. He had wanted to achieve something visible and tangible, and it was hard for him to resign himself to the idea that politics, like history, is an emerging process. He was succumbing to a kind of impatience, thinking that he alone could find a solution to the problem. He thought he could but saw with enforced patience that the world and history are ruled by a time of their own, as are our lives, in which we can creatively intervene but never achieve complete control. He ended his piece with the beautiful image of planting something, of putting the seed in, of watering the earth, and of giving the plant the time that is essential to it. One cannot fool a plant any more than one can fool history, was how he put it. I suppose the same is true for ourselves. One cannot force the hearts or minds of other people, or get them to do what we want them to do at the precise moment we want it. We can only wait and, perhaps like the Portuguese nun, convert our tribulations into lasting prose.

CYNTHIA OZICK

The Break

FROM ANTAEUS

I WRITE THESE WORDS at least a decade after the terrifying operation that separated us. Unfortunately, no then-current anesthesia, and no then-accessible surgical technique, was potent enough to suppress consciousness of the knife as it made its critical blood-slice through the area of our two warring psyches. It is the usual case in medicine that twins joined at birth are severed within the first months of life. Given the intransigence of my partner (who until this moment remains recalcitrant and continues to wish to convert me to her loathsome outlook), I had to wait many years until I could obtain her graceless and notoriously rancorous consent to our divergence.

The truth is I have not spoken to her since the day we were wheeled, side by side as usual, on the same stretcher, into the operating room. Afterward it was at once observed (especially by me) that the surgery had not altered her character in any respect, and I felt triumphantly justified in having dragged her into it. I had done her no injury — she was as intractable as ever. As for myself, I was freed from her proximity and her influence. The physical break was of course the end, not the beginning, of our rupture; psychologically, I had broken with her a long time ago. I disliked her then, and though shut of her daily presence and unavoidable attachment, I dislike her even now. Any hint or symptom of her discourages me; I have always avoided reading her. Her style is clotted, parenthetical, self-indulgent, long-winded, periphrastic, in every way excessive — hard going altogether. One day it came to me: why bother to keep up this fruitless connection?

We have nothing in common, she and I. Not even a name. Since our earliest school years she has masqueraded as Cynthia, a Latin fancifulness entirely foreign to me. To my intimates I am Shoshana, the name given me at birth: Hebrew for Lily (anciently mistransliterated as Susanna).

To begin with, I am honest; she is not. Or, to spare her a moral lecture (but why should I? what has she ever spared *me*?), let me put it that she is a fantasist and I am not. Never mind that her own term for her condition is, not surprisingly, realism. It is precisely her "realism" that I hate. It is precisely her "facts" that I despise.

Her facts are not my facts. For instance, you will never catch me lying about my age, which is somewhere between seventeen and twenty-two. She, on the other hand, claims to be over sixty. A preposterous declaration, to be sure — but see how she gets herself up to look the part! She is all dye, putty, greasepaint. She resembles nothing so much as Gravel Gertie in the old Dick Tracy strip. There she is, done up as a white-haired, dewlapped, thick-waisted, thick-lensed hag, seriously myopic. A phenomenal fake. (Except for the nearsightedness, which, to be charitable, I don't hold against her, being seriously myopic myself.)

Aging is certainly not her only pretense. She imagines herself to be predictable; fixed; irrecoverable. She reflects frequently — tediously — on the trajectory of her life, and supposes that its arc and direction are immutable. What she has done she has done. She believes she no longer has decades to squander. I know better than to subscribe to such fatalism. Here the radical difference in our ages (which began to prove itself out at the moment of surgery) is probably crucial. It is her understanding that she is right to accept her status. She is little known or not known at all, relegated to marginality, absent from the authoritative anthologies that dictate which writers matter.

She knows she does not matter. She argues that she has been in rooms with the famous and felt the humiliation of her lesserness, her invisibility, her lack of writerly weight or topical cachet. In gilded chambers she has seen journalists and cultural consuls cluster around and trail after the stars; at conferences she has been shunted away by the bureaucratic valets of the stars. She is aware that she has not written enough. She is certainly not read. She sees with a perilous clarity that she will not survive even as "minor."

I will have none of this. There was a time — a tenuous membrane still hung between us, a remnant of sentiment or nostalgia on my part — when she was fanatically driven to coerce me into a similar view of myself. The blessed surgery, thank God, put an end to all that. My own ambition is fresh and intact. I can gaze at her fearfulness, her bloodless perfectionism and the secret crisis of confidence that dogs it, without a drop of concern. You may ask, Why am I so pitiless? Don't I know (I know to the lees) her indiscipline, her long periods of catatonic paralysis, her idleness, her sleepiness? Again you ask, Do you never pity her? Never. Hasn't she enough self-pity for the two of us? It is not that I am any more confident or less fearful; here I am, standing at the threshold still, untried, a thousand times more diffident, tremulous, shy. My heart is vulnerable to the world's distaste and dismissiveness. But oh, the difference between us! I have the power to scheme and to construct — a power that time has eroded in her, a power that she regards as superseded, useless. Null and void. Whatever shreds remain of her own ambitiousness embarrass her now. She is resigned to her failures. She is shamed by them. To be old and unachieved: ah.

Yes, ah! Ah! This diminution of hunger in her disgusts me; I detest it. She is a scandal of sorts, a superannuated mourner: her Promethean wounds (but perhaps they are only Procrustean?) leak on her bed when she wakes, on the pavement when she walks. She considers herself no more than an ant in an anthill. I have heard her say of the round earth, viewed on films sent back from this or that space shuttle, that Isaiah and Shakespeare are droplets molten into that tiny ball, and as given to evaporation as the pointlessly rotating ball itself. Good God, what have I to do with any of that? I would not trade places with her for all the china in Teaneck.

Look, there is so much ahead! Forms of undiminished luminescence: specifically, novels. A whole row of novels. All right, let her protest if it pleases her — when *she* set out, the written word was revered; reputations were rooted in the literariness of poets, novelists. Stories are electronic nowadays, and turn up in pictures: the victory, technologically upgraded, of the comic book. The writer is at last delectably alone, dependent on no acclaim. It is all for the sake of the making, the finding, the doing: the *Ding-an-Sich*. The wild *interestingness* of it! I will be a novelist yet! I feel myself

GRACE PALEY

Six Days: Some Rememberings

FROM ALASKA QUARTERLY REVIEW

I WAS IN JAIL. I had been sentenced to six days in the Women's House of Detention, a fourteen-story prison right in the middle of Greenwich Village, my own neighborhood. This happened during the American War in Vietnam, I have forgotten which important year of the famous sixties. The civil disobedience for which I was paying a small penalty probably consisted of sitting down to impede or slow some military parade.

I was surprised at the sentence. Others had been given two days or dismissed. I think the judge was particularly angry with me. After all, I was not a kid. He thought I was old enough to know better, a forty-five-year-old woman, a mother and teacher. I ought to be too busy to waste time on causes I couldn't possibly understand.

I was herded with about twenty other women, about 90 percent black and Puerto Rican, into the bullpen, an odd name for a women's holding facility. There, through someone else's lawyer, I received a note from home, telling me that since I'd chosen to spend the first week of July in jail, my son would probably not go to summer camp, because I had neglected to raise the money I'd promised. I read this note and burst into tears, real running-down-the-cheek tears. It was true: thinking about other people's grown boys, I had betrayed my little son. The summer, starting that day, July 1, stood up before me day after day, steaming the city streets, the after-work crowded city pool.

I guess I attracted some attention. You — you white girl you — you never been arrested before? A black woman about a head taller than I put her arm on my shoulder. — It ain't so bad. What's your time sugar? I gotta do three years. You huh?

Six days.

Six days? What the fuck for?

I explained, sniffling, embarrassed.

You got six days for sitting down front of a horse? Cop on the horse? Horse step on you? Jesus in hell, cops gettin crazier and stupider and meaner. Maybe we get you out.

No, no, I said. I wasn't crying because of that. I didn't want her to think I was scared. I wasn't. She paid no attention. Shoving a couple of women aside — Don't stand in front of me, bitch. Move over. What you looking at? — she took hold of the bars of our cage, commenced to bang on them, shook them mightily, screaming — Hear me now, you motherfuckers, you grotty pigs, get this house-wife out of here! She returned to comfort me. — Six days in this low-down hole for sitting front of a horse!

Before we were distributed among our cells, we were dressed in a kind of nurse's aide scrub uniform, blue or green, a little too large or a little too small. We had had to submit to a physical in which all our hiding places were investigated for drugs. These examinations were not too difficult, mostly because a young woman named Andrea Dworkin had fought them, refused a grosser, more painful examination some months earlier. She had been arrested protesting the war in front of the U.S. Mission to the UN. I had been there too, but I don't think I was arrested that day. She was mocked for that determined struggle at the Women's House, as she has been for other braveries, but according to the women I questioned, certain humiliating, perhaps sadistic customs had ended — for that period at least.

My cellmate was a beautiful young woman, twenty-three years old, a prostitute who'd never been arrested before. She was nerv-ous, but she had been given the name of an important long-termer. She explained in a businesslike way that she *was* beautiful, and would need protection. She'd be O.K. once she found that woman. In the two days we spent together, she tried *not* to talk to the other women on our cell block. She said they were mostly street whores and addicts. She would never be on the street. Her man wouldn't allow it anyway.

I slept well for some reason, probably the hard mattress. I don't seem to mind where I am. Also I must tell you, I could look out

the window at the end of our corridor and see my children or their
friends, on their way to music lessons or Greenwich House pottery.
Looking slantwise I could see right into Sutter's Bakery, then on
the corner of Tenth Street. These were my neighbors at coffee
and cake.

Sometimes the cell block was open, but not our twelve cells.
Other times the reverse. Visitors came by: they were prisoners,
detainees not yet sentenced. They seemed to have a strolling
freedom, though several, unsentenced, unable to make bail, had
been there for months. One woman peering into the cells stopped
when she saw me. Grace! Hi! I knew her from the neighborhood,
maybe the park, couldn't really remember her name.

What are you in for? I asked.

Oh nothing — well a stupid drug bust. I don't even use — oh
well forget it. I've been here six weeks. They keep putting the trial
off. Are you O.K.?

Then I complained. I had planned not to complain about anything while living among people who'd be here in these clanging
cells a long time; it didn't seem right. But I said, I don't have
anything to read and they took away my pen and I don't have paper.

Oh you'll get all that eventually, she said. Keep asking.

Well they have all my hairpins. I'm a mess.

No no she said, you're O.K. You look nice.

(A couple of years later, the war continuing, I was arrested in
Washington. My hair was still quite long. I wore it in a kind of bun
on top of my head. My hairpins gone, my hair straggled wildly
every which way. Muriel Rukeyser, arrested that day along with
about thirty other women, made the same generous sisterly remark. No no Grace, love you with your hair down, you really ought
to always wear it this way.)

The very next morning, my friend brought me *The Collected
Stories of William Carlos Williams.* — These O.K.?

God! O.K. — Yes!

My trial is coming up tomorrow, she said. I think I'm getting off
with time already done. Over done. See you around?

That afternoon, my cellmate came for her things — I'm moving
to the fourth floor. Working in the kitchen. Couldn't be better. We
were sitting outside our cells, she wanted me to know something.
She'd already told me, but said it again. — I still can't believe it.

This creep, this guy, this cop, he waits he just waits till he's fucked and fine, pulls his pants up, pays me, and arrests me. It's not legal. It's not. My man's so mad, he like to kill *me,* but he's not that kind of — he's not a criminal type, *my* man. She never said the word pimp. Maybe no one did. Maybe that was our word.

I had made friends with some of the women in the cells across the aisle. How can I say "made friends." I just sat and spoke when spoken to, I was at school. I answered questions — simple ones. Why I would do such a fool thing on purpose? How old were my children? My man any good? Then, you live around the corner? That was a good idea, Evelyn said, to have a prison in your own neighborhood, so you could keep in touch, yelling out the window. As in fact we were able to do right here and now, calling and being called from Sixth Avenue, by mothers, children, boyfriends.

About the children: One woman took me aside. Her daughter was brilliant, she was in Hunter High School, had taken a test. No she hardly ever saw her, but she wasn't a whore — it was the drugs. Her daughter was ashamed, the grandmother, the father's mother made the child ashamed. When she got out in six months it would be different. This made Evelyn and Rita, right across from my cell, laugh. Different, I swear. Different. Laughing. But she *could* make it, I said. Then they really laughed. Their first laugh was a bare giggle compared to these convulsive roars. Change her ways? That dumb bitch Ha!!

Another woman, Helen, the only other white woman on the cell block, wanted to talk to me. She wanted me to know that she was not only white but Jewish. She came from Brighton Beach. Her father, he should rest in peace, thank God, was dead. Her arms were covered with puncture marks almost like sleeve patterns. But she needed to talk to me, because I was Jewish (I'd been asked by Rita and Evelyn — was I Irish? No, Jewish. Oh, they answered). She walked me to the barred window at the end of the corridor, the window that looked down on West Tenth Street. She said, How come you so friends with those black whores? You don't hardly talk to me. I said I liked them, but I liked her too. She said, If you knew them for true, you wouldn't like them. They nothing but street whores. You know, once I was friends with them. We done a lot of things together, I knew them fifteen years Evy and Rita maybe twenty, I been in the streets with them, side by side, Amsterdam,

Lenox, West Harlem; in bad weather we covered each other. Then
one day along come Malcolm X and they don't know me no more,
they ain't talking to me. You too white. I ain't all that white. Twenty
years. They ain't talking.

My friend Myrt called one day, that is called from the street,
called — Grace Grace. I heard and ran to the window. A police-
man, the regular beat cop, was addressing her. She looked up, then
walked away before I could yell my answer. Later on she told me
that he'd said, I don't think Grace would appreciate you calling
her name out like that.

What a mistake! For years, going to the park with my children,
or simply walking down Sixth Avenue on a summer night past the
Women's House, we would often have to thread our way through
whole families calling up — bellowing, screaming to the third,
seventh, tenth floor, to figures, shadows behind bars and screened
windows — How you feeling? Here's Glena. She got big. Mami
mami you like my dress? We gettin you out baby. New lawyer
come by.

And the replies, among which I was privileged to live for a few
days — shouted down. — You lookin beautiful. What he say? Fuck
you James. I got a chance? Bye bye. Come next week.

Then the guards, the heavy clanking of cell doors. Keys. Night.

I still had no pen or paper despite the great history of prison
literature. I was suffering a kind of frustration, a sickness in the
way claustrophobia is a sickness — this paper-and-penlessness was
a terrible pain in the area of my heart, a nausea. I was surprised.

In the evening, at lights out (a little like the army or on good
days a strict, unpleasant camp), women called softly from their
cells. Rita hey Rita sing that song — Come on sister sing. A few
more importunings and then Rita in the cell diagonal to mine
would begin with a ballad. A song about two women and a man.
It was familiar to everyone but me. The two women were prison
sweethearts. The man was her outside lover. One woman, the
singer, was being paroled. The ballad told her sorrow about having
been parted from him when she was sentenced, now she would
leave her loved woman after three years. There were about twenty
stanzas of joy and grief.

Well, I was so angry not to have pen and paper to get some of it down that I lost it all — all but the sorrowful plot. Of course she had this long song in her head, and in the next few nights she sang and chanted others, sometimes with a small chorus.

Which is how I finally understood that I didn't lack pen and paper but my own memorizing mind. It had been given away with a hundred poems, called rote learning, old-fashioned, backward, an enemy of creative thinking, a great human gift, disowned.

Now there's a garden where the Women's House of Detention once stood. A green place, safely fenced in, with protected daffodils and tulips; roses bloom in it too, sometimes into November.

The big women's warehouse and its barred blind windows have been removed from Greenwich Village's affluent throat. I was sorry when it happened; the bricks came roaring down, great trucks carried them away.

I have always agreed with Rita and Evelyn that if there are prisons, they ought to be in the neighborhood, near a subway — not way out in distant suburbs, where families have to take cars, buses, ferries, trains, and the population that considers itself innocent forgets, denies, chooses to never know that there is a whole huge country of the bad and the unlucky and the self-hurters, a country with a population greater than that of many nations in our world.

CHARLES SIMIC

The Necessity of Poetry

FROM CREATIVE NONFICTION

LATE NIGHT on MacDougal Street. An old fellow comes up to me and says: "Sir, I'm writing the book of my life and I need a dime to complete it." I give him a dollar.

Another night in Washington Square Park, a fat woman with a fright wig says to me: "I'm Esther, the Goddess of Love. If you don't give me a dollar, I'll put a curse on you." I give her a nickel.

One of those postwar memories: a baby carriage pushed by a humpbacked old woman, her son sitting in it, both legs amputated.

She was haggling with the greengrocer when the carriage got away from her. The street was steep so it rolled downhill with the cripple waving his crutch, his mother screaming for help, and everybody else laughing as if they were in the movies. Buster Keaton or somebody like that about to go over a cliff.

One laughed because one knew it would end well. One was surprised when it didn't.

I didn't tell you how I got lice wearing a German helmet. This used to be a famous story in our family. I remember those winter evenings just after the war with everybody huddled around the stove, talking and worrying late into the night. Sooner or later, somebody would bring up my German helmet full of lice. They thought it was the funniest thing they ever heard. Old people had tears of laughter in their eyes. A kid dumb enough to walk around with a German helmet full of lice. They were crawling all over it. Any fool could see them!

I sat there saying nothing, pretending to be equally amused, nodding my head while thinking to myself, what a bunch of idiots! All of them! They had no idea how I got the helmet, and I wasn't about to tell them.

It was in those first days just after the liberation of Belgrade, I was up in the old cemetery with a few friends, kind of snooping around. Then, all of a sudden, we saw them! A couple of German soldiers, obviously dead, stretched out on the ground. We drew closer to take a better look. They had no weapons. Their boots were gone, but there was a helmet that had fallen to the side of one of them. I don't remember what the others got, but I went for the helmet. I tiptoed so as not to wake the dead man. I also kept my eyes averted. I never saw his face, even if sometimes I think I did. Everything else about that moment is still intensely clear to me.

That's the story of the helmet full of lice.

Beneath the swarm of high-flying planes we were eating watermelon. While we ate the bombs fell on Belgrade. We watched the smoke rise in the distance. We were hot in the garden and asked to take our shirts off. The watermelon made a ripe, cracking noise as my mother cut it with a big knife. We also heard what we thought was thunder, but when we looked up, the sky was cloudless and blue.

My mother heard a man plead for his life once. She remembers the stars, the dark shapes of trees along the road on which they were fleeing the Austrian army in a slow-moving ox-cart. "That man sounded terribly frightened out there in the woods," she says. The cart went on. No one said anything. Soon they could hear the river they were supposed to cross.

In my childhood women mended stockings in the evening. To have a "run" in one's stocking was catastrophic. Stockings were expensive, and so was electricity. We would all sit around the table with a single lamp, my grandmother reading the papers, we children pretending to do our homework, while watching my mother spreading her red-painted fingernails inside the transparent stocking.

There was a maid in our house who let me put my hand under her skirt. I was five or six years old. I can still remember the dampness of her crotch and my surprise that there was all that hair there. I couldn't get enough of it. She would crawl under the table where I had my military fort and my toy soldiers. I don't remember what was said, if anything. Just her hand, firmly guiding mine to that spot.

They sit on the table, the tailors do. At least, they used to. A street of dim shops in Belgrade where we went to have my father's coat narrowed and shortened so it would fit me. The tailor got off the table and stuck pins in my shoulder. "Don't squirm," my mother said. Outside it was getting dark. Large snowflakes fell.

Years later in New York, on the same kind of afternoon, a dry-cleaning store window with an ugly, thick-legged woman on the chair in a white dress. She's having the hems raised by a gray-headed Jewish tailor, who kneels before her as if he is proposing marriage.

There was an expensive-looking suitcase on the railroad tracks, and they were afraid to come near it. Far from any station, it was on a stretch of track bordered by orchards where they had been stealing plums that afternoon. The suitcase, she remembers, had colorful labels, of what were probably world-famous hotels and ocean liners. During the war, of course, one heard of bombs, special ones, in the shape of toys, pens, soccer balls, exotic birds — so why not suitcases? For that reason they left it where it was.

"I always wondered what was in it," my wife says. We were talking about the summer of 1944, of which we both had only a few clear recollections.

The world was going up in flames and I was studying violin. The baby Nero sawing away . . .

My teacher's apartment was always cold. A large, almost empty room with a high ceiling already in shadow. I remember the first few screechy notes my violin would make and my teacher's stern words of reprimand. I was terrified of that old woman. I also loved her because after the scolding she would give me something to eat. Something rare and exotic, like chocolate filled with sweet liqueur. We'd sit in that big empty room, almost dark now. I'd be eating and she'd be watching me eat. "Poor child," she'd say, and I thought it had to do with my not practicing enough, my being dim-witted when she tried to explain something to me, but today

I'm not sure that's what she meant. In fact, I suspect she had something else entirely in mind. That's why I'm writing this, to find out what it was.

When my grandfather was dying from diabetes, when he had already had one leg cut off at the knee and they were threatening to do the same to the other, his old buddy Savo Lozanic used to visit him every morning to keep him company. They would reminisce about this and that and even have a few laughs.

One morning my grandmother had to leave him alone in the house, as she had to attend the funeral of a distant relative. That's what gave him the idea. He hopped out of bed and into the kitchen, where he found candles and matches. He got back into his bed, somehow placed one candle above his head and the other at his feet, and lit them. Finally, he pulled the sheet over his face and began to wait.

When his friend knocked, there was no answer. The door being unlocked, Savo went in, calling from time to time. The kitchen was empty. A fat gray cat slept on the dining room table. When Savo entered the bedroom and saw the bed with the sheet and lit candles, he let out a wail and then broke into sobs as he groped for a chair to sit down.

"Shut up, Savo," my grandfather said sternly from under his sheet. "Can't you see I'm only practicing?"

Another story about time. This one about the time it took the people to quit their cells after beginning to suspect that the Germans were gone. In that huge prison in Milan all of a sudden you could hear a pin drop. Eventually they thought it best to remove their shoes before walking out.

My father was still tiptoeing hours later crossing a large empty piazza. There was a full moon above the dark palaces. His heart was in his mouth.

"It was just like an opera stage," he says. "All lit up, nobody in the audience, and nobody in the orchestra pit. Nevertheless, I felt like singing. Or perhaps screaming?"

He did neither. The year was 1944.

The streets are empty, it's raining, and we are sitting in the Hotel Sherman bar listening to the bluesy piano. I'm not yet old enough to order a drink, but my father's presence is so authoritative and intimidating that when he orders for me the waiters never dare to ask about my age.

We talk. My father remembers a fly that wouldn't let him sleep one summer afternoon fifty years ago. I tell him about an old gray overcoat twice my size, which my mother made me wear after the war. It was wintertime. People on the street would sometimes stop and watch me. The overcoat trailed the ground and made walking difficult. One day I was standing on the corner waiting to cross when a young woman gave me a small coin and walked away. I was so embarrassed.

"Was she pretty?" my father asks.

"Not at all," I tell him. She looked like a hick, maybe a nun.

"A Serbian Ophelia," my father thinks.

It's possible. Anything is possible.

The huge crowd cheering the dictator; the smiling faces of children offering flowers in welcome. How many times have I seen that? And always the same blond little girl curtsying! Here she is surrounded by the high boots of the dignitaries and a couple of tightly leashed police dogs. The monster himself is patting her on the head and whispering in her ear.

I look in vain for someone with a troubled face.

The exiled general's grandson was playing war with his cheeks puffed to imitate bombs exploding. The grim daughter wrote down the old man's reminiscences. The whole apartment smelled of bad cooking.

The general was in a wheelchair. He wore a bib and smoked a cigar. The daughter smiled for me and my mother in a way that made her sharp little teeth show.

I liked the general better. He remembered some prime minister pretending to wipe his ass with a treaty he had just signed, the captured enemy officers drinking heavily and toasting some cabaret singer from their youth.

It's your birthday. The child you were appears on the street wearing a stupid grin. He wants to take you by the hand, but you won't let him.

"You've forgotten something," he whispers. And you, quiet as a mutt around an undertaker, since, of course, he (the child) doesn't exist.

There was an old fellow at the *Sun Times,* who was boss when I first came and worked as a mail clerk, who claimed to have read everything. His father was a janitor at the university library in Urbana, and Stanley, for that was his name, started as a kid. At first I didn't believe any of it; then I asked him about Gide, whom I was then reading. He recited for me the names of the major novels and their plots. What about Isaac Babel, Alain Fournier, Aldous Huxley, Ford Madox Ford? The same thing. It was amazing! Everything I had read or heard of he had already read. You should be on a quiz show, Stanley, people who overheard us said. Stanley had never been to college and had worked for the newspaper most of his life. He had a stutter, so I guess that explains why he never married or got ahead. So, all he did was read books. I had the impression that he loved every book he read. Only superlatives for Stanley, one book better than the other. If I started to criticize, he'd get pissed off. Who do I think I am? Smartass, he called me, and wouldn't talk to me about books for a few days. Stanley was pure enthusiasm. I was giddy myself at the thought of another book waiting for me to read at home.

The night of my farewell dinner in Chicago, I got very drunk. At some point, I went to the bathroom and could not find my way back. The restaurant was large and full of mirrors. I would see my friends seated in the distance, but when I hurried toward them, I would come face to face with myself in a mirror. With my new beard I did not recognize myself immediately and almost apologized. In the end, I gave up and sat at an old man's table. He ate in silence, and I lit a cigarette. Time passed. The place was emptying. The old man finally wiped his mouth and pushed his full, untouched wineglass toward me. I would have stayed with him indefinitely if one of the women from our party hadn't found me and led me outside.

Did I lie a little? Of course. I gave the impression that I had lived for years on the Left Bank and often sat at the tables of the famous cafés watching the existentialists in their passionate arguments. What justified these exaggerations in my eyes was the real possibil-

ity that I could have done something like that. Everything about
my life already seemed a fluke, a series of improbable turns of
events, so in my case fiction was no stranger than truth. Like when
I told the woman on the train from Chicago that I was a Russian.
I described our apartment in Leningrad, the terrors of the long
siege during the war, the deaths of my parents before a German
firing squad which we children had to witness, the DP camps in
Europe. At some point during the long night I had to go to the
bathroom and simply laugh.

How much of it did she believe? Who knows? In the morning
she gave me a long kiss in parting, which could have meant anything.

My father and his best friend talking about how some people
resemble animals. The birdlike wife of so and so, for example. The
many breeds of dogs and their human look-alikes. The lady who
is a cow. The widow next door who is a tigress, etc.

"And what about me?" says my father's friend.

"You look like a rat, Tony," he replies without a moment's hesitation, after which they just sit drinking without saying another
word.

"You look like a young Franz Schubert," the intense-looking woman
told me as we were introduced.

At that same party, I spoke to a lawyer who insisted we had met
in London two years before. I explained my accent to a doctor by
telling him that I was raised by a family of deaf-mutes.

There was a girl there, too, who kept smiling sweetly at me
without saying anything. Her mother told me that I reminded her
of her brother, who was executed by the Germans in Norway. She
was going to give me more details, but I excused myself, telling
everyone that I had a sudden and terrible toothache that required
immediate attention.

I got the idea of sleeping on the roof in Manhattan on hot nights
from my mother and father. That's what they did during the war,
except it wasn't a roof but a large terrace on the top floor of a
building in downtown Belgrade. There was a blackout, of course.
I remember immense starry skies, and how silent the city was. I
would begin to speak, but someone — I could not tell for a moment who it was — would put a hand over my mouth.

Like a ship at sea we were with stars and clouds up above. We were sailing full speed ahead. "That's where the infinite begins," I remember my father saying, pointing with his long, dark hand.

If my father has a ghost, he's standing outside some elegant men's store on Madison Avenue on a late summer evening. A tall man studying a pair of brown suede Italian shoes. He himself is impeccably dressed in a tan suit, a blue shirt of an almost purple hue with a silk tie the color of rusty rose. He seems in no hurry. At the age of fifty-three, with his hair thinning and slicked back, he could be an Italian or a South American. Belle Georgio, one waitress in Chicago used to call him. No one would guess by his appearance that he is almost always broke.

I'm packing parcels in the Lord & Taylor basement during the Christmas rush with a bunch of losers. One fellow is an inventor. He has a new kind of aquarium with piped music, which makes it look as if the fish are doing water ballet, but the world is not interested. Another man supports three ex-wives, so he has a night job in addition to this one. His eyes close all the time. He's so pale, he could pass for a stiff in an open coffin.

Then there's Felix, a mousy fellow a bit older than I who claims to be a distant relative of the English royal family. One time he brought the chart of his family tree to make us stop laughing and explained the connection. What does not make sense is his poverty. He said he was a writer but wouldn't tell us what kind. "Are you writing porno?" one Puerto Rican girl asked him.

Her name was Rosie. She liked boxing. One time she and I went on a date to watch the fights at the Garden. We sat in the Spanish section. "Kill him! Kill him!" she screamed all evening without interruption. At the end she was so tired she wouldn't even have a drink with me, and had to rush home.

At a poetry reading given by Allen Tate, I met a young poet who was attending a workshop given by Louise Bogan at NYU. I sat in a few times and accompanied my new friends for beers after class. One day I even showed two of my poems to Bogan. One was called "Red Armchair," and it had to do with an old chair thrown out on the sidewalk for the trashmen to pick up. The other poem I don't remember. Bogan was very kind. She fixed a few things but was generally encouraging, which surprised me, since I didn't think much of the poems myself.

The other critique of my poetry came later that fall and it was devastating. I had met a painter in a bar, an older fellow living in poverty with a wife and two small kids in a cold-water flat in the Village, where he painted huge, realistic canvases of derelicts in the manner of 1930s socialist realism. A skyscraper and underneath a poor man begging. The message was obvious, but the colors were nice.

Despite the difference in our ages, we saw each other quite a bit, talking art and literature, until one day I showed him my poems. We were sitting in his kitchen with a bottle of whiskey between us. He leaned back in the chair and read the poems slowly, slowly while I watched him closely. At some point I began to detect annoyance in him and then anger. Finally, he looked at me as if seeing me for the first time and said something like: "Simic, I thought you were a smart kid. This is pure shit you're writing!"

I was prepared for gentle criticism in the manner of Louise Bogan, even welcomed it, but his bluntness stunned me. I left in a daze. I was convinced he was right. If I'd had a pistol, I would have shot myself on the spot. Then, little by little, mulling over what he had said, I got pissed off. There were some good things in my poems, I thought. "Fuck him," I shouted to some guy who came my way in the street. Of course, he was right, too, and it hurt me that he was, but all the same.

I came out of my daze just as I was entering Central Park on Fifty-ninth Street. I had walked more than sixty blocks totally oblivious of my surroundings. I sat on a bench and reread my poems, crossing out most of the lines, attempting to rewrite them then and there, still angry, still miserable, and at the same time grimly determined.

There was this old guy in Washington Square Park who used to lecture me about Sacco and Vanzetti and the great injustice done to them. We'd share a bench from time to time, and I'd hear him say again and again how if shit was worth money the poor would be born without assholes. He wore gray gloves, walked with a cane, tipped his hat to ladies, and worried about me. "A kid just off the boat," he'd say to someone passing by. "Sure to get screwed if he doesn't watch out."

I went to see Ionesco's *Bald Soprano* with Boris. It was being presented at the small theater in the Village. There were only six people in the audience, and that included the two of us. They gave the performance anyway. When it came to the love scene with the woman who has three noses, the actors got carried away on the couch. Their voices went down to a whisper as they started undressing each other. Boris and I just looked at each other. The other four people had suddenly become invisible. I have no recollection of the rest of the play except that at the exit the streets were covered with newly fallen snow.

I was five minutes late from lunch at the insurance company where I was working and my boss chewed me out for being irresponsible in front of twenty or thirty other drudges. I sat at my desk for a while fuming, then I rose slowly, wrapped my scarf around my neck and put my gloves on in plain view of everybody, and walked out without looking back. I didn't have an overcoat and on the street it was snowing, but I felt giddy, deliriously happy at being free.

We were on our third bottle of wine when he showed me the pictures of his girlfriend. To my surprise, the photographs spread out on the table were of a naked woman shamelessly displaying herself. Leaning over my shoulder, he wanted me to note each detail, her crotch, her ass, her breasts, until I felt aroused. It was an odd situation. My host's pregnant wife was asleep in the next room. The photographs were spread all over the dining room table. There must've been close to a hundred of them. I looked and listened. From time to time, I could hear the wife snore.

Approaching Manhattan on the train at night, I remember the old Polish and Ukrainian women wielding their mops in the brightly lit towers. I'd be working on some ledger that wouldn't balance, and they'd be scrubbing floors on their knees. They were fat and they all wore flowered dresses. The youngest would stand on a chair and dust off the portrait of the grim founder of the company. The old black man who ran the elevator would bow to them like a headwaiter in a fancy restaurant as he took them from one floor to the next. That would make them laugh. You'd see they had teeth missing. More than a few teeth missing.

It was a window with a view of a large office with many identical desks at which men and women sat working. A woman got up with papers in hand and walked the length of the floor to where a man rose to meet her at the other end. He waved his arms as he talked, while she stood before him with her head lowered, and I went on tying my necktie in the hotel room across the street. I was about to turn away from the window when I realized that the man was yelling at the woman, and that she was sobbing.

Here's a scene for you. My father and I are walking down Madison, when I spot a blue overcoat in a store called the British American House. We study it, comment on the cut, and my father suggests I try it on. I know he has no money, but he insists since it's beginning to snow a little and I'm only wearing a tweed jacket. We go in, I put it on, and it fits perfectly. Immediately, I'm in love with it. We ask the price and it's $200 — which was a lot of money in 1959. Too bad, I think, but then my father asks me if I want it. I think maybe he's showing off in front of the salesman or he's come into some money he hasn't told me about. Do you want it? he asks again while the salesman goes to attend to another customer. You've no money, George, I remind him, expecting him to contradict me or come to his senses. "Don't worry" is his reply.

I've seen him do this before and it embarrasses me. He asks for the boss and the two of them sequester themselves for a while. I stand around waiting for us to be kicked out. Instead, he emerges triumphant and I wear the overcoat into the street. A born con man. His manner and appearance inspired such confidence that with a small down payment and promise to pay the rest in a week or two, he'd get what he wanted. This was in the days before credit cards and credit bureaus, when store owners had to make such decisions on the spot. They trusted him, and he eventually did pay whatever he owed. The crazy thing was that he pulled this stunt only in the best stores. It would never occur to him to ask for credit from a grocer, and yet he often went hungry despite his huge salary.

My father had phenomenal debts. He borrowed money any

chance he had and paid his bills only when absolutely necessary. It was nothing for him to spend the rent money the night before it was due. I lived in terror of my landlords and landladies while he seemingly never worried. We'd meet after work and he'd suggest dinner in a French restaurant and I'd resist, knowing it was his rent money he was proposing to spend. He'd describe the dishes and wines we could have in tantalizing detail, and I'd keep reminding him of the rent. He'd explain to me slowly, painstakingly, as if I were feeble-minded, that one should never worry about the future. We'll never be so young as we are tonight, he'd say. If we are smart, and we are, tomorrow we'll figure out how to pay the rent. In the end, who could say no? I never did.

On the street corner the card trickster was shuffling his three cards, using a large cardboard box as a table. The cards, the quick hands fluttered. It looked like a cockfight. Five of us watching without expression, our heads, in the meantime, buzzing with calculations and visions of riches. The day was cold so we all had to squint.

Tough guys, he said, time to place your bets.

I became more and more lucid the later it got. This was always my curse. Everybody was already asleep. I tried to wake my dearest, but she drew me down on her breasts sleepily. We loved, slowly, languidly, and then I talked to her for hours about the necessity of poetry while she slept soundly.

JOHN EDGAR WIDEMAN

Father Stories

FROM THE NEW YORKER

*One day neither in the past nor in the future, and not at this moment,
either, all the people gathered on a high ridge that overlooked the rolling
plain of earth, its forests, deserts, rivers unscrolling below them like a
painting on parchment. Then the people began speaking, one by one, telling
the story of a life — everything seen, heard, and felt by each soul. As the
voices dreamed, a vast, bluish mist enveloped the land and the seas below.
Nothing was visible. It was as if the solid earth had evaporated. Now there
was nothing but the voices and the stories and the mist; and the people
were afraid to stop the storytelling and afraid not to stop, because no one
knew where the earth had gone.*

*Finally, when only a few storytellers remained to take a turn, someone
shouted: Stop! Enough, enough of this talk! Enough of us have spoken! We
must find the earth again!*

*Suddenly, the mist cleared. Below the people, the earth had changed. It
had grown into the shape of the stories they'd told — a shape as wondrous
and new and real as the words they'd spoken. But it was also a world
unfinished, because not all the stories had been told.*

*Some say that death and evil entered the world because some of the people
had no chance to speak. Some say that the world would be worse than it is
if all the stories had been told. Some say that there are no more stories to
tell. Some believe that untold stories are the only ones of value and we are
lost when they are lost. Some are certain that the storytelling never stops;
and this is one more story, and the earth always lies under its blanket of
mist being born.*

I begin again because I don't want it to end. I mean all these
father stories that take us back, that bring us here, where you

are, where I am, needing to make sense, to go on if we can and should.

Once, when you were five or six, all the keys to the camp vehicles disappeared. Keys for trucks, vans, rental cars, a schoolbus, a tractor, boats — the whole fleet necessary each summer to service the business of offering four hundred boys an eight-week escape in the Maine woods. In the innocence of the oasis that your grandfather had created — this gift of water, trees, a world apart — nobody bothered to lock things; keys were routinely left in the ignition for the next driver. Then, one day, the keys were gone. For hours, everybody searched high and low. I thought of you as I climbed into the cab of the dump truck to check for a key that might have fallen to the floor or slipped into some crevice or corner of the raw, gasoline-reeking interior. You because countless times I'd hoisted you into the cab, tucked you in the driver's seat. Nothing you enjoyed more than turning a steering wheel, roaring and vrooming engine noise while you whipped the wheel back and forth, negotiating some endless, dramatic highway only you could see. You were fascinated by that imaginary road and the wheels that rolled you there. Even before you could talk, you'd flip your toy trucks and cars on their sides or upside down so you could spin the wheels, growl motor noise.

You never admitted taking the keys, and nobody pressed you very hard after they were found, in a heap in the sand under the boat dock. But years later, Junie, the head caretaker, mentioned that he'd seen you making your usual early-morning rounds from vehicle to vehicle the day the keys were missing, and confided to me a suspicion he had felt then but had kept to himself till you were gone and were unlikely to return for a long time. Turns out your grandfather had been suspicious, too. He didn't miss much that happened in the camp, either, and had observed what Junie had observed. I recall being rather annoyed when your grandfather suggested that I ask you if you might have noticed keys anywhere the day they disappeared. Annoyed and amazed, because you were hardly more than a baby. No reason for you to bother the keys. I'd instructed you never to touch them, and that was one of the conditions you'd promised to honor in return for the privilege of installing yourself behind steering wheels. I trusted you. Questioning my trust insulted us both. Besides, the missing keys implied a plot, a prank, sabotage, some scheme premeditated and methodically perpetrated by older campers or adults, and you were just a kid. You were my son. His grandson. So he gently hinted I might casually check with you, not because you were a suspect but because you had access and had been noticed at the scene, and so perhaps might be able to assist the searchers with a clue.

I don't remember your grandfather's ever mentioning the keys again until we'd lost you and all of us were searching once more for answers. And since each of us had then begun to understand that answers were not around us, not in the air, and not exclusively in you, but inside us all, when your grandfather repeated ten years later his suspicions about the keys, it sounded almost like a confession, and we both understood that some searches never end.

A small army of adults, stymied, frustrated, turning the camp inside out. A couple of hours of mass confusion, pockets, drawers, memories rifled, conspiracy theories floated, paranoia blossoming, numb searches and re-searches. Minor panic when duplicate keys weren't stashed where they should be; righteous indignation and scapegoating; the buzz, the edge for weeks afterward whenever keys were mentioned, picked up, or set down in the camp office. The morning of the lost keys became one of those incidents, significant or not in themselves, that lend a name, a tone to a whole camp season: the summer of baby goats in the nature lodge, the hurricane summer, the summer a boy was lost for a night on Mount Katahdin, the summer you-remember-who bit your grandfather's finger, the summer two counselors from a boys' camp nearby were killed in a high-speed crash late at night, the summer the Israeli nurses swam topless, the summer you left and never returned.

If you'd ambled up on your short, chunky legs and handed me the lost keys, it wouldn't have convinced me you'd taken them. Nor would a confession have convinced me. Nothing you might have said or done could have solved the mystery of the keys. No accident or coincidence would have implicated you. Without a reason, with no motive, no *why*, the idea of your removing the keys remained unthinkable.

You were blond then. Huge brown eyes. Hair on your head of many kinds, a storm, a multiculture of textures: kinky, dead straight, curly, frizzy, ringlets; hair thick in places, sparse in others. All your people, on both sides of the family, ecumenically represented in the golden crown atop your head.

You cried huge tears, too. Heartbreaking, slow, sliding tears that formed gradually in the corners of your dark eyes — gleaming, shapely tears before they collapsed and inched down your cheeks. Big tears, but you cried quietly, almost privately, even though the proof of your unhappiness was smearing your face. Then again, when you needed to, you could bellow and hoot — honking Coltrane explorations of anger, temper, outrage. Most of the time, however, you cried softly, your sobs pinched off by deep, heaving sighs, with a rare, high-pitched, keening wail escaping in spite of whatever was disciplining you to wrap your sorrow so close to yourself.

I'm remembering things in no order, with no plan. These father stories. Because that's all they are.

Your mother said that the story she wishes she could write, but knows is so painful she hesitates to tell it to herself, would be about her, of course, and you, yes, but also about her father, your grandfather: what he built, who he was, his long, special life, how many other lives he touched, the place he created out of nothing, in the woods, along the lake that I'm watching this morning, and that watches me as I write.

It is her father she has returned to all these summers in Maine. What he provided, no strings attached. His gift of water, trees, weather, a world apart, full of surprise, a world unchanging. Summers in Maine were the stable, rooted part of her.

One morning, as I sit on the dock staring at the lake, a man and a boy float past in a small boat. They have turned off the putt-putt outboard motor hanging over the stern and are drifting in closer to the rocky shoreline, casting their fishing lines where the water is blackish green from shadows of tall pines lining the lake. A wake spreads languidly behind the boat, one wing plowing the dark water, its twin unfurling like a bright flag dragged across the surface. No sound except birdsong, the hiss of a fishing line arcing away from the boat, then its plopping like a coin in the bottom of a well. The weather has changed overnight. Wind from the west this morning — a cooling, drying wind lifting the mist before dawn, turning the sky unwaveringly blue at this early hour. A wind shunting away last week's mugginess and humidity, though it barely ruffles the skin of the water in this inlet. Gray bands of different shades and textures stripe the lake's center, panels of a fan lazily unfolding, closing, opening. Later, the west wind will perk up and bring chill gusts, stir a chop into the water. Smooth and quiet now for the man and the boy hunkered down in their boat. They wear baseball caps, layers of shirts and jackets, the same bulky shape twice; one form is larger than the other, and each is a slightly different color, but otherwise the two are identical, down to the way their wrists snap, their lines arc up and away from the boat. The man's lure lands further away than the boy's each time, in scale with the hunched figures drifting past in the boat.

I will see the boat again, about an hour later, when the water is louder, when ripples driven from the west are forming scalloped waves. The boy, alone then, whips the boat full throttle in tight, spray-sluicing circles, around and around, gouging deep furrows. The nose of the boat high in the air, he hunches over the screaming engine, gunning it in short, sprinting bursts, then in sharp turns, around and around, as if he were trying to escape a swarm of hornets.

The wind is forgetting it's July. I wish for extra insulation under my hooded sweatshirt and nylon windbreaker. Trees are a baffle for the wind and conjure its sound into colder, stronger, arctic messages shuttling through the upper atmosphere. In the same way, your mother's hair when it's long and loose, catching all the colors of light, falling down around her bare shoulders, carries within itself that wind rush of surf crashing far away, the muffled roar of a crowd in a vast, distant stadium.

You'd twist thick clumps of her chestnut hair in your fist, clutch it while she held you and you sucked the thumb of your other hand. For hours. For hours if she'd let you.

Maybe all things happen, including ourselves, long before we see, hear, know they are happening. Memory, then, isn't so much archival as it is a seeking of vitality, harmony, an evocation of a truer, more nearly complete present tense. All of this, of course, relates to personality — the construction of a continuous narrative of self. Our stories. Father stories.

*

Do you remember your fear of leaves? Of course you do. The teasers in our family would never let you forget.

Once, in Laramie, Wyoming, after dinner, just as a full-moon night was falling and the wide, straight-arrow streets were as empty and still as Long Lake at dawn, I was riding you on my shoulders — a rare moment, the two of us together, away from your mother and brother — when, suddenly, you cried out. The street we were on had a ceiling. Branches from trees planted in people's yards hung over fences lining the sidewalk, forming a canopy overhead. I panicked. Thought I'd knocked you against a low branch or you'd got your hair tangled — or, worse, been scratched in the eye or the face. Your fingers dug into my scalp. You didn't want to let go as I tried to unseat you from my shoulders, slide you down into the light from a streetlamp to see what was the matter.

You'd given me a couple of good yanks, so I was both mad and scared when I finally pulled you down, cradling you in my arms to get a clear look at your face.

No tears. No visible damage. Yet you were wild-eyed, trembling uncontrollably. The leaves had been after you. Probably not touching you but, worse, a blanket of quivering, rustling, mottled dread suddenly hovering above you. Surrounding you, rendering you speechless. Terrorized beyond words or tears, you'd gripped my hair and kicked my chest. I'd thought you were roughing me up because you wanted to play. Grabbed your wrists and squeezed them tight to hold you as I galloped down the quiet Laramie street, doing my best imitation of the bucking bronco on Wyoming license plates. You were rendered even more helpless with your hands clamped in mine, struggling to free yourself while I thought we were having fun. Your father snorting and braying, jiggedy-jig, jiggedy-jig, suddenly in league with your worst enemy, and nowhere to run, nowhere to hide — he was rushing you to your doom. No wonder your fingers tried to rip my hair out when I released your wrists. Holding on, reining me in, pounding on my skull, fighting back the only way you knew how, short of pitching yourself down from a dizzying height, down, down to the pavement, itself strewn with shadowy leaves.

When I was a kid, I harbored a morbid fear of feathers. Feathers. Not a single feather or a few loose feathers, like the ones I'd stick in my naps to play Indian, but feathers in a bunch, attached to birds who could wriggle them, flutter them, transform them into loose flesh, rotting, molting, the unnatural sign of death-in-life and life-in-death, the zombie, mummy, decaying corpses of movies and my nightmares. Feathers a kind of squirmy skin hanging off the bone, all the more horrible because feathers seemed both dry and sticky with blood.

My feathers, your leaves. One afternoon at the Belmar on Home-wood Avenue, in Pittsburgh, in one of those Bible-days epic movies, a man was tortured nearly to death, his bloody body flung off a fortress wall. He landed on a heap of corpses in a ditch. As the camera pans the mangled bodies, the sound of huge wings beating thumps through the Belmar's crackly speakers. After the Techni-color glare of carnage under a desert sun, the camera is blinded an instant by the black swoop of vultures. They land atop the corpses, feathers rippling, glinting as the birds begin their slow-motion, ponderously delicate lope toward the choicest morsels of meat — eyeballs, tongues, exposed guts — toward the not-quite-dead-yet man sprawled on a bed of other victims.

Then a closeup of the man's face. As he spots the vultures and screams, I scream. I know I did. Even though I couldn't hear myself, because everybody in the Belmar joined in one shrieking whoop of fear and disgust. And I never forgot the scene. Never. Never forgot, never forgave. Hated pigeons. They became my scapegoats, or scapebirds. I'd hurt them any chance I got. Trapped one in a box and tormented it. Fully intended to incinerate the crippled one who wound up on the stone steps in the hallway of my dorm freshman year until my roommate shamed me out of it when I asked to borrow his lighter and some fluid and he de-manded to know for what.

Pigeons were brown and dirty. They shat everywhere. Spoiled things. Their cooing from the eaves of our roof on Finance Street could startle you awake. They sneaked around, hid in dark corners, carried disease, like rats. Far too many of the useless creatures. I focused my fear and hate of feathers on them. Went out of my way to cause them difficulties.

Once, I was so angry at your mother's pain I thought I was angry at her. She was sharing out loud for the first time how torn apart she'd felt that summer you never came back. How she feared her father's gift had been blighted forever. Woods, lake, sky a mirror reflecting absence of father, absence of son, the presence of her grief.

I couldn't deal with the pain in her voice, so I made up another story. Presumed to tell her she was letting her pain exclude other ways of trying to make sense, with words, with stories, with the facts as given and the facts as felt, make sense of the enormity of what happens and doesn't happen, the glimmers of it we paste together trying to find peace. One different story would be the day she meets her father again in this place and what he might have to say to her and why he needed to see her and what he might remind her of and why it would need to be here, on a path through the thick pine woods where light can surprise you, penetrating in smoky shafts where it has no business being, where it sparkles, then shifts instantly, gone faster than the noises of creatures in the underbrush you never see. I make up her father, as I'm making up mine. Her father appearing to her in a suit of lights because that, too, could transpire, could redeem, could set us straight in a world where you never know what's going to happen next and often what happens is bad, is crushing, but it's never the worst thing, never the best, it's only the last thing, and not even exactly that, except once, and even then death is not exactly the last thing that happens, because you never know what's going to happen next. For better or worse, cursed and blessed by this ignorance, we invent, fill it, are born with the gift, the need, the weight of filling it with our imaginings. That are somehow as real as we are. Our mothers and fathers and children. Our stories.

I hope this is not a hard day for you. I hope you can muster peace within yourself and deal with the memories, the horrors of the past eight years. It must strike you as strange — as strange as it strikes me — that eight years have passed already. I remember a few days after hearing you were missing and a boy was found dead in the room the two of you had been sharing, I remember walking down toward the lake to be alone, because I felt myself coming apart: the mask I'd been wearing, as much for myself as for the benefit of other people, was beginning to splinter. I could hear ice cracking, great rents and seams breaking my face into pieces, carrying away chunks of numb flesh. I found myself on my knees, praying to a tree. In the middle of some absurdly compelling ritual that I'd forgotten I carried the memory of. Yet there I was on my knees, digging my fingers into the loose soil, grabbing up handfuls, sinking my face into the clawed earth as if it might heal me. Speaking to the roots of a pine tree as if its shaft might carry my message up to the sky, send it on its way to wherever I thought my anguish should be addressed.

I was praying to join you. Offering myself in exchange for you. Take me. Take me. Free my son from the terrible things happening to him. Take me in his place. Let them happen to me. I was afraid you were dying or already dead or suffering unspeakable tortures at the hands of a demon kidnapper. The tears I'd held back were flowing finally, a flood that brought none of the relief I must have believed that hoarding them would earn me when I let go at last. Just wetness burning, clouding my eyes. I couldn't will the spirit out of my body into the high branches of that tree. What felt familiar, felt like prayers beside my bed as a child, or church people moaning in the amen corner, or my mother weeping and whispering *hold on, hold on* to herself as she rocks side to side and mourns, or some naked priest chanting and climbing toward the light on a bloody ladder inside his chest — these memories of what might have been visions of holiness could not change the simple facts. I was a man who had most likely lost his son, and hugging trees and burying his face in dirt and crying for help till breath slunk out of his body wouldn't change a thing.

A desperate, private moment, one of thousands I could force myself to dredge up if I believed it might serve some purpose. I share that one example with you to say that the eight years have not passed quickly. The years are countless moments, many as intense as this one I'm describing to you, moments I conceal from myself as I've hidden them from other people. Other moments, also countless, when terrible things had to be shared, spoken aloud, in phone calls with lawyers, depositions, interviews, conferences, in the endless conversations with your mother. Literally endless, because often the other business of our lives would seem merely a digression from the dialogue with you, about you. A love story finally, love of you, your brother and sister, since no word except love makes sense of the ever-present narrative our days unfold.

Time can drag like a long string, studded and barbed, through a fresh wound, so it hasn't gone quickly. The moment-to-moment, day-by-day struggles imprint my flesh. But the eight years are also a miracle, a blink of the eye through which I watch myself wending my way from there to here. In this vast house of our fathers and mothers.

*

Your mother didn't need my words or images to work out her grief. She needed time. Took the time she needed to slowly, gradually, painstakingly unravel feelings knotted in what seemed for a while a hopeless tangle. No choice, really. She's who she is. Can give nothing less than her whole heart to you, to this place, inseparable from all our lives, that her father, your grandfather, provided.

For a while, I guess it must have felt impossible. And still can, I know. She may have doubted her strength, her capacity to give enough, give everything, because everything seemed to be tearing her apart, breaking her down. She needed time. Not healing time, exactly, since certain wounds never heal, but time to change and more time to learn to believe, to understand she could go on, was going on, for better or worse. She could be someone she'd never dreamed she could be. Her heart strong, whole, even as it cracks and each bit demands everything.

The fullness of time. The fullness of time. That phrase has haunted me since I first heard it or read it, though I don't know when or how the words entered my awareness, because they seem to have always been there, like certain melodies, for instance, or visual harmonies of line in your mother's body that I wondered how I'd ever lived without the first time I encountered them, although another recognition clicked in almost simultaneously, reminding me that I'd been waiting for those particular notes, those lines, a very long time. They'd been forming me before I formed my first impressions of them.

The fullness of time. Neither forward nor backward. A space capacious enough to contain your coming into and going out of the world, your consciousness of these events, the wrap of oblivion bedding them. A life, the passage of a life: the truest understanding, measure, experience of time's fullness. So many lives, and each different, each unknowable, no matter how similar to yours, your flesh and not your flesh, lives passing, like yours, into the fullness of time, where each of these lives and all of them together make no larger ripple than yours, all and each abiding in the unruffled innocence of the fullness that is time. All the things that mattered so much to you or them sinking into a dreadful, unfeatured equality that is also rest and peace, time gone: but more, always more, the hands writing, the hands snatching, hands becoming bones, then dust, then whatever comes next, what time takes and fashions of you after the possibilities, permutations, and combinations — the fullness in you — are exhausted, played out for the particular shape the fullness has assumed for a time in you, for you. You are never it but what it could be, then is not: you not lost but ventured, gained, stretched, more, until the dust is particles and the particles play unhindered, unbound, returned to the fullness of time.

I know my father's name, Edgar, and some of his fathers' names, Hannibal, Tatum, Jordan, but I can't go back any further than a certain point, except that I also know the name of a place, Greenwood, South Carolina, and an even smaller community, Promised Land, nearly abutting Greenwood, where my grandfather, who, of course, is your great-grandfather, was born, and where many of his brothers are buried, under sturdy tombstones bearing his name, our name, "Wideman," carved in stone in the place where the origins of the family name begin to dissolve into the loam of plantations owned by white men, where my grandfathers' identities dissolve, where they were boys, then men, and the men they were fade into a set of facts, sparse, ambiguous, impersonal, their intimate lives unretrievable, where what is known about a county, a region, a country and its practice of human bondage, its tradition of obscuring, stealing, or distorting black people's lives, begins to crowd out the possibility of seeing my ancestors as human beings. The powers and principalities that originally restricted our access to the life that free people naturally enjoy still rise like a shadow, a wall between my grandfathers and me, my father and me, between the two of us, father and son, son and father.

So we must speak these stories to one another.

Love.

TOBIAS WOLFF

Civilian

FROM THE THREEPENNY REVIEW

I WAS DISCHARGED in Oakland the day after I stepped off the plane. The personnel officer asked me if I would consider signing up for another tour. I could go back as a captain, he said. Captain? I said. Captain of *what*?

He didn't try to argue with me, just made me watch him take his sweet time fiddling with the file folders on his desk before handing over my walking papers and separation pay. I went back to the bachelor officers' quarters and paced my room, completely at a loss. For the first time in four years I was absolutely free to follow my own plan. The trouble was, I didn't have one. When the housekeeping detail asked me to leave I packed up and caught a taxi to San Francisco.

For over a week I stayed at a hotel in the Tenderloin, hitting the bars, sleeping late, and wandering the city, sharply aware that I was no longer a soldier and feeling that change not the way I'd imagined, as freedom and pleasure, but as aimlessness and solitude. It wasn't that I missed the army. I didn't. But I'd been a soldier since I was eighteen, not a good soldier but a soldier, and linked by that fact to other soldiers, even those long dead. When, browsing through a bookstore, I came across a collection of letters sent home by Southern troops during the Civil War, I heard their voices as those of men I'd known. Now I was nothing in particular and joined to no one.

In the afternoons I put myself through forced marches down to the wharf, through Golden Gate Park, out to the Cliff House. I walked around the Haight, seedier than a year before, afflicted like the faces on the street with a trashed, sullen quality. Sniffling guys in big overcoats hunched in doorways, hissing at passersby, though not at me: a clue that I was radiating some signal weirdness of my own. No hug patrols in evidence. I went there once and didn't go back.

As I walked I kept surprising myself in the windows I passed, a gaunt hollow-eyed figure in button-down shirt and khakis and one of my boxy Hong Kong sport coats. Without cap or helmet, my head seemed naked and oversized. I looked newly hatched, bewildered, without history.

There might have been some affectation in this self-imposed quarantine. I didn't have to stay in a seedy room in San Francisco, broodingly alone; I could have gone on to Washington. My mother and brother gave every sign of wanting to welcome me home, and so did my friends, and my ex-fiancée Vera. She had parted ways with my successor, Leland, soon after they took up together, and her most recent letters had spoken of her wish to try again with me. All I had to do was get on a plane and within hours I would be surrounded by the very people I'd been afraid of not seeing again. But I stayed put.

I thought of my friends and my family as a circle, and this was exactly the picture that stopped me cold and kept me where I was. It didn't seem possible to stand in the center of that circle. I did not feel equal to it. I felt morally embarrassed. Why this was so I couldn't have said, but a sense of deficiency, even blight, had taken hold of me. In Vietnam I'd barely noticed it, but here, among people who did not take corruption and brutality for granted, I came to understand that I did, and that set me apart. San Francisco was an open, amiable town, but I had trouble holding up my end of the conversation. I said horrifying things without knowing it until I saw the reaction. My laugh sounded bitter and derisive even to me. When people asked me the simplest questions about myself I became cool and remote. Lonesome as I was, I made damn sure I stayed that way.

One day I took a bus over to Berkeley. I had the idea of applying for school there in the fall, and it occurred to me I might get a break on admission and fees because of my father being a California resident. It wasn't easy to collect hard intelligence about the old man, but since the state had kept him under lock and key for over two years, and on parole ever since, I figured his home of record was one thing we could all agree on.

I never made it to the admissions office. There was some sort of gathering in Sproul Plaza, and I stopped to listen to one speaker and then another. Though it was sunny I got cold in the stiff bay breeze and sat down by a hedge. The second speaker started reading a list of demands addressed to President Johnson. People were walking around, eating, throwing Frisbees for dogs with hand-kerchiefs around their necks. On a blanket next to me, a bearded guy and a languorous Chinese girl were passing a joint back and forth. The girl was very beautiful.

Microphone feedback kept blaring out the speaker's words, but I got the outline. Withdrawal of our troops from Vietnam. Recognition of Cuba. Immediate commutation of student loans. Until all these demands were met, the speaker said he considered himself in a state of unconditional war with the United States government.

I laughed out loud.

The bearded guy on the blanket gave me a look. He said some-thing to the Chinese girl, who turned and peered at me over the top of her sunglasses, then settled back on her elbows. I asked him what he thought was so interesting and he said something curt and dismissive and I didn't like it, didn't like this notion of his that he could scrutinize me and make a judgment and then brush me off as if I didn't exist. I said a few words calculated to let him know that he would be done with me when I was done with him, and then he stood up and I stood up. His beautiful girlfriend pulled on his hand. He ignored her. His mouth was moving in his beard. I hardly knew what he was saying, but I understood his tone perfectly and it was intolerable to me. I answered him. I could hear the rage in my voice and it pleased me and enraged me still more. I gave no thought to my words, just said whatever came to me. I hated him. If at that moment I could have turned his heart off, I would have. Then I saw that he had gone quiet. He stood there looking at me. I heard the crazy things I was saying and realized, even as I continued to yell at him, that he was much younger than I'd thought, a boy with ruddy cheeks his beard was too sparse to hide. When I managed to stop myself I saw that the people around us were watching me as if I were pathetic. I turned away and walked toward Sather Gate, my face burning.

I got to Manhattan Beach just after sundown, and surprised my father once again. He was in his bathrobe, about to pop some frozen horror into the oven. I told him to keep it on ice and let me stand him to dinner at the restaurant where we'd eaten the year before. He said he wasn't feeling exactly jake, thought he might be coming down with something, but after we had a few drinks he let himself be persuaded of the tonic potential of a night on the town.

So we gave it another try, and this time we got it right. Again we stuffed ourselves with meat and drink, and again my father grew immense with pleasure and extended his benevolence to everyone in range. The old rich rumble entered his voice; the stories began, stories of his youth and the companions of his youth, rioters whose deeds succeeded in his telling to the scale of legend. He found occasion to invoke the sacred names (Deerfield; New Haven; Bones; the Racquet Club), but this time I managed to get past the lyrics and hear his music, a formal yet droll music in which even his genuine pretensions sounded satirical. I let him roll. In fact I egged him on. I didn't have to believe him; it was enough to look across the table and see him there, swinging to his own beat.

I had come back to Manhattan Beach, I surely understood even then, because there could no longer be any question of judgment between my father and me. He'd lost his claim to the high ground, and so had I. We could take each other now without any obligation to approve or disapprove or model our virtues. It was freedom, and we both grabbed at it. It was the best night we'd ever had.

I paid the next morning. So did he, and then some. Late into the day he was still in bed, flushed and hot, and I finally realized that he really had been coming down with something. I called his doctor, who stopped by the apartment on his way home that evening, diagnosed the flu, and prescribed something to bring the fever down. He wouldn't let me pay, not after my father sneaked it in that I was just back from Vietnam. I followed the doctor to the door, insisting, wagging my wallet, but he wouldn't hear of it. When he left I went back to the old man's bedroom and found him laughing, and then I started laughing too. Couple of crooks.

That night and the next day he was too sick to do much of anything but sleep. In his sleep he moaned and talked to himself. I came into his room now and then, and stood over him in the dim slatted light cast by the streetlamp. Big as he was, he looked as if he'd been toppled, felled. He slept like a child, knees drawn up almost to his chest. Sometimes he whimpered. Sometimes he put his thumb in his mouth. When I saw him like that he seemed much older than his sixty years, closer to the end and more alone than I wanted to think about.

Then he started coming out of it. He liked being babied, so he wore his invalid droop and mopery as long as I let him. When I helped him in and out of bed he groaned piteously and walked as if his joints had rusted shut. He had me buy him an ice bag, which he wore like a tam-o'-shanter, his eyes tremulous with self-pity. All day long he called out his wishes in a small desolate voice — cheese and crackers, please, some Gouda on stone-ground Wheat Thins would be swell, with a little tabasco and red onion, if I wouldn't mind. Palm hearts with cream cheese, *por favor,* and this time could I skip the paprika and just sprinkle a little onion salt on them? Thanks a mil! Ginger ale, old son, over ice, and would it be too much trouble to *crush* the ice?

He was relentless and without shame. Once he pushed me too far and I said, "Jesus, Duke, suffer in silence awhile, okay?" This was the first time in my life I'd called him by that name, and the sound of myself saying it made me cringe. But he didn't object. It probably reassured him that I was ready to vacate any outstanding claims on him as his child and accept a position as his crony. I never called him Duke again. I wanted to feel as if I still had a father out there, however peculiar the terms.

He started feeling better after the second day, and I was almost sorry. I liked taking care of him. I'd blitzed the apartment with cleansers, stocked his cabinets with cans of stew and hash and clam chowder and the treats he favored — Swedish flatbread, palm hearts, macadamia nuts. I had a new muffler put on the Cadillac. While he was laid up sick, the smallest acts felt purposeful and worthwhile, and freed me from the sodden sensation of uselessness. Out running errands, I found myself taking pleasure in the salt smell and hard coastal light, the way the light fired the red-tiled roofs and cast clean-edged shadows as black as tar. In the afternoons I brought a chair and a book out to the sidewalk and faced the declining sun, chest bared to the warmth, half listening for the old man's voice through the open window at my back. I was reading *Portnoy's Complaint.* My brother Geoffrey had sent it to me some time before and I'd never been able to get past the first few pages, but now it came to life for me. I read it in a state of near collapse, tears spilling down my cheeks. It was the first thing I'd finished in months.

My father took note of my absorption. He wanted to know what was so fascinating. I let him have it when I was through, and that evening he told me it was the most disgusting thing he'd ever read — not that he'd finished it. Come on, I said. He had to admit it was funny. Funny! How could such a thing be funny? He was baffled by the suggestion.

"Okay," I said. "What do you think *is* funny, then?"

"What b-book, you mean?"

"Book. Movie. Whatever."

He looked at me suspiciously. He was stretched out on the couch, eating a plate of scrambled eggs. *"Wind in the Willows,"* he said. Now there was a book that showed you didn't have to be dirty to be humorous. He happened to have a copy on hand and would be willing to prove his point.

More than willing; I knew he was dying to read it aloud. He'd done this before, to Geoffrey and me, one night in La Jolla seven years earlier. It was a dim memory, pleasant and rare in that it held the three of us together. Of the book itself I recalled nothing except an atmosphere of treacly Englishness. But I couldn't say no.

He started to read, smiling rhapsodically, the ice bag on his head. I was bored stiff, until Toad of Toad Hall made his entrance and began his ruinous love affair with the automobile. "What dust clouds shall spring up behind me as I speed on my reckless way!" he cried. "What carts shall I fling carelessly into the ditch in the wake of my magnificent onset!" Toad had my attention. I found him funny, yes, but also familiar in a way that put me on guard.

Toad is arrested for stealing a car, and in the absence of any remorse is sentenced to twenty years in a dungeon. He escapes dressed as a washerwoman and manages to commandeer the very car he was imprisoned for stealing, after the owner offers a lift to what he thinks is a weary old crone. Toad pins the Samaritan with an elbow and seizes the wheel. "Washerwoman indeed!" he shouts. "Ho, ho! I am the Toad, the motor-car snatcher, the prison-breaker, the Toad who always escapes! Sit still, and you shall know what driving really is, for you are in the hands of the famous, the skillful, the entirely fearless Toad."

By now I knew where the déjà vu came from. My father was Toad.

He wasn't playing Toad, he *was* Toad, and not only Toad the audacious, Toad the shameless and incorrigible, but, as the story gave occasion, goodhearted Toad, hospitable Toad, Toad for whom his friends would risk their very lives. I'd never seen my father so forgetful of himself, so undefended, so confiding.

He read the whole book. It took hours. I got up now and then to grab a beer and refill his glass of ginger ale, stretch, fix a plate of crackers and cheese, but quietly, so he wouldn't break stride. The night deepened around us. Cars stopped going by. We were entirely at home, alone in an island of lamplight. I didn't want anything to change.

But Toad couldn't keep up the pace. The hounds of respectability were on his neck, and finally they brought him down. He had no choice but to make a good act of contrition and promise to keep the peace, live within his means, be good.

My father closed the book. He put it down and looked over at me, shaking his head at this transparent subterfuge. He wasn't fooled. He knew exactly what Toad's promise was worth.

I'd meant only to touch down in Manhattan Beach, but day followed day and I was still there. In the afternoons I sat by the water and read. At night I went to a bar down the road, then came home and sat up with the old man, listening to music and shooting the breeze. We talked about everything except Vietnam and prison. Only once did he mention his life there, when I asked about a livid scar on his wrist. He told me he'd been cut in a fight over which television program to watch, and that stupid as it sounded he'd had no choice, and didn't regret it. I never heard him mention another inmate, never heard him say "the joint" or even "Chino." He gave the impression it hadn't touched him.

I was drinking too much. One night he asked me if I didn't want to give the old noggin a breather, and I stalked out and came back even drunker than usual. I wanted it understood that he could expect nothing of me, as I expected nothing of him. He didn't bring it up again. He seemed to accept the arrangement, and I found it congenial enough that I could even imagine going on in this way, the two of us in our own circle, living on our own terms. I had nearly six thousand dollars in the bank, a year's worth of unspent salary and hazardous duty pay. If I enrolled in the local community college I could milk another three hundred a month from the G.I. Bill. They didn't check to see if you actually went to class — all you had to do was sign up. I could get a place of my own nearby. Start writing. By the time my savings and subsidies ran out, I'd have a novel done. Just a thought, but it kept coming. I mentioned it to the old man. He seemed to like the idea.

It was a bad idea, conceived in laziness and certain to end miserably for both of us. Instead of posing as a student I needed to *be* a student, because I was uneducated and lacked the discipline to educate myself. Same with the novel. The novel wouldn't get written, the money would all get spent, and then what? I had intimations of the folly of this plan, though I persisted in thinking about it.

I'd been in town about a week when I met a woman on the beach. She was reading and I was reading, so it seemed natural to compare notes. Her name was Jan. She did speech therapy in the local schools. She had four or five years on me, maybe more. Her nose was very long and thin and she wore her blond hair mannishly close. She was calm, easy to talk to, but when I asked her out she frowned and looked away. She picked up a handful of sand, let it run through her fingers. "All right," she said.

Grand Illusion was showing at the local art theater. We got there early and strolled to the end of the street and back until they opened the doors. Jan wore a white dress that rustled as she walked and made her skin look dark as chocolate. She had the coolness and serenity of someone who has just finished a long swim. As we were going inside I noticed that her zipper had slipped a few inches. Hold on, I said, and slowly pulled it up again, standing close behind her, my nose almost in her hair.

I had seen *Grand Illusion* before, many times. My friend Laudie and I had memorized Pierre Fresnay's death scene with Erich von Stroheim and used to play it out to impress our dates. But that night I couldn't even follow the plot, I was so conscious of this woman beside me, her scent, the touch of her shoulder against mine, the play of light on her bare arms. At last I figured do or die and took her hand. She didn't pull away. A little while later she laced her fingers through mine.

When the lights came on I was awkward and so was she. We agreed to stop somewhere for a drink. She didn't have any place in mind, so I took her to the bar where I'd been going, an alleged discotheque frequented by former servicemen and some still in uniform. The moment I saw Jan inside the place, in her white dress and cool, manifest sanity, I saw it for what it was — a dive. But she claimed she liked it and insisted on staying.

We'd just gotten our drinks when a hand fell on my shoulder.

"Hey, Cap'n, you trying to keep this lovely lady all to yourself? No fuckin way, man."

Dicky. Dicky and his sidekick, Sleepy.

Chairs scraped. Lighters and cigarettes and glasses descended on the table, a pitcher of beer. They were with us. Jan kept trying not to stare at Dicky, and kept failing. Dicky was clean-shaven, but he had a big curly mustache tattooed above his lip. I couldn't tell whether his intention was serious or jocose, if he actually thought he resembled a person with a mustache or was just riffing on the idea. He claimed to have been with a Marine recon team near the DMZ, even to have operated in North Vietnam. I didn't know what Sleepy's story was.

They were there every night, hopping tables. The last time I'd seen them they were trying to break into Sleepy's car after he'd locked the keys inside. Dicky rigged up a wire of some kind, and when that didn't work right away he went into a rage and smashed out the driver's window, but not before he'd kicked some dents into the door panel and broken off the radio antenna. Sleepy stood there with the rest of us who'd come out of the bar to watch, and didn't say a word.

Dicky caught Jan looking at him. He looked back at her. "So," he said, "how'd you get to know this cabron? Hey, just kidding, the cap'n here's numero fuckin uno."

I told him we'd been to see a film together.

"*Film?* You saw a *film?* What happen, your specs get dirty? Hey, Sleepy, you hear that? The captain says he saw a film, I say, What happen, your specs dirty?"

"I laughed," Sleepy said. "Didn't you hear me laugh?"

"No, I didn't hear you laugh. Speak up, asshole! So what film did you see, Cap'n?" For some reason sweat was pouring out of his hair and down his face.

I gave Dicky the short description of *Grand Illusion*.

He was interested. "That was some bad shit, man, Whirl War One. All that bobwire and overcoats and shit, livin like a buncha

moles, come out, take a look around, *eeeeeeerrr, boom,* your fuckin
head gets blown off. No way, man. No fuckin way. I couldn't get
behind that shit *at all.* I mean, millions of assholes going south,
right? Millions! It's like you take the whole city of L.A., tell em,
Hey, muchachos, here's the deal, you just run into that bobwire
over there and let those other fuckers put holes in you. Big Bertha,
man. And poison gas, what about that mustard shit, you think you
could handle that?"

Jan had her eyes on me. "Were you a captain?"

I'd told her I'd just come back from Vietnam, but nothing else.
I shook my head no.

"But I tell you straight," Dicky said, "no bullshit. If they'd of had
me and my team back in Whirl War One we coulda turned that
shit around *real* fast. When Heinrich starts waking up in the morning with Fritz's dick in his hand, maybe they decide to do their
yodeling and shit at home, leave these other people the fuck alone,
you hear what I'm saying?"

Sleepy's chin was on his chest. He said, "I hear you, man."

"What were you, then?" Jan said to me.

"First lieutenant."

"Same thing," Dicky said. "Lieutenant, cap'n, all the same —
hang you out to dry every fuckin one of em."

"That's not true."

"The fuck it isn't. Fuckin officers, man."

"I didn't hang anybody out to dry. Except maybe another officer,"
I said. "A captain, as a matter of fact."

Dicky ran a napkin over his wet face and looked at it, then at
me. Jan was also looking at me.

As soon as I started the story I knew I shouldn't tell it. It was the
story about Captain Kale wanting to bring the Chinook into the
middle of the hooches, and me letting him do it. I couldn't find
the right tone. My first instinct was to make it somber and regretful, to show how much more compassionate I was than the person
who had done this thing, how far I had evolved in wisdom since
then, but it came off sounding phony. I shifted to a clinical,
deadpan exposition. This proved even less convincing than the
first pose, which at least acknowledged that the narrator had a
stake in his narrative. The neutral tone was a lie, also a bore.

How do you tell such a terrible story? Maybe such a story
shouldn't be told at all. Yet finally it will be told. But as soon as

you open your mouth you have problems, problems of recollection, problems of tone, ethical problems. How can you judge the man you were, now that you've escaped his circumstances, his fears and desires, now that you hardly remember who he was? And how can you honestly avoid judging him? But isn't there, in the very act of confession, an obscene self-congratulation for the virtue required to see your mistake and own up to it? And isn't it just like an American boy, to want you to admire his sorrow at tearing other people's houses apart? And in the end who gives a damn, who's listening? What do you owe the listener, and which listener do you owe?

As it happened, Dicky took the last problem out of my hands by laughing darkly when I confessed that I'd omitted to offer Captain Kale my ski goggles. He grinned at me, I grinned at him. Jan looked back and forth between us. We had in that moment become a duet, Dicky and I, and she was in the dark. She had no feel for what was coming, but he did, very acutely, and his way of encouraging me was to show hilarity at every promissory detail of the disaster he saw taking shape. He was with me, even a little ahead of me, and I naturally pitched my tune to his particular receptivities, which were harsh and perverse and altogether familiar, so that even as he anticipated me I anticipated him and kept him laughing and edgy with expectation.

And so I urged the pilot on again, and the Chinook's vast shadow fell again over the upturned faces of people transformed, by this telling, into comic gibbering stick-men just waiting to be blown away like the toothpick houses they lived in. As I brought the helicopter down on them I looked over at Jan and saw her watching me with an expression so thoroughly disappointed as to be devoid of reproach. I didn't like it. I felt the worst kind of anger, the anger that proceeds from shame. So instead of easing up I laid it on even thicker, playing the whole thing for laughs, as cruel as I could make them, because after all Dicky had been there, and what more than that could I ever hope to have in common with her?

When I got to the end Dicky banged his forehead on the table to indicate maximum mirth. Sleepy leaned back with a startled expression and gave me the once-over. "Hey," he said, "great shirt, I used to have one just like it."

*

I called Vera the next morning from a pancake house, my pockets sagging with quarters. It was the first time I'd heard her voice in over a year, and the sound of it made everything in between seem vaporous, unreal. We began to talk as if resuming a conversation from the night before, teasing, implying, setting each other off. We talked like lovers. I found myself shaking, I was so maddened not to be able to see her.

When I hung up, the panic of loneliness I'd come awake to that morning was even worse. It made no sense to me that Vera was there and I was here. The others too — my mother, my friends, Geoffrey and Priscilla. They had a baby now, my nephew Nicholas, born while I was in Vietnam. I still hadn't laid eyes on him.

I made up my mind to fly home the next day.

That last night, the old man and I went out to dinner. For a change of pace we drove down to Redondo Beach, to a stylish French restaurant where, as it happened, they required a coat and tie. Neither of us had a tie, so they supplied us with a pair of identical clip-ons, mile-wide Carnaby Street foulards with gigantic red polka dots. We looked like clowns. My father had never in his life insulted his person with such a costume, and it took him awhile to submit to it, but he came around. We had a good time, quietly, neither of us drinking much. Over coffee I told him I was leaving.

He rolled with it, said he'd figured it was about time I checked in with my mother. Then he asked when I'd be coming back.

"I'm not sure," I said.

"If you're thinking of going to school here, you'll want to give yourself plenty of time to look around, find some digs."

"Dad, I have to say, I've been giving that a lot of thought."

He waited. Then he said, "So you won't be going to school here."

"No. I'm sorry."

He waved away the apology. "All for the b-best, chum. My view exactly. You should aim higher." He looked at me in the kindest way. He had beautiful eyes, the old man, and they had remained beautiful while his face had gone to ruin all around them. He reached over and squeezed my arm. "You'll be back."

"Definitely. That's a promise."

"They all come back for Dr. Wolff's famous rest cure."

"I was thinking maybe next summer. As soon as I get myself really going on something."

"Of course," he said. "Filial duty. Have to look in on your old pop, make sure he's keeping his nose clean." He tried to smile but couldn't, his very flesh failed him, and that was the closest I came to changing my mind. I meant it when I said I'd be back, but it sounded like a bald-faced lie, as if the truth was already known to both of us that I would not be back and that he would live alone and die alone, as he did, two years later, and that this was what was meant by my leaving. Still, after the first doubt I felt no doubt at all. Even that brief hesitation began to seem like mawkish shamming.

He was staring at my wrist. "Let's have a look at that watch."

I handed it over, a twenty-dollar Seiko that ran well and looked like it cost every penny. My father took off his Heuer chronograph and pushed it across the table. It was a thing of beauty. I didn't hold back for a second. I picked it up, hefted it, and strapped it on.

"Made for you," he said. "Now let's get these g-goddamned ties off."

Geoffrey noticed the chronograph a few nights after I got home. We were on his living room floor, drinking and playing cards. He admired the watch and asked how much it set me back. If I'd had my wits about me I would have lied to him, but I didn't. I said the old man had given it to me. "The old man gave it to you?" His face clouded over and I thought, Ah, nuts. I didn't know for sure what Geoffrey was thinking, but I was thinking about all those checks he'd sent out to Manhattan Beach. "I doubt if he paid for it," I said. Geoffrey didn't answer for a while. Then he said, "Probably not," and picked up his cards.

Vera's family owned a big spread in Maryland. After a round of homecoming visits, I left Washington and moved down there with her to help with the haying and see if we couldn't compose ourselves and find a way to live together. We did not. In the past she'd counted on me to control my moods so that she could give free rein to her own and still have a ticket back. Now I was as touchy and ungoverned as Vera, and often worse. She began to let her basset hound eat at the table with her, in a chair, at his own place setting, because, she said, she had to have *some* decent company.

We were such bad medicine together that her mother, the most forbearing of souls, went back to Washington to get away from us. That left us alone in the house, an old plantation manor. Vera's family didn't have the money to keep it up, and the air of the place was moldy and regretful, redolent of better days. Portraits of Vera's planter ancestors hung from every wall. I had the feeling they were watching me with detestation and scorn, as if I were a usurping cad, a dancing master with oily hair and scented fingers.

While the sun was high we worked outside. In the afternoons I went upstairs to the servants' wing, now empty, where I'd set up an office. I had begun another novel. I knew it wasn't very good, but I also knew that it was the best I could do just then and that I had to keep doing it if I ever wanted to get any better. These words would never be read by anyone, I knew, but even in sinking out of sight they made the ground more solid under my hope to write well.

Not that I didn't like what I was writing as I filled up the pages. Only at the end of the day, reading over what I'd done, working through it with a green pencil, did I see how far I was from where I wanted to be. In the very act of writing I felt pleased with what I did. There was the pleasure of having words come to me, and the pleasure of ordering them, reordering them, weighing one against another. Pleasure also in the imagination of the story, the feeling that it could mean something. Mostly I was glad to find out that I could write at all. In writing you work toward a result you won't see for years, and can't be sure you'll ever see. It takes stamina and self-mastery and faith. It demands those things of you, then gives them back with a little extra, a surprise to keep you coming. It toughens you and clears your head. I could feel it happening. I was saving my life with every word I wrote, and I knew it.

In the servants' quarters I was a man of reason. In the rest of the house, something else. For two months Vera and I tied knots in each other's nerves, trying to make love happen again, knowing it wouldn't. The sadness of what we were doing finally became intolerable, and I left for Washington. When I called to say my last goodbye she asked me to wait, then picked up the phone again and told me she had a pistol in her hand and would shoot herself if I didn't promise to come back that same night.

"Vera, really, you already pulled this."

"When?"

"Before we got engaged."

"That was you? I thought it was Leland." She started to laugh. Then she stopped. "That doesn't mean I won't do it. Toby? I'm serious."

"Bang," I said, and hung up.

*

A week later I traveled to England with friends. When they returned home I stayed on, first in London, then in Oxford, reading,
hitting the pubs, walking the countryside. It was restful: the green-
ness, the fetishized civility, the quaint, exquisite class consciousness
I could observe without despair because as a Yank I had no place
in it. My money stretched double, and nobody talked about Vietnam. Every afternoon I went back to my room and wrote. I saw
little to complain of in this life except that it couldn't go on. I
knew I had to make a move, somehow buy into the world outside
my window.

Some people I'd met encouraged me to take the Oxford entrance exams in early December. That left four and a half months
to prepare myself in Latin, French, English history and literature.
I knew I couldn't do it alone, so I hired university tutors in each
of the test areas. After they'd made it clear how irregular this
project was, how unlikely, they warmed to it. They took it on in
the spirit of a great game, strategizing like underdog coaches,
devising shortcuts, second-guessing the examiners, working me
into the ground. After the first few weeks my Latin tutor, Miss
Knight, demanded that I take a room in her house so she could
crack the whip even harder. Miss Knight wore men's clothing and
ran an animal hospital out of her kitchen. When she worked in
the garden birds flew down and perched on her shoulder. She very
much preferred Greek to English, and Latin to Greek, and said
things like "I can't *wait* to set you loose on Virgil!" She cooked my
meals so I wouldn't lose time, and drilled me on vocabulary and
grammar as I ate. She kept in touch with my other tutors and
proofread my essays for them, scratching furiously at the pompous
locutions with which I tried to conceal my ignorance and uncertainty. All those months she fed her life straight into mine, and
because of her I passed the examination and was matriculated into
the university to read for an honors degree in English language
and literature.

Oxford: for four years it was my school and my home. I made
lifelong friends there, traveled, fell in love, did well in my studies.
Yet I seldom speak of it, because to say "When I was at Oxford . . ."
sounds suspect even to me, like the opening of one of my father's
bullshit stories. Even at the time I was never quite convinced of
the reality of my presence there. Day after day, walking those
narrow lanes and lush courtyards, looking up to see a slip of cloud

drifting behind a spire, I had to stop in disbelief. I couldn't get used to it, but that was all right. After every catch of irreality I felt an acute consciousness of good luck; it forced me to recognize where I was, and give thanks. This practice had a calming effect that served me well. I'd carried a little bit of Vietnam home with me in the form of something like malaria that wasn't malaria, ulcers, colitis, insomnia, and persistent terrors when I did sleep. Coming up shaky after a bad night, I could do wonders for myself simply by looking out the window.

It was the best the world had to give, and yet the very richness of the offering made me restless in the end. Comfort turned against itself. More and more I had the sense of avoiding some necessary difficulty, of growing in cleverness and facility without growing otherwise. Of being once again adrift.

I was in the Bodleian Library one night, doing a translation from the West Saxon Gospels for my Old English class. The assigned passage was from the Sermon on the Mount. It came hard, every line sending me back to the grammar or the glossary, until the last six verses, which gave themselves up all at once, blooming in my head in the same words I'd heard as a boy, shouted from evangelical pulpits and the stages of revival meetings. They told the story of the wise man who built his house upon a rock, and the foolish man who built his house upon the sand. "And the rain descended, and the floods came, and the winds blew, and beat upon that house; and it fell; and great was the fall of it."

I'd forgotten I'd ever known these words. When they spoke themselves to me that night I was surprised, and overcome by a feeling of strangeness to myself and everything around me. I looked up from the table. From where I sat I could see the lights of my college, Hertford, where Jonathan Swift and Evelyn Waugh had once been students. I was in a country far from my own, and even farther from the kind of life I'd once seemed destined for. If you'd asked me how I got here I couldn't have told you. The winds that had blown me here could have blown me anywhere, even from the face of the earth. It was unaccountable. But I *was* here, in this moment, which all the other moments of my life had conspired to bring me to. And with this moment came these words, served on me like a writ. I copied out my translation in plain English, and thought that, yes, I would do well to build my house upon a rock, whatever that meant.

ELAINE SCARRY

Counting at Dusk
(Why Poetry Matters
When the Century Ends)

FROM FINS DE SIÈCLE

WHY SHOULD THE END of a century mark poetry so deeply?
Why should it in particular mark lyric so deeply? There are strong
reasons why it should *not* mark it at all, since, as Helen Vendler
writes, the subject is "unsuitable" to lyric: fin de siècle "derives from
the time span of epic narration, and lyric generically prefers the
moment to the narrative span." But not only is it marked: its being
marked is awaited, expected. "The world is waiting for the poet,"
Allen Grossman keeps telling us in the late twentieth century. If
the mounting number of poetry readings in the 1990s is indicative,
the world is, if not waiting for the poet, at least newly alert to its
need for poetry. This seems true of other final decades. "Is any
new poetry in the wind?" Thomas Hardy suddenly asks in the last
line of the last letter he wrote in the winter of 1899. And Wordsworth
in the 1790s openly sets out at once to incite and to fulfill the
expectation for the new: his poems, he repeatedly presses in the
"Preface" to the *Lyrical Ballads,* are "an experiment"; they are
"materially different from those upon which general approbation
is at present bestowed"; they differ from "the popular Poetry of
the day"; he is creating something original and therefore has "the
task of *creating* the taste by which he is to be enjoyed"; he is called
upon both "to clear and often to shape his own road."

Why poetic practice should be so marked is partially explained

by what happens in the wake of numbers. But it is also in part
explained by the direct experience of numbers themselves. Mathe-
maticians have described the acute pleasure they take in the practice of their trade and have likened it to certain forms of aesthetic
pleasure. Solving the proof for the square root of 2, writes Seymour
Papert, entails the delight of watching the numeral 2 flit from side
to side across the equal sign, now appearing as a number, now
disappearing and returning as a superscript: the process bears a
strong resemblance, he says, to the pleasure one feels at a theatrical play, with its rhythm of entrances and exits, its disappearances
and unforeseen returns.

Even the simpler and more widely practiced sequence of counting has this drama. The numbers mount (6, 7, 8, 9), then suddenly
disappear into a nullity (0), which brings an alteration in the next
column (10), introducing numerical activity in a place where there
had been none before. It is as though the sequence of units
suddenly becomes a lever able to act on the space adjacent to itself,
shifting the location of drama from its own habitually perturbed
territory to its normally undisturbed neighbor. The ones column
is so hyperactive that it hardly occasions attention. Activity in the
tens column brings notice: when it is one's own age (30, 40, 50,
60), it may even be treated as a grand event. The hundreds column
is still more portentous: objects of every color are priced at $4.99
or $499 not because anyone fails to see that one more unit will
affect the hundreds column but precisely because everyone sees
that one more unit will affect the hundreds column. We accept it
as a legitimate display of restraint: our merchant-guardians have
prohibited numerical activity from straying recklessly into the next
column ($5.00, $500). The sudden disturbance in the hundreds
or the thousands column — 1699 to 1700, 1799 to 1800, 1899 to
1900, 1999 to 2000 — brings a slight thrill even when it is only
occurring on an odometer, even, that is, when it involves only one's
own solitary encapsulated vehicle. How much more so when it is
a calendar: it is as though here and there all over the world,
everyone with their widely divergent genres of vehicles (horseback,
muleback, camelback, carriage), their different road surfaces (tar-
mac, sand, water), their habits of motion, were simultaneously,
despite their prior unmindfulness of one another, to look down at
the odometer strapped to their ankle, or bike handle, or car, and

see that it was about to turn from 1999 to 2000 and know that in
many places elsewhere everyone had reached the same interval.
(The numerical would temporarily cease to be a background calibration but would seem instead the point of arrival, the destination
toward which everyone had all along been heading.) This experience — happening just as one started up a long hill, just as another
arrived at a son's wedding, just as another practiced a new song,
just as another crossed Simplon Pass, just as another rushed to be
beside someone injured, just as another wondered if the odometer
was working — would seem highly particularized and intimate yet
would carry the vertigo of collective fate normally occasioned only
by earth-imperiling or -saving events. Thus even if the new century
properly begins in 2001, part of the deep experiential turn will
come in 1999 and the interim year 2000.

If one were to say, "Many people will notice this numerical
change," should one add, "Even poets," or should one instead say,
"Especially poets"?

Counting has its own cadence; cadence imposes the constraint
of counting. So does lineation. Thus the names of poetic forms
are persistently numerical — couplets, quatrains, terza rima, octave, sestet, sestina, ottava rima, iambic pentameter, hexameter,
triolet — because the poetic voice seldom ceases to count. At the
end of the century, verse may become explicitly calendric. Set in
the jubilee year 1300, Dante's *Divine Comedy* has 100 cantos. Composed in 1595, Spenser's *Epithalamion* has 24 stanzas and 365 long
lines. Shakespeare's sonnets of the 1590s, Margreta de Grazia
persuasively shows, present themselves as a book of hours. Written
in 1594, *Romeo and Juliet* absorbs into its structure what Walter
Pater sees as a heightened form of the nocturne. But quite apart
from the ends of the century, poetry is deeply calendric. Pater, for
example, calls attention to the way the nocturne of Provençal
poetry is always subdivided according to the hour at which it was
to be sung ("Some were to be sung at midnight — songs inviting
to sleep, the *serena,* or *serenade;* others at break of day — waking
songs, the *aube,* or *aubade*"), just as Spenser urged that the eclogue
was always a genre devoted to the calendar year; and even without
these recognizable temporal names (day, night, week, month, year)
poetry has in common with the calendar the unceasing act of
numerical counting. In any sonnet, in other words, regardless of

the decade, the iambs, the pentameter line, the octave and the sestet establish at its interior a calendric sequence of moments and hours, its inevitable daybreak, its anticipated nightfall. The point is not, then, that poetry *becomes* numerical at the fin de siècle. Exactly the reverse: it is the very persistence of the act of counting, its ongoing inseparability from the poetic act, which ensures that this external event in the realm of counting — the turning over of the calendar — is likely to be noticed. For a person with high numerical sensitivity, any activity in the hundreds column is likely to be perceived not as an abstract experience but as something occurring in one's own interior. Hardy said, for example, that the shift from the nineteenth to the twentieth century changed the way the words of a song felt in his mouth and the way coins weighed in his hands. For Coleridge, similarly, the turn from 1799 to 1800 registered itself in the intimate space between fingertips and eyes: "How many Thousand Letter-writers," he wrote to William Godwin in early January, "will in the first fortnight of this month write a 7 first, & then transmogrify it into an 8 — in the dates of their Letters! I like to catch myself doing that which involves any identity of the human Race." In each case the calendar binds the intimate to the collective: the song in Hardy's mouth was the national anthem; Coleridge saw in the conversion of his 7s into 8s the numerical rehabilitation of the whole species.

The etymological identity of *meter* with *measure*, the intimacy between poetry and the act of counting, and hence the heightened poetic attention to numbers at the moment when the calendar turns over are vividly illustrated in Wordsworth's extraordinary last letter of 1799. Written to Coleridge on December 24 and December 27, it provides an account of the arrival of Wordsworth and his sister Dorothy at their Grasmere cottage, their rapid attempts to domesticate and inhabit it (clearing away smoke, learning the flues, making curtains), their plans for building an enclosed garden in the summer, and then, most elaborately, a detailed description of their four-day winter journey that had brought them to this cottage, from Sockburn to Grasmere, at least forty-five miles of it on foot, occasionally supplemented for small intervals by horses, pony carts, and a post chaise. Perhaps not surprisingly, the letter is a stunning piece of description: moonlight falling on snow-covered meadows on their first morning; the orange light of the second dawn reflected in a brook in an otherwise dark valley, the brightness of the orange brook "varying according to the agitation of the current"; their eventual climb over "stones of all colours . . . encased in the clearest ice" to arrive beneath the vaulted "cieling of a huge cave" where a powerful stream of water hurls rocks before falling into a spray of dissolving snow, the intricate secret interior of "this Arabian scene" seeming in its cascading details to bring into the world the dream world of Kubla Khan. The letter documents with exquisite precision the sensory perceptions of the present (a "keen frosty morning," a succession of light snowfalls on their faces and backs, their numb feet aching with cold during the last two miles of "hard frozen road" on the first day's walk, his sister's "raging toothache" as she later sits sewing the cottage curtains). Yet it continually trips the calendar forward. The Grasmere cottage already has, at least in speculative form, the small enclosed garden that they would later make in the summer of 1800 and fill with honeysuckle, roses, and the red blossoms of runner bean vines. So, too, key locations in the Sockburn-Grasmere walk are continually tripped forward out of the winter of 1799 into the summer of the 1800s (detouring in one case through an earlier fin de siècle). Of the waterfall they see at sunset on the first day he writes: "such a performance as you might have expected from some giant gardiner employed by one of Queen Elizabeth's Courtiers, if this same giant gardiner had consulted with Spenser and they two had finish'd the work together." And his long description of the huge cave entered on the second day climaxes once more into a garden, compressing into itself "all that summer and winter can produce of delicate beauty":

> The rock in the centre of these falls where the water was most abundant, deep black, the adjoining parts yellow white purple violet and dove colour'd, or covered with water-plants of the most vivid green, and hung with streams and fountains of ice and icicles that in some places seemed to conceal the verdure of the plants and the variegated colours of the rocks and in some places to render their hues more splendid. I cannot express to you the enchanted effect produced by this Arabian scene of colour as the wind blew aside the great waterfall behind which we stood and hid and revealed each of these faery cataracts in irregular succession or displayed them with various gradations of distinctness, as the intervening spray was thickened or dispersed. In the luxury of our

imaginations we could not help feeding on the pleasure which in the
heat of a July noon this cavern would spread through a frame exqui-
sitely sensible.

As the Grasmere garden and orchard are glimpsed through the
curtained smoke of the troublesome winter chimneys, so here
again the 1800s' first July is half displayed, half concealed in the
curtain of waters.

Yet this conflation of the delicate and the miraculous is steadily
paced, for Wordsworth periodically erupts into the prosaic act (or
actually, the poetic act) of counting: 12 miles on foot on day 1, 3
of those in the dark, 2 of those with hurt feet; 21 miles on day 2,
occurring in segments of $\frac{1}{4}$ mile, $1\frac{1}{2}$ miles, 2 miles (the distance
traveled with the help of the ponies and carts), 10 miles in $2\frac{1}{4}$
hours, 7 miles in 1 hour 35 minutes; on day 3, 11 miles in 3 hours.
Periods of rest are measured as well: 1 hour at the domed cave;
$\frac{1}{4}$ hour "close by Garsdale chapel." Even the landscape structures
itself into countable objects: 2 fields, 2 banks, 2 rocky banks, 1st
waterfall, 2d waterfall, 3d waterfall (its "water fell at least ten yards
from us"), 2 winding rocky banks, 3 festoons embedded in the
rock, 3 diminutive waterfalls near the 3d large waterfall. He per-
forms throughout the letter a dedicated labor of measurement: it
is as though he were to speak aloud the poetry of *An Evening Walk*
(1793) or *Descriptive Sketches* (1793) but periodically break from its
language into a vocalization of the stress counts, alternating between phrases and numbers the way dancers in the rigor of training sometimes count aloud.

The fin de siècle has been, over a sequence of centuries, devoted
to the aesthetic, not just to poetry but to literature more broadly,
and not just to literature but to music and to the visual arts.
William Godwin, for example, said that 1799–1800 marked "a
great epocha, or division in [his] life" because it was at that
moment that he "began to read [not poetry but more inclusively]
the old English authors." The 1690s were dedicated, as Leo Braudy
makes clear, not just to poetry but to sentimental drama. The
1590s saw not just the sudden proliferation of sonnet sequences
but also the less overtly lyric genres of epigram and satire, neatly
trimmed to fit the period: "A crackdown in censorship [in 1599]
which called for the banning and burning of satirical works," writes

Margreta de Grazia, "[brought] the genre to an abrupt halt." Still, while other genres have flourished at the centuries' turn, it is also the case that some, such as drama, have done so by absorbing poetry into their own lineaments: Austin Clarke, for example, points out that the drama of the 1590s (Shakespeare's comedies and histories), the 1790s (the five-act blank-verse tragedies of Coleridge, Wordsworth, and later, Byron and Shelley), and the 1890s (Yeats's many verse plays, Hardy's 125-scene *Dynasts*) has consistently been dedicated to poetic theater. Perhaps more to the point, since at least the 1390s, when Chaucer wrote the *Canterbury Tales* (most tales between 1392 and 1395; several, such as the Nun's Priest's Tale, between 1396 and 1400), final decades have produced a legacy of poets — Chaucer, Spenser, Shakespeare, Donne, Dryden, Blake, Coleridge, Wordsworth, Hardy, Yeats — who cannot, by any method of counting, be calculated as one tenth of the calendar's cut. In many of these cases, the poet's major work appeared during the nineties or at the century's turn: Chaucer's *Canterbury Tales,* Spenser's *Faerie Queene* and *Epithalamion,* Shakespeare's sonnets and twenty-two of the plays, many of Donne's songs and sonnets, Blake's *Songs of Innocence and Experience* as well as many of the prophetic books, the *Lyrical Ballads* of Wordsworth and Coleridge. In other instances, the nineties have had a decisive impact on the poetry even when the poems themselves were written over several decades: it is in the 1890s, for example, that Hardy suddenly gives up novel writing and dedicates himself to poetry, a dedication from which he then never swerved. Yeats's major poems, though not written in the 1890s, are — as Helen Vendler shows — themselves rewritings of his earlier fin-de-siècle lyrics.

Special pleading for the primacy of poetry at the ends of centuries does not seem wholly out of place, because it has often been during these very periods that such special pleading has itself taken place. In 1595, Sidney's *Defence of Poesy* was published, placing poetry above the other arts, as well as above philosophy and history. In 1694, Dryden asserted the primacy of poetry over painting (poems were there in the Garden; painting came after the Fall) in a poem written to a painter. In his dedication to his translation of Virgil's *Aeneid,* also written in 1694, the poem is superior not only to painting but to all other human outcomes: "An Heroic Poem, truly such, is undoubtedly the greatest Work which the Soul of Man is capable to perform." For Dryden, the poet displaces not just the painter and other artists but, as Leo Braudy so crucially shows, the monarch as a site of cultural authority. Whereas access to the monarchy is limited to inheritance, access to poetry is achievable through education and "taste"; hence it is distributed to an ever widening population. The stress on the special position of the poet occurs at the end of other centuries as well. Oscar Wilde, both in an 1885 review and in the 1890 essay "The Critic as Artist," designates the poet "the supreme artist." Whether poetry, painting, or sculpture was the superior art was still at issue at the end of the nineteenth century. That artists, rather than monarchs, were the center of cultural authority was noncontroversial and hence not even addressed. (The "cultural life" of Dryden's assertion, notes Braudy, has been long.) At the turn from the nineteenth to the twentieth century, the question was not whether art was authoritative but only how "totalizing" that authority might become. If art could always, Yeats wrote in 1901, aspire to the intensity and dedication of current productions at Stratford-on-Avon, it would grow "serious as the Ten Commandments."

It has been the argument here that poetry's persistent attention to "numbering" may be one reason why it is so marked by the end of the century. Certainly the relation between numbered and unnumbered language — verse and prose — is itself a fin-de-siècle topic: Sidney addresses it (1595); Dryden addresses it (1697, 1700); Wordsworth addresses it (1800); Pater addresses it in his 1889 essay "Style," which also discusses Dryden's and Wordsworth's century-apart accounts. The metrical experimentation that occurs at the ends of centuries reinforces attention to the subject: the first three books of *The Faerie Queene* appeared in 1590; the next three in 1596; *Epithalamion* in 1595. Spenser's metrical virtuosity and experimentation were already richly evident in the 1579 *Shepheardes Calender;* and although that work greatly predates the fin de siècle, it surely validates the connection between metrical and calendric counting. A short 1899 treatise by William Johnson Stone called *On the Use of Classical Meters in English* assesses William Webbe's 1586 *Discourse on English Poetry,* George Puttenham's 1589 *Art of English Poesie,* and the influence of Abraham Fraunce's experiments in hexameter on the poetry of Sidney and Spenser. Stone identifies the 1589 era as "the most fruitful period of metrical experiments." He argues that the metrical experimentation of the Elizabethans then disappeared for a long period and that its "revival" only took place with "Southey and his school" — that is, in the 1790s. More recent theorists of meter, I. A. Richards and Paul Fussell, have speculated that it is because the beat in poetry takes place at a more accelerated rate than one's own heartbeat that it elicits a sense of excitement. Perhaps the overtness with which calendric counting takes place at the end of the nineties (the century, according to Jorie Graham, "clicking by") causes this same press of rapidity and excitement. Wordsworth's long December 1799 letter — alternating all along between numbering and describing — suddenly surrenders at the very end to the exhilaration and exclamation of uninterrupted counting:

> We were in high spirits, and off we drove, and will you believe me when I tell you that we walked the next ten miles . . . thanks to the wind that drove behind us and the good road, in two hours and a quarter, a marvellous feat of which D. will long tell. Well! we rested . . . and then off to Sedbergh 7 miles farther in an hour and thirty five minutes, the wind was still at our backs. . . . I must hurry on, next morning we walked to Kendal, 11 miles, a terrible up and down road, in 3 hours, and after buying and ordering furniture, the next day by half past four we reached Grasmere in a post chaise. So ends my long story. God bless you. W. W.

The acceleration incited by the mounting proximity of Grasmere seems redoubled by the rush to post the letter — "I must hurry on" — and place it in Coleridge's hands before the 7s turned to 8s.

A second reason why the turn of the century may impress itself on poetry is the peculiarly difficult relation between the human will and fin-de-siècle engagements with the calendar. Allen Grossman's 1990 *Summa Lyrica* (subtitled *A Primer of the Commonplaces in Speculative Poetics*) opens by identifying the central aspiration of poetry: "The function of poetry is to obtain for everybody a kind of success at the limits of the autonomy of the will. . . . Poetry serves to obtain a kind of outcome . . . precisely at those points where the natural will is helpless." Many of the major descriptive terms associated with the fin de siècle — lassitude, malaise, enervation — suggest the way the calendar (although itself a humanly invented artifact) imperils the individual will. When, in contrast, one draws a picture of the human will based on the *poetic* legacy of final decades, a very different portrait emerges: the many poems already invoked here — poems, for example, by Chaucer, Sidney, Shakespeare, Spenser, Blake, Coleridge, Wordsworth — suggest that the end of the century inspires inaugurating linguistic acts, words, lines, passages, plays that invigorate the language not just of the next century but of a period far into the future. The end of the century, in other words, far from contracting one's belief in one's own agency, seems instead to prompt the desire to reconstitute the world linguistically. A related area of linguistic endowment which becomes especially marked in final decades is the contractual. Margreta de Grazia speaks of the way millenarianism sometimes inspires political reform, "most consequentially by Parliamentarians"; and Leo Braudy focuses on the way in which the publication of Locke's *Two Treatises of Government* in the 1690s, coupled with a shift to parliamentary rather than monarchic power, inaugurates a world whose beneficiaries resided in (not the next but) the next three centuries. Thomas Paine's *Rights of Man* of the 1790s is, as Martin Green observes in *Prophets of a New Age,* the same kind of attempt to inaugurate a new world, to provide the tools by which a new world might successfully get built; and Green persuasively argues that the 1890s are also characterized by people who take on themselves responsibility for the next century, figures such as Gandhi, whose work in the nineties was dedicated to the parliamentary and constitutional.

Final decades, then, at once disempower and reinvigorate the human will, a coupling that bears out Yeats's observation that "only the greatest obstacle that can be contemplated without despair rouses the will to full intensity." The peculiar combination of enervation and revivification is observable even in a much smaller unit of time such as the transition to a new year: the end of the old year comes upon us like winter, something that we can (however vigorous or vague our preparation) do nothing to alter. Yet the widespread custom of "New Year's resolutions" demonstrates the way that ending simultaneously revivifies the will, incites the will to confidence. The century's end provides a far more enervating problem for at least four reasons: the radius of the will, the impossibility of sequence, the disappearance of adjacency, and the loss of self-description. (And it is these problems, rather than the mystery of how they are overcome by poets and political actors, which are briefly unfolded below.)

First, the scale of the period — one hundred years — places it outside the radius of the human will. Thomas Hardy, for example, was normally comfortable with endings. He inhabited them. As a child he each evening sat alone by a staircase wall that had been painted "Venetian red" to watch its hue intensify in the setting sun and recite ("with great fervency") the hymn "And now another day is gone." As an adult, he recorded the precise sequence in which the trees in any given year dropped their leaves: "The order in which the leaves fall this year is: Chestnuts; Sycamores; Limes; Hornbeams, Elm; Birch; Beech." Yet, unlike these other calendric units, the century's end could never be comfortable, because the hundred-year unit was itself uninhabitable. He returns to its uninhabitability again and again, not only in his overt elegy for the nineteenth century, "Darkling Thrush" — dated December 31, 1900, and originally titled "By the Century's Deathbed" — but also in a set of poems that describe his house either one hundred years prior to or posterior to his own inhabiting of it. "Domicilium," the first poem he ever wrote, includes in its description of his childhood cottage at Bockhampton an oak from a seed "dropped by some bird a hundred years ago"; and the later poem, "The Strange House: Max Gate, A.D. 2000," describes, as its subtitle specifies, the house he lived in as an adult a century after his presence there. In 1867 he wrote a poem entitled "1967": "In five-score summers! All new eyes,/New minds, new modes, new fools, new wise." And throughout the late 1890s he returns often to the hundred-year unit, or its close approximation: the seventy-six-year-long orbit of Halley's comet ("The Comet at Yell'ham"); the 110th anniversary of the midnight on which Gibbon wrote the last sentence of *Decline and Fall* ("Lausanne: In Gibbon's Old Garden: 11–12 P.M.").

The hundred-year period is anomalously called "a period" because, *experientially*, the one thing it can never be is periodic: like a comet, the fin de siècle may arc through one's lifetime once, but it is highly unlikely to do so two or three times. Therefore it asserts sequence while placing the sequential beyond us. Those who live inside the year 2000 may refer to it as the jubilee year, as Hillel Schwartz shows was true of 1300, 1500, 1600, 1700, and 1900, but one will not use the word with any palpable sense of the accrued weight that comes with its return. On January 1, 2001, people may well exchange New Century greetings and New Century gifts, as they did on January 1, 1701, and again in 1801, and again in 1901; but though we will know that it is an end-of-century practice, there will be no felt fact of it as a practice, no sense of the committedness that accompanies the habitual and the rhythmic, the inhabitably arhythmetic. Like Ashbery's "The Plural of Jack-in-the-Box," it is even hard to determine exactly how to write the plural of fin de siècle.

Against this impossibility of experiential sequence is the poet's own act of lifting forward, making sensuously available, the phenomenon of sequence. "When one reads Blake," Yeats wrote in 1897, "it is as though the spray of an inexhaustible fountain of beauty was blown into our faces." Yeats, in the *Autobiographies,* says that he and a friend entered the nineties by undertaking a four-year project of studying Blake's prophetic books: "We took it as almost a sign of Blake's personal help when we discovered that the spring of 1889, when we first joined our knowledge, was one hundred years from the publication of *The Book of Thel,* the first published of the 'Prophetic Books,' as though it were firmly established that the dead delight in anniversaries." Given this sensitivity to hundred-year periods, and to the decade of the nineties to which the *Autobiographies* are primarily devoted, it seems plausible that he thought of himself as writing about the 1390s, the 1590s, and the 1790s when, near the end of the first book, he summarizes the trajectory of English literature by imagining Chaucer's pilgrims climbing onto an Elizabethan stage, then reemerging once more in romantic poetry: "Chaucer's personages had disengaged themselves from Chaucer's crowd, forgot their common goal and shrine, and after sundry magnifications became each in turn the centre of some Elizabethan play, and had after split into their elements and so given birth to romantic poetry."

This bridging back across ends of centuries appears in other writers as well. When Pater attends to Dryden's and Wordsworth's accounts of the relation between prose and verse, he consciously notes that Wordsworth is writing one hundred years after Dryden, and he is surely not unmindful of the fact that he in turn is writing one hundred years after Wordsworth. Again, Hardy in the year 1900, one hundred years after the "Preface" to the *Lyrical Ballads,* makes diary entries attempting to clarify Wordsworth's use of the

word "imagination," as well as charts displaying his own conception
of the overlays and separations between the three terms Wordsworth
sorted out: verse, the language of common speech, and poetic
diction. Florence Emily Hardy records these diary entries shortly
before her all-capitalized break in the biography, "END OF THE
NINETEENTH CENTURY."

This sequencing is important because with the experiential impossibility of sequence comes a third disempowering event, the
falling away of the century that used to be adjacent to our own:
the nineteenth century, the thing by which we knew ourselves if
only because it steadily neighbored us with its differences, will
suddenly be out of our reach, interrupted by this other overfull
thing, this big thing in the way, the twentieth century, which will
seem strangely intrusive in its adjacency, even when it is constituted
by our own acts and objects, our wars and our poems. The beloved
predecessor — with its Shelleys and Brontës and Austen and Eliot
— will slip over the horizon, blocked from view by this other
crammed-full thing, and be demoted to the nonprecursor status,
the diffuse pastness, of the eighteenth century or the Renaissance.

With this comes a fourth disempowering event, the loss of the
power of self-description. The time allotted to any population to
give an account of themselves eventually runs out; soon it becomes
other people's turn to describe them. Even the names by which
we are called will probably not be of our own choosing. The
arithmetic is, in this regard, once more exceptional: it provides a
reliable vehicle of self-representation, since it ensures some measure of continuity between what one calls oneself — "twentieth
century" — and what one is called by later peoples. In contrast,
the nonarithmetic names by which an era designates itself — modern and postmodern, for example — are unlikely to be the ones
by which the period will be designated three centuries later. Even
if people name themselves by a favorite invention of the period —
age of air, jet age, atomic age, computer age, century of cinema,
high tech — it is unlikely to stand; we usually now refer to the "age
of steam" only when we are talking about steam-drawn trains and
how the people of the period quaintly called themselves by that
name. Even the dynastic names — ones coming from the governor
(Elizabethan) or from an attribute of the government (Augustan,
Restoration) — tend to come long after the fact: the *Oxford English*

Dictionary's first recorded use for "Elizabethan" (1558–1603) is 1807; for "Georgian" (1714–1820) is 1855; for "Restoration" (1660 and following) is 1728. Even if a period is self-named, as were the Victorians and again the twentieth-century Georgians, the cluster of connotations may change radically as soon as the self-namers are gone: the Victorians named themselves but had not in mind the dismissive connotations the word had acquired by 1918, when Pound would speak of "the odour of defunct Victoriana," or by 1934, when the word appeared in *Webster's* defined as "prudish, strict; old-fashioned, out-dated." Perhaps (like people not only in Victorian Britain but in the "Victorian" United States and "Victorian" Germany) we will all in the twentieth century eventually be named for a British queen: we could be called the Second Elizabethans. Or perhaps like early-twentieth-century Georgian Green, we will come to be identified by what is eventually perceived as the century's characteristic color (Second Elizabethan Neon).

This elegy to the lost power of self-naming simply summarizes the more important and complicated surrender of the power of self-description. The last chance for self-description puts a special pressure on language and on the great wielders of language, as Barbara Smith's *Poetic Closure* and Frank Kermode's *Sense of an Ending* have made so enduringly visible. Even the ending of a solitary life incites this special attention to language. In his 1992 *Last Words,* Karl Guthke examines the many-centuries-long cultural preoccupation with the last sentence that people have spoken before dying, the thick tradition of both authentic and inauthentic narratives about the final words of Montaigne, Goethe, Socrates, and hundreds of others. The long history of anthologizing those final words began in the seventeenth century and then became more generalized and accelerated from the mid-nineteenth century forward. It is even the case that the law in many countries — possibly all countries, writes Guthke — gives a special status to dying words. Hearsay, for example, is ordinarily inadmissible in Anglo-American law; but if the hearsay is spoken by a person immediately before death (naming the murderer, for example), an exception is made; the testimony is counted as legitimate evidence and is admissible in a court of law. At issue here is the exit line of an individual person, not the exit lines of entire populations inhabiting a given century. But something of the same pressure toward acute self-description must surely be at work in the larger sphere, and this cultural desire to find appropriate "final" sentences partly explains the rapt attention to poets, to those whose powers of language are most rigorous. Even, then, in the midst of fin-de-siècle pluralism, the free-for-all of open voices, there is the sense of the circle drawing back, the clearing being made, to hear the voice of Seamus Heaney or Jorie Graham. And as the approaching "turn" increases the longing for language, so language (continually recontextualized into the ever greater lateness of the nineties) itself undergoes a magnification, a "latening." In 1896, the question was whether *Jude the Obscure* was the best or worst book of the year. By 1899, the question was whether it was the best or worst book of the century.

The four forms of disempowering the will — the radius of one hundred years, the impossibility of experiencing sequence, the disappearance of the predecessor, the loss of the power of self-description — all entail the past and present. An even greater problem is the future. What the twentieth century will have been can still be greatly changed by what now occurs in the final few years; but most of its canvas is filled. The future century, in contrast, is vast and open. The knownness of the past and unknownness of the future is, of course, a source of disablement not just in final decades but in all decades: Allen Grossman speaks of the ongoing "asymmetry of consciousness," its inclusion of what is over, its noninclusion of what has not yet happened. But the turning of a century draws attention to and heightens (latens) the discomfort of that asymmetry. "Here we are in a new reign, & with a general sense of the unknown lying round us," writes Hardy in February 1901. Here we are, he might have written, borrowing Jorie Graham's 1991 title, in the "Region of Unlikeness."

So we return to the calendric nature of poetry and the poet's desire "to obtain a kind of outcome . . . precisely at those points where the natural will is helpless," to enter the calendar, to alter it, to make it an active verb ("I . . . shall calendar an evening spent with you on so interesting a subject among my noctes atticae," writes Coleridge to Godwin in the January 1800 letter about 7s and 8s), to place the century within the radius of the human will.

Like the *Canterbury Tales,* Chaucer's *Treatise on the Astrolabe* was written in the final decade of the 1300s. It is, in fact, the only work by Chaucer which is explicitly dated in its own interior: March 12, 1391, recurs several times. It is addressed to the ten-year-old child Lewis who would come of age in the next century, when Chaucer, who died in 1400, would no longer be present. The treatise moves lovingly over the concrete surface of the astrolabe — "forget not thys, litel Lowys" — requiring the child to commit its intricately detailed surface to memory. It places within his grasp, confers as legacy, the ability to locate horizon and zenith, the twenty-four hours of the day, the rise and fall of the stars, the movements of the moon. Bright, beautiful toy, it enables its user not simply to distinguish and demarcate day and night but to find the precise moment when night becomes dawn, or when evening gives way to night; "to knowe the spryng of the dawneyng" and to "fynd in the bordure the ende of the evenyng, that is verrey nyght." Like Donne's compasses of the 1590s or Blake's compasses of the 1790s, Chaucer's astrolabe is a material locus of empowerment: it places the person in an active or volitional relation to the calendar.

Perhaps poetry written in the final decade of a century should be seen under the rubric (borrowed from Wordsworth) of the "evening voluntary," for much of it is devoted to finding the precise moment when one thing ends and another begins: to "fynd in the bordure the ende of the evenyng, that is verrey nyght." The poems that Wordsworth entitled "Evening Voluntaries" were written in the 1830s. But their care to calibrate the passage of growing night —

> Look for the stars, you'll say that there are none;
> Look up a second time, and, one by one,
> You mark them twinkling out . . .
>
> (I, lines 3–5)

— recurs again and again throughout the poetry of the 1790s, such as *Descriptive Sketches*, which presents the same scene at "Sunset," "Twilight," and "Morning," and *An Evening Walk*, whose opening argument maps the poem's passage across "Sunset," "Twilight Objects," "Twilight Sounds," "Western Lights," "Night," "Moonlight," and "Night Sounds." It is descriptive of the work of many others as well: William Blake's 1796 watercolor drawings of Young's *Night Thoughts* (he made more than five hundred of them); Thomas Hardy's turn-of-the-century poems about crossing the transition line of midnight; Frank Bidart's two long poems of 1991, "In the First Hour of the Night" (a poem that initiates the act of counting, for it is the start of a series of long poems about the successive hours of the night) and "In the Western Night," a poem whose title, says Seamus Heaney, "can evoke the balm and romance of the Pacific Coast of California and at the same time intimate the burnt-out categories of European civilization in the late twentieth century." In its musical context, the voluntary (a term first used in 1597) is a devotional composition usually marking the terminal points, the beginning or end, of a religious service: it is "voluntary" in that its inclusion is at the discretion of the organist, who is wholly at liberty to originate the piece, which is at once "inspirational" and "improvisational."

It is not just the calendar whose interior is entered and altered (the calendar is, after all, from its outset a human construct) but the natural events behind it: stars, sky, blossoms are themselves hybridized with human artfulness. The garden — call it the garden voluntary — is to the calendar year what the evening voluntary is to the calendar day. The attempt to recuperate the human will is most overt in those centuries in which garden and calendar are allied with the monarch, either in portraits of the ruler given by poets or in the ruler's own self-portrait. Elizabeth, for example, was perceived as the eglantine rose, and the poetic hybridization of queen with flower extends, as Roy Strong writes in *The Renaissance Garden in England,* from the April eclogue in Spenser's 1579 *Shepheardes Calender* to John Davies's twenty-six *Hymnes to Astraea* of 1600, in which the letters of her name, ELIZABETH REGINA, provide the starting places for a crossweave of calendar and flowers: *E* generates the line *"Empresse of flowers . . .";* *T* becomes *"The new fresh* Houres *and Graces";* *R* starts the line *"Roses and lillies did them draw."* For William III in the 1690s, the garden served as a form of self-portrait, as historians John Harris, William Stearn, and John Discon Hunt have shown. In that decade, he lavished £88,000 on his gardens, a figure estimated to be half of all expenses on his palaces. Appropriately, he was perceived by contemporaries (if not as rose or lily, still) as a gardener — as much "a *Gard'ner* as he was a *Soldier."* Queen Mary, who originated the post of "Queen's Botanist," shared William's devotion; and together they inspired in the British population the fever of personal gardens which is described in Peter Greenaway's film about the 1690s,

The Draughtsman's Contract. Even, then, by the 1690s the garden is distributed to a widening population: by the 1790s and the 1890s it is not the monarch's garden but the cottage garden that is central.

The fin-de-siècle entry of the artist into the realm of blossoms has its most visually familiar registration in the omnipresent, stylized plants of art nouveau, many of whose practitioners were deeply influenced by the Swiss-French artist Eugène Grasset, whose range of flower designs is compressed in *La plante et ses applications ornamentales* (1896). Grasset's practice, amidst that of William Morris and many other British and Continental designers, is of particular interest because his work makes visible the inseparability of garden and calendar. The twelve prints of the 1896 *La Belle Jardinière*, for example, were originally commissioned as a calendar for the Parisian department store Bon Marché. Shoulder deep in huge red poppies and white lilies (their cups supporting her as though she were only another flower in their midst), the beautiful gardener of July repeats in the folds and form of her dress and scarf the breezy shapes of the blossoms. As though to merge garden voluntary with evening voluntary, the tissue of her dress (as is true in the other eleven months as well) is imprinted with an abstract skywriting of celestial signs. Grasset had ten years earlier done a calendar for Bon Marché based exclusively on plants and zodiac signs. His plant-filled cover illustrations during the 1890s for magazines such as *L'illustration* and *Harpers* were themselves calendric, since such magazines came in weekly or monthly installments. Plants, flowers, and gardens appeared throughout the visual and verbal arts of the nineties (Yeats's *The Rose* was published in 1893, *The Wind Among the Reeds* in 1899) in Britain and other countries. It is not accidental, for example, that almost a third of Carl Schorske's classic study *Fin-de-siècle Vienna* is devoted to chapters with titles such as "The Transformation of the Garden" and "Explosion in the Garden."

But the devotion to blossoms, at least in England, typifies other final decades as well. Wordsworth's Grasmere letter of late December 1799 — its curtain of water falling over rocks colored dove, violet, yellow, purple, black and "covered with water-plants of the most vivid green" — is suggestive of the place of gardens at the century's turn, as well as backward through the preceding decade. Among the illuminated plates of Blake's *Book of Thel* and *Songs of*

Innocence and Experience, there is barely a page where the poem is not companioned by the arching illustration of a tree, plant, flower that seems to wish to enclose, shelter (or at least coinhabit the space of) the linguistic events. Often — as in the pages for "Infant Joy" and "The Blossom" — the dramatic personae themselves reside along the inner surface of the delicate blossom; and always, always, the letters of the poems break into the "leafy flourishes," "tendrils," and "trailing vines" the commentators have described with such precision: "The italic capitals of *'BOOK,'* " begins David Erdman's commentary on *The Book of Thel,* "are alive with sinuous leaves that make buds of the three plump letters and form, against the *'K,'* a calyx from which curved stamens rise in a pattern repeated in the soaring forms rising from blossoms of a similar shape at page bottom." Back in behind Blake one can sense the presence of what Jerome McGann calls the "vocal landscapes" and "the luscious pages" of the Della Cruscans.

This desire to yoke acts of linguistic origination or verbal creation with vegetation occurs in the 1690s, the 1590s, and forward into the 1990s as well. Dryden's belief, announced in 1694, that poetry originated with the Garden was no doubt influenced by the fact that he himself had spent the year translating Virgil's *Pastorals* and *Georgics.* Throughout the 1590s appear the "honeysuckle villains" of Shakespeare's histories and the "luscious woodbine" of the comedies. The fictive persons often come to seem hybrids of verse and flowers, not only in the most flower-filled of all the plays, *A Midsummer Night's Dream* (1594–95), in which three of the characters are blossoms, but even in the tragedies at the century's turn and a few years afterward. Ophelia, as her brother sees, is continuous with the columbine and meadow rue, the blue-veined pansies and violets that might seem only her "fantastic garlands," just as Lear is continuous with the nettles and cuckoo flowers of his wildflower crown. To inhabit the creative word is, for Shakespeare almost as much as for Blake, to inhabit a blossom: "Where the bee sucks, there suck I / In a cowslip's bell I lie," says Ariel on behalf of a poet for whom the whole of England is a "sea-walled garden" and islands are apples that can be closed in a hand or a pocket, seeding other islands the following year.

The evening voluntary and the garden voluntary, though never confined to the ends of centuries, continually recur there. It is as though in ordinary times we are content to permit the construct of the calendar to exist in a loose analogic relation to the events of sky and ground which lie behind it (barely remembering that Sunday is Sun-day, Monday is Moon-day, that spring began as "spring of the leaf"), or as though the calendar were a huge semitransparent curtain very loosely draped in front of, and hence often swinging away from, those celestial and material events. And it is as though the turning of the century, in contrast, could only be accomplished by somehow, for a time, bringing the calendar into more precise alignment with those anterior events, pulling the curtain back (like Wordsworth's waterfall), or making it fully transparent, or pinning its contours to the thick shapes and sounds that lie, now newly exposed, behind. Or perhaps the calendar isn't draped over the events at all but can, by cutting those events open, be found inside: like Seamus Heaney cutting open roots, "And, at the centre, a dark watermark. / O calendar customs!" Seamus Heaney — for whom the felt experience of the poem's coming into being is like a plant and the poem's effect is like the wet cutting blades of holly and ice — repeatedly locates poetic consciousness at ground level. As a child, he first recognized that he was to be a poet on a day when, covered with nets and twigs, he mimed a thicket and spoke as a "shaking bush"; and his poems repeatedly place him underground, or prone on the ground (looking up at the sky through a mat of sweet pea), or even when standing on the ground, submerged and surrounded ("waist-deep in cow-parsley"). This sense of poetic making as occurring in the space from which plants grow is reaffirmed in the way he pictures the formation of other poets. His account of poetic making in Hardy centers on the child's head thrown back onto a grassy space, and his account of poetic making in Wordsworth centers on a picture (drawn from Dorothy's 1802 diary) of Dorothy and William lying prone on the ground, heads back, faces skyward: "Phrases like 'diurnal course' and 'diurnal roll' are underwritten by sensation and take their lifeline from moments like this." The calendar is verified.

At evening, in the garden, the century ends but the world stays fresh. In its connotations of coolness, moisture, and sweetness, that which is fresh primarily addresses the senses of touch and taste. It derives from the old Germanic *frisk*, "fresh of temperature, hence unfaded, unwithered, also recent," and describes that which is "newly made, cool." It is connected to the Italian word *fresco*, "to paint upon a fresh, still moist plaster." Its early meaning as "unsalted" or "sweet" generates a set of connotations that include "pure, sweet, eager" or "eager and ardent," bringing to mind Seamus Heaney's observation that "blooming" means "impatient" as well as "flourishing." At the ends of centuries "the fresh" ceases to be exclusively adjectival and begins to occupy all grammatical positions. It first appears as a noun in 1596 when the word "freshet" ("fresh water flowing into the sea") is formed, and 1596 is also the year when the noun "freshman" is first recorded. Its first appearance as the verb "to freshen" occurs in 1697.

The sense that the ends of centuries have been bound up with poems, constitutions, and gardens is perhaps as much a performative as a descriptive: here, in the 1990s, in our own final decade, "let it be the case that there will be . . ." or "I wish that there might be . . ." poems, constitutions, and gardens. Writing to the author of *Political Justice* in September 1800, Coleridge sent kisses to Godwin's two little girls, then expressed the "wish" that they might all three move to a house near his own, then (seeing the unlikelihood of this outcome) observed that the linguistic construction "I wish" is "privileged" to have almost anything following it. The end of the century is a period in which the performative and the descriptive often become for a time indistinguishable.

Poetry, says Allen Grossman, is not just the wish we make but the promise we make "against our vanishing." In Blake's *Book of Thel* (1789), the young girl Thel (whose name is the Greek word for "wish" or "will") speaks first to a Lily and then to a Little Cloud. The cloud asks, "Fearest thou because I vanish and am seen no more / Nothing remains?" This conversation between girl and sky continues in Yeats's *A Vision* (1934): "My imagination goes some years backward," he writes, "and I remember a beautiful young girl singing at the edge of the sea in Normandy words and music of her own composition. . . . [She] sang with lifted head of the civilizations that there had come and gone, ending every verse with the cry: 'O lord, let something remain.'" Thel and the beautiful Normandy singer are in turn joined by other singers on other waterways (the river Avon, the coast of Galway); for Yeats, in his turn-of-the-century essay on Stratford-on-Avon, describes the vivacity of the "strange procession of kings and queens" he has just seen in a group of plays (all written between 1590 and 1599), *King John, Richard II, Second Part of Henry IV, Henry V, Second Part of Henry VI,* and *Richard III.* Watching them, he says, "I have felt as I have sometimes felt on grey days on the Galway shore, when a faint mist has hung over the grey sea and the grey stones, as if the world might suddenly vanish and leave nothing behind, not even a little dust under one's feet." And in his essay on Edmund Spenser written a year later (1902), he discovers that his constant dread that a company of people will "then suddenly vanish" has its origins in another end-of-century work, the vision of Scudamour in *The Faerie Queene.* The edge of the calendar itself becomes a shoreline on which a company of people gathers — Thel, the beautiful Normandy singer, Spenser, Shakespeare, and Yeats — making the shared promise "against our vanishing."

Biographical Notes

JOEL AGEE is the author of *Twelve Years: An American Boyhood in East Germany.* His stories and essays have appeared in *The New Yorker, Harper's,* and other magazines. He is also known as a translator of German literary works, among them Elias Canetti's *The Secret Heart of the Clock* and Rainer Maria Rilke's *Letters on Cézanne.* He has received a Guggenheim Fellowship and a grant from the National Endowment for the Arts. The essay in this volume is part of a book in progress, titled *In the House of My Fear.*

HAROLD BRODKEY is the author of two volumes of short stories, *First Love and Other Sorrows* and *Stories in an Almost Classical Mode,* and two novels, *The Runaway Soul* and *Profane Friendship.* His stories and essays have appeared in all the leading magazines, especially *The New Yorker.* He is currently at work on an AIDS memoir.

JOSEPH BRODSKY, exiled from the Soviet Union in 1972, is Andrew Mellon Professor of Literature at Mount Holyoke College. His books include two collections of poetry, *A Part of Speech* and *To Urania,* a volume of essays, *Less than One,* and *Watermark,* a long essay about Venice. He received the Nobel Prize for Literature in 1987. A new collection of poetry, *So Forth,* and a new volume of essays, *On Grief and Reason,* are scheduled to be published this fall.

DUDLEY CLENDINEN has been a columnist for the *St. Petersburg Times,* a national correspondent for the *New York Times,* assistant managing editor for features of the *Atlanta Journal and Constitution,* and assistant managing editor for writing of the *Baltimore Sun* papers. He is the editor of a book of essays, *The Prevailing South: Life and Politics in a Changing*

Culture. His own essays have been published in a book of photographs, *Homeless in America*, and reprinted in a college English text, the *Simon & Schuster Book of Writing*, and have appeared on the op-ed page of the *New York Times*, in *The New Yorker*, in the *Media Studies Journal* at Columbia University, and in *Lear's*, *GQ*, and *Men's Health*. Married for twenty years, he is now divorced and is the father of a daughter. He is at work, with Adam Nagourney, on a narrative history of the modern gay rights movement, to be published in 1996.

BERNARD COOPER is the author of *Maps to Anywhere* and *A Year of Rhymes*. He received the 1991 PEN/USA Ernest Hemingway Award and a 1995 O. Henry prize. "Burl's" is from a collection of memoirs to be published in 1996 entitled *Truth Serum*, parts of which have appeared in *Harper's Magazine*, *The Los Angeles Times Magazine*, and *The Paris Review*. His work was also included in *The Best American Essays 1988*.

W. S. DI PIERO is the author of several books of poetry, the most recent being *Shadows Burning*, and two volumes of essays, *Memory and Enthusiasm: Essays 1975–1985* and *Out of Eden: Essays on Modern Art*. The essay printed here appears in his new collection, *Shooting the Works*. He was born and grew up in South Philadelphia and now lives in the Bay area.

JOSEPHINE FOO's collage book of poems and pictures, *Endou*, has recently been published with a grant from the National Endowment for the Arts. Her poems and essays have appeared in *Premonitions: An Anthology of Asian American Poems*, *The American Voice*, *The Asian Pacific American Journal*, *Kalliope*, *Amerasia Journal*, and others. Winner of the Eve of St. Agnes Prize for Poetry in 1994, sponsored by *Negative Capability*, she holds degrees from Vassar College and Brown University and is currently at the University of Pennsylvania Law School.

WILLIAM H. GASS is the author of seven books of fiction and nonfiction, including *Omensetter's Luck*, *In the Heart of the Heart of the Country*, *On Being Blue*, and *The World Within the Word*. He is the David May Distinguished University Professor in the Humanities and director of the International Writers Center at Washington University in St. Louis. His most recent collection of essays, *Habitations of the Word*, won the 1986 National Book Critics Award for criticism. His most recent novel, *The Tunnel*, was published this year.

HENRY LOUIS GATES, JR., is W.E.B. Du Bois Professor of the Humanities and chair of the Afro-American Studies Department at Harvard University, as well as director of the W.E.B. Du Bois Institute for Afro-American Research at Harvard. He received his Ph.D. in English literature from the University of Cambridge. Among his books are *The*

Signifying Monkey: A Theory of Afro-American Literary Criticism; Figures in Black: Words, Signs, and the Racial Self; and *Loose Canons: Notes on the Culture Wars.* "In the Kitchen" appears in his most recent book, *Colored People: A Memoir,* which has been awarded the Lillian Smith Prize for Southern Literature and the *Chicago Tribune's* Heartland Award for Non-Fiction. Well known for his work in recovering black writers from obscurity, Dr. Gates is the series editor of the forty-volume Schomberg Library of Nineteenth-Century Black Women Writers as well as the Amistad literary series entitled Critical Perspectives Past and Present, and coeditor of *Transition* magazine. He has been the recipient of a MacArthur Fellowship as well as numerous prizes, including a Polk Award for Social Commentary.

EDWARD HOAGLAND has published seven collections of essays, most recently *Balancing Acts;* five books of fiction, including *Seven Rivers West;* and two travel books, *Notes from the Century Before: A Journal from British Columbia* and *African Calliope: A Journey to the Sudan,* both of which have been reissued this year. He also writes criticism and is the editor of the Penguin Nature Classics series. He is a member of the American Academy of Arts and Letters.

DIANA KAPPEL-SMITH is the author and illustrator of three books of natural history essays: *Wintering, Night Life: Nature from Dusk to Dawn,* and *Desert Time: A Journey through the American Southwest.* Her work has appeared in *New Woman, Orion,* and the *Smithsonian,* among other publications. She is working on essays about experiences that "metamorphose" people's relationship with nature and on a series of children's picture books about a wizard whose creative powers get him into trouble. She isn't working on these things as hard as she should because sailboat racing is too much fun.

MAXINE KUMIN is the author of ten collections of poems and three of essays. Her most recent book is *Women, Animals, and Vegetables,* which includes the essay in this volume. Her *New and Selected Poems* will appear in the spring of 1996. She and her husband live on a farm in New Hampshire, where they raise horses and vegetables.

JAMES A. MCPHERSON is the author of *Hue and Cry, Railroad,* and *Elbow Room.* His articles and short stories have appeared in numerous periodicals, including *The Atlantic Monthly, Esquire, The Yale Review, Ploughshares,* and *The Iowa Review.* A graduate of Morris Brown College and Harvard Law School, he has received a Guggenheim Fellowship, a Pulitzer Prize, and a MacArthur Prize Fellows Award and is a member of the Academy of Arts and Sciences. Two new books, *Crabcakes* and a collection of essays, *Pompey's Line,* are forthcoming. He is a professor of English at the University of Iowa.

EDNA O'BRIEN's most recent novel is *House of Splendid Isolation.* Born in Ireland, she divides her time between Ireland, London, and New York.

CYNTHIA OZICK is the author of four novels — *Trust, The Cannibal Galaxy, The Shawl,* and *The Messiah of Stockholm* — and several collections, including *The Pagan Rabbi and Other Stories, Bloodshed and Three Novellas,* and *Levitation: Five Fictions.* She has published two collections of essays, *Art and Ardor* and *Metaphor and Memory.* A new collection of essays, *Fame and Folly,* is in preparation. *The Shawl,* a play directed by Sidney Lumet, will be produced in New York in the fall of 1995.

GRACE PALEY is the author of several collections of stories as well as of two books of poetry and one volume of poems and prose pieces, *Long Walks and Intimate Talks.* She has long been a feminist and antiwar activist. She has taught at Columbia University, Sarah Lawrence, Dartmouth, and the City College of New York. She is the recipient of many awards and honors, including the 1993 Vermont Award for Excellence in the Arts, the 1992 REA Award for Short Stories, and the 1989 Edith Wharton Award. In 1989, Mario Cuomo declared her the first official New York State Writer. Her *Collected Stories* was published in 1994.

ELAINE SCARRY is professor of English at Harvard University and senior fellow at the Society of Fellows. She has written *The Body in Pain* and is now completing a book about war and the social contract entitled *The Master of Consent.* Her essays about the way the material world resists language are collected in *Resisting Representation.* She is the editor of *Fins de Siècle,* where the essay "Counting at Dusk" originally appeared.

CHARLES SIMIC's first volume of poetry was published in 1967, and fifteen others have followed. His most recent book of poems is *A Wedding in Hell.* The essay in this volume is included in his new book of essays and memoirs, *The Unemployed Fortune Teller,* and he has two other collections from the same publisher. Mr. Simic won a Pulitzer Prize for Poetry in 1990.

JOHN EDGAR WIDEMAN is a two-time winner of the PEN/Faulkner Award and has been a nominee for the National Book Critics Circle Award. His novels include *A Glance Away, Hurry Home, The Lynchers, Sent for You Yesterday, Reuben,* and *Philadelphia Fire.* Along with several short story collections, Wideman has written two memoirs, *Brothers and Keepers* and, most recently, *Fatheralong,* which was a National Book Award finalist and which includes "Father Stories." He teaches at the University of Massachusetts in Amherst.

TOBIAS WOLFF is the author of several books, including *This Boy's Life* and *In Pharoah's Army: Memoirs of the Last War,* from which this essay is taken. His next book, a collection of stories, will be published in the spring of 1996.

Notable Essays of 1994

SELECTED BY ROBERT ATWAN

JOEL AGEE
Progress and the Prayer Wheel. *Yale Review,* April.

MARCIA ALDRICH
Questions. *Northwest Review,* no. 2.

DOROTHY ALLISON
Gun Crazy. ZYZZYVA, Summer.

ELIJAH ANDERSON
The Code of the Streets. *Atlantic Monthly,* May.

CAROL ASCHER
My Father's Violin. *Shenandoah,* Winter.

JULENE BAIR
Dirt. *Apalachee Quarterly,* no. 40/41.

STEPHEN BARTHELME
Louisiana, Home of the Blues. *Apalachee Quarterly,* no. 42.

RICK BASS
The End of the Season. *Sports Afield,* December.

STEPHEN BATCHELOR
A Democracy of the Imagination. *Tricycle,* Winter.

MICHAEL BERUBE
Life As We Know It. *Harper's Magazine,* December.

NEAL BOWERS
Plagiarism and Silence. *American Scholar,* Autumn.

JANE BRADLEY
Spellbound at Chincoteague. *Literary Review,* Summer.

JIMMY BRESLIN
Monsters of the Heart. *Esquire,* October.

JENNIFER BRICE
Grease Monkey. *Manoa,* Winter.

T. ALAN BROUGHTON
Some Notes on the Art of Lying. *New England Review,* Spring.

JANE BROX
This Deliberate Dream. *Georgia Review,* Spring.

MELISSA CAPERS
Sins. *Western Humanities Review,* Spring.

JOHN CHRISTIE
Found Places of Peace. *Hopewell Review.*

EDIE CLARK
Paul's Stone. *Yankee,* May.

GEOFFREY CLARK
The Best I Can Wish You. *Northeast Corridor,* no. 1/2.

RICHARD SELZER
  The Language of Pain. *Wilson Quarterly*, Autumn.
DAVID SHIELDS
  Almost Famous. *Witness*, vol. 8, no. 1.
LESLIE MARMON SILKO
  Fences Against Freedom. *Hungry Mind Review*, Fall.
CHARLES SIMIC
  Don't Squeeze the Tomatoes. *Antaeus*, Spring.
LOUIS SIMPSON
  Waterloo, the Story of an Obsession. *Hudson Review*, Summer.
PETER STARK
  The Man Who Loved Winter. *We Alaskans*, October 30.
MICHAEL STEINBERG
  Trading Off: A Memoir. *Missouri Review*, no. 1.
ALEXANDER STILLE
  Latin Fanatic. *American Scholar*, Autumn.
DOROTHEA STRAUS
  Women Studies. *Confrontation*, Fall.
MARY SWANDER
  Leap Frog. *Cream City Review*, Spring.

BARRY TARGAN
  The Equalization Fallacy. *Sewanee Review*, Summer.
KERRY TEMPLE
  Last Call of the Wild. *Notre Dame Magazine*, Autumn.
SALLIE TISDALE
  Meat. *Antioch Review*, Summer.

JONATHAN VEITCH
  Angels of the Assembly Line. *Southwest Review*, Autumn.
MICHAEL VENTURA
  Living in the Red Zone. *Los Angeles Times Magazine*, February 13.

NANCY L. WALKER
  Snowbound. *So to Speak*, Spring/Summer.
DONOVAN WEBSTER
  Out There Is a Bomb with Your Name. *Smithsonian*, February.
SHARON WHITE
  Winter: Kelly, Wyoming. *Quarterly West*, Summer/Fall.
LEON WIESELTIER
  Against Identity. *New Republic*, November 28.
PATRICIA J. WILLIAMS
  Hate Radio. *Ms.*, March–April.
TERRY TEMPEST WILLIAMS
  Elements of Love. *New England Review* ["Earth," Winter; "Fire," Spring; "Water," Summer; "Air," Fall].
S. L. WISENBERG
  Holocaust Girls/Lemon. *Ploughshares*, Fall.
GREGORY WOLFE
  The Christian Writer in a Fragmented Culture. *Image*, Fall.

JIANYING ZHA
  Beijing: A City Without Walls. *Antioch Review*, Summer.

Special issues of 1994:

"Old Friends, New Neighbors: A Celebration of the American Essay," *American Literary Review*, Fall (editor, W. Scott Olsen).
"Mentors," *Ohio Review*, no. 51 (editor, Wayne Dodd).
"Intimate Exile," *Ploughshares*, Fall (editor, Rosellen Brown).
"American Cities," *Witness*, vol. 8, no. 2 (editor, Peter Stine).
"Poets Writing Prose," *Creative Nonfiction*, no. 2 (editor, Lee Gutkind).